THE
PERSISTENCE OF
RACISM
IN AMERICA

THE PERSISTENCE OF RACISM IN AMERICA

Thomas Powell

UNIVERSITY
PRESS OF
AMERICA

Lanham • New York • London

Copyright © 1992 by
University Press of America®, Inc.
4720 Boston Way
Lanham, Maryland 20706

3 Henrietta Street
London WC2E 8LU England

Library of Congress Cataloging-in-Publication Data

Powell, Thomas F.
The persistence of racism in America / Thomas Powell.
p.   cm.
Includes bibliographical references and index.
1. United States—Race relations.   2. Racism—United States.
I. Title.
E184.A1P664   1992   305.8'00973—dc20   91–46949 CIP

ISBN 0–8191–8587–6 (cloth : alk. paper)
ISBN 0–8191–8588–4 (pbk. : alk. paper)

To Stuart Gerry Brown, my wonderful adviser for more than thirty years;
to Roy A. Price, without whom, nothing;
and to my friends and early teachers in the 353 Project.

Table of Contents

Preface

Racism is a disposition involving beliefs or attitudes or both. Such beliefs and attitudes require examination, and they must be distinguished from forms of behavior: i.e., the *treatment* of others. This work does not explicitly attempt to explain slavery, discrimination, segregation, or any form of exploitation. Its subject is not African-American or other minority experience in America, but the "reasons why" racism is such a persistent part of the culture.

Racism rose from a quiet inclination in the sixteenth century to an epidemic in the nineteenth and twentieth centuries. The history of racism is necessary to an understanding of its persistence, but the history of racism itself does not explain its persistence. What *else* have people believed and felt, related to views on "race"? What other dispositions permit or support or complement racist beliefs and attitudes? Why did racism spread and intensify after the Civil War, when justification or rationalization of slavery was no longer at issue? Why has racism retained such powerful appeal, when the scientific community and educated people in general have rejected it intellectually for decades? What accounts for the seemingly stubborn popular refusal to abandon racism? Why is it so appealing, congenial, or simply acceptable to so many? To address such questions about America since the Civil War, it is necessary to consider how the beliefs and attitudes of Americans took shape from the beginning, and to consider some other developments concomitant with racism.

Politicians and others often adopt a self-congratulatory position of righteous indignation about racism, identifying it as a disgrace because it betrays basic American values. No doubt that is enjoyable, but rounding up the usual suspects, whether anonymous or as conspicuous as Hitler, is not helpful in understanding the subject. The standard explanation since Gunnar Myrdal's *An American Dilemma*

(1944) has been that there is an "ever-raging conflict" in the hearts of Americans, between an "American Creed" and "Christian precepts" on the one hand, and irrational prejudices on the other.   But racism is not just an aberration or a contradiction of basic American values. Rather, racist beliefs and attitudes are inextricably bound up with our firmest traditional value assumptions and convictions about ourselves; and they "work" as pragmatic "truth" for many Americans. This book is mainly about how white Americans have thought and felt about themselves in relation to others. It is not a lament or a simplistic denunciation of America as a "racist society," but an attempt to explain how we got where we are in this regard.

* * * * *

A book about beliefs, attitudes, and value assumptions has to be a "book about books" to a great extent, unless the writer is a powerful original thinker. This writer, sad to say, is not one of those; so in what follows I am indebted in various ways and degrees to hundreds of authors. Many primary sources are used, some classics and some rather unusual sources, perhaps; but I am heavily indebted to the authors of many works interpreting American experience from different vantage points. Whole chapters depend upon the analyses of scholars like Winthrop Jordan, David Potter, Stephen Jay Gould, Cynthia Eagle Russett, Reginald Horsman, Richard Huber, Richard Weiss, Warren I. Susman, Donald B. Meyer, Christopher Lasch, Daniel J. Singal, Philip Rieff, John Rawls, Robert Nozick, and the leading authority on individualism, Steven Lukes. The organization of my bibliography into four sections is intended to acknowledge authors of course, but also to guide readers with different kinds and levels of interest.

I am grateful for encouragement from Anne Powell, Anthony Crain, and Tony Annunziata, and for help from Jean Dittmar and Kate Edwards. Special thanks are due Christine Margelli for her fine editing and layout work. Some important political understandings from Stephen Holmes are reflected in the study, and Ivan Brady and Jean L. Hooker have provided valuable counsel. My efforts have been assisted by the National Endowment for the Humanities, on the subject of individualism, and on racism by the Faculty Research Committee, State University of New York, Oswego.

Any errors in the work should, of course, be attributed to someone else.

One

The Subject of Racism

Many authors have contributed valuable analysis and interpretation of racism; but only a consideration of the subject in relation to the broader culture can deal with the question, "Why do so many white Americans continue to hold racist views?" Descriptions of racism's effects, and exhortations to rid the culture of it, are constantly heard. A popular response to any social ill in America is to announce a "war" against it. This approach suggests that we might mount a successful campaign to abolish racism, because its persistence merely shows lack of information, or misunderstanding. Like most popular "solutions," this one takes into consideration some aspects of reality, but overlooks a great deal.

Studies of racism commonly relate the subject to discrimination and exploitation: associations which are unavoidable, perhaps, but which lead to confusion. Racism serves to *justify* aggressive behavior such as discrimination and other forms of abuse. These forms of behavior are *expressions* of racism, not aspects of racism itself as a clearly defined subject. Similarly, segregation institutionalizes aversion to others, which is related to racism but is a separately definable subject. What, then, is racism? As used here, the word means some degree of working assumption that others are inherently inferior or disagreeably different in their fundamental behavioral, mental or moral characteristics or capacities. Guarded language is necessary because difficulties immediately arise regarding the ways in which we make assumptions.

First, our working assumptions are beliefs which we have adopted or accepted in varying ways and degrees. Beliefs are convictions or positions presented on the basis of reason and evidence. People do not adopt beliefs "for no reason" or without cause, but for reasons and with causes presented by their culture. Racism is not a perspective or belief system suited to rigorous thinking, nevertheless, our society includes a very significant proportion of people who consciously believe blacks to be generally inferior or objectionable as associates. Their numbers include professors who are taken very seriously, and many journalists and officials who see the question of inferiority as "open" and who want to deal with all claims "objectively."

These commentators believe or profess to believe that the First Amendment to the Constitution obliges us to treat all opinions as if they were "created equal" with regard to their validity, rather than obliging us to acknowledge equal rights to express beliefs *regardless* of their validity. The assertion that all opinions must be seriously considered seeks to confer legitimacy on racist beliefs in the name of righteous open-mindedness. The history of racism illustrates how the relatively or seemingly rigorous thinkers who have held to it have wanted desperately for it to be valid, and have been proportionately resourceful in framing their arguments. But as we come closer to the present, we also see that racism as formal *belief* or intellectual persuasion has lost respectability among educated people, in widening circles since the 1920s or '30s.

In every phase of its history, racism has provided several levels of explanation which accommodate constituencies with different expectations of what constitutes a convincing argument. At some level, belief gives way to what is more accurately termed *attitude*. Masses of people have accepted or taken racist positions without examining arguments or thinking beyond a point at which they feel comfortable or pleased. After all, intellectual rigor is neither necessary nor important in a popular bias, and many people do not claim it for their views. Attitudes are emotive rather than cognitive, simply dispositions on the basis of feeling rather than reason or evidence. People hold attitudes "for no *reason*" in the sense of systematic analysis, but their views can still be analyzed and understood. A much larger number of people now hold racist attitudes than hold racist beliefs, since such beliefs no longer exert the authority from philosophy and science which they held in earlier generations. Racist attitudes in themselves are sufficient to account for a great deal of racist expression, since these attitudes evidently meet both the small intellectual demands and the large emotional needs of great numbers of people.

We can address racism as a position based on beliefs or attitudes, or both, recognizing that we survey a broad spectrum of justifications for various kinds and degrees of racism; and that the justifications themselves range from highly academic to virtually incoherent. The extremely academic and the extremely illiterate positions exhibit the odd similarity of being virtually unintelligible, the former because of their arcane language and intricate methodological twists. But our central question, as to how racism persists with such force, now assumes a more specific sort of meaning for a historical essayist: it asks how beliefs and attitudes took their shapes over time, and what accounts for their appeal. Such questioning cannot produce (apodeictic) demonstration of irrefutable *causation*, but it can provide (deictic) explanation through *description*.

Already an implicit basis for both beliefs and attitudes is acknowledged: interest. People have always been receptive to claims which imply their own importance. To put the matter another way, "What kinds of beliefs and attitudes are most difficult for people to give up?" Those we find pleasant or otherwise useful are most tenaciously held. Racism entails prejudice with regard to important kinds of performance. This means that assumptions must be made about what constitutes estimable or acceptable performance; and such assumptions are cultural. Our culture includes religious, moral and prescriptive norms, and also convictions about what is attractive, appropriate, etc. Racist norms have suited interests, met needs and served purposes in this society. They enable people to "feel good about themselves," and also to justify any other benefits derived from actively treating other people as inferior.

Where interest appears, our cultural disposition is to regard beliefs and attitudes as matters of choice, voluntarily adopted out of egoism, conscious self-regard, or as the path of least resistance. We tend very strongly to assume autonomy, real choice, entailing individual responsibility and deserving. Leading ethical theorists like John Rawls and Robert Nozick now draw opposed political inferences from the view that nobody deserves anything; but racism has always blamed the alleged deficiencies of character and ability of blacks and others on their not being both *able and willing* to meet cultural standards. Being able has generally entailed being willing, since the main thrust of the culture is to assume that behavioral disposition or "determination" is volitional, chosen by the actor. *Willing* itself has appeared as a kind of ability, and if absence or ineffective it is considered an inherent lack, such as near-sightedness or slow reflexes, a natural handicap.

With the education solution, or war on racism approach, reformers tend to treat racists very much as blacks and other minorities have been treated. Racists are criticized for deficiencies of character or intellect or both, and thought to deserve blame, disdain or contempt insofar as they are not convinced and therefore not willing to come around or measure up to more enlightened expectations. This approach assumes that beliefs or attitudes (or both) are susceptible of revision or reversal on the basis of reason and evidence; and that racist views are held only in perverse or obtuse defiance of reason and evidence. While it is obvious that systematic beliefs are often invoked as *reasons*, to undergird popular racist attitudes, it seems more commonly the case that beliefs dissipate into tacit assumptions, inchoate underlying cultural *supports* of popular attitudes, quite independent of the reasons that support the beliefs.

For example, reasons for the widespread belief that blacks are generally less capable than whites developed over centuries, and they are quite complex. The attitude that blacks' understanding is not to be relied upon may draw support from such a belief, but shows no further concern with explanation, or with whether the underlying belief is justified. It has proved a congenial attitude for many whites, not successfully challenged as far as they are concerned, and not refuted because an attitude *cannot* be refuted, but only rejected. Most whites are now convinced not to express either such beliefs or such attitudes in public; but racism has to do with *holding* the beliefs or attitudes or both, not whether or how they find expression.

We should resist any inclination to assume that slave-holders, exploiters, segregationists and racists have been or are somehow morally different from educated, modern citizens. By far the safer assumption, and the one to serve as a point of departure in this treatment of racism, is that people have believed and felt, and continue to believe and feel, what they "need" in order to pursue happiness, or what *seems* to serve them in that pursuit. People try to be practical and to promote their own sense of well-being, and Americans in particular have notably appreciated practicality. A utilitarian disposition, in the broadest and most fundamental sense of that adjective, has dominated American thinking. Pragmatism is widely known as "the American philosophy," and instrumentalism, expediency, success, and "winning" form the very core of America's consequentialist orientation to meaning itself. For that reason, racism is widely thought of as having arisen to justify slavery. But the fact that racism not only persisted but intensified after slavery was abolished suggests that material as well as other advantages were still expected from racism.

The early history of racism is inextricably bound up with the history of slavery and of segregation and discrimination; but also with the most cherished ideas and values of the culture. The history of racism itself is therefore only part of the explanation of racism's persistence. That persistence is linked with American adaptations of Christianity; with the utilitarian mind-set and its accompanying habits of thought; with the rise of capitalism and of political liberalism; with natural rights philosophy; with personal freedom, self-reliance, moral responsibility; with democracy, several forms of individualism, romanticism, and social and intellectual movements which seem at first to have little or nothing to do with racism. The persistence of racism would be easy to understand if it could be accounted for just by poor science, ignorance, and self-interested rationalization. It is in fact difficult to grasp, and its explanation is hard to accept, because our most cherished conceptions of reality have made it seem justified, attractive, and even necessary.

An able sociologist like David T. Wellman, studying recent and contemporary American experience, can accurately conclude that the "solutions" to racism which are commonly suggested are really no solutions at all, because they propose no fundamental changes. Wellman writes that racist ". . . thinking . . . justifies policies and institutional priorities that perpetuate racial inequality, and it does so in distinctively American terms."[1] He is perfectly correct; but since he is a student of sociology rather than intellectual history, he does not delineate how the beliefs and attitudes of racism have complemented and perhaps even been required by the "policies and institutional priorities" which continue to dominate our society. Such an explanation is the purpose here, with emphasis on "distinctively American terms" which permit or even dictate a sort of innocent, well-meaning complicity in the continuing force of racism.

Only in the weird ideological surrealism of recent experience has it become clear how racism has always been supported by American religious, social, economic and political thought, and even by our formal philosophy. Of course we often adopt false beliefs by reasoning validly from wrong premises which are useful, pleasant and attractive. Irrational beliefs result very often from rational treatment of false assumptions. On the other hand, as Stephen Jay Gould once pointed out in an essay ostensibly on baseball, the inverse process is also common: we accurately perceive patterns (such as behavioral characteristics of different groups) and then draw unwarranted inferences from them, or impute false "meaning" to them. Once beliefs are adopted or attitudes formed, irrationality usually takes the form of defensive rationalization, which both uses and abuses logic.

Racist characterizations assert common, categorical deficiencies or undesirable traits. Of course exceptions to racist generalizations are routinely made; but they do not affect the frame of reference that accepts racism, because they are made on *individual* grounds, pointing to the exceptional and impressive traits of individuals. Anti-racist arguments also generalize. They assert equal ability, merit, and deserving. But ability, merit and deserving are predominantly seen in our society as individual traits only. Groups may reasonably be disdained on the grounds that their individual members commonly exhibit undesirable traits; and "superior" groups accordingly comprise individuals who tend to share estimable traits. (The word "superior" is never used.) To address racism by accommodating groups or categories of people is to run head-on into America's foremost article of traditional faith: that virtue is individual. In short, racism rests firmly on American individualism, with its cherished values of will-power and individual responsibility for shaping one's own life.

To defend our very selves, we defend beliefs in terms of which we have come to perceive and define the self, self-respectfully, comfortably and pleasantly. We invest our lives in beliefs, quite literally. Since changing such "vested" beliefs is painful, threatening identity itself, we hold onto our beliefs and associated attitudes with utmost tenacity. We find or contrive the "reasons" we need in order to "be ourselves"; and that is what we call pragmatic, practical and necessary. Radical empiricism, the epistemology of pragmatism, requires following the evidence wherever it leads. But *will*, for lack of any better term, is also a real factor: an established sense of interest influences the choice of what kinds of evidence we follow, by choosing what kinds of questions we ask. Even choices of questions are "determined." We *are determined* to choose what will *be determined* as belief: what we are "resolved" to believe, or insist upon. "Naturally," we choose what works: i.e., what feels good, satisfies us, fulfills us, makes us happy. We accept and perpetuate explanations that appeal to us.

How does racism gain such massive support, even though the most tortuous convolutions of logic and belief have been required to try to reconcile it with religious values and ideas of democracy and fairness? Racist characterizations became comfortable for the majority, conducive to the greatest happiness of the greatest number. Pragmatism, our national philosophy, enabled and encouraged people to believe what served their interests. Varying forms and degrees of racism still work as truth, and as palliatives, as "therapy." They are satisfying; and since they are usually held subjectively, they cannot be refuted, but only opposed. To attack racism through public policy is to challenge America's "faith in the individual," and to be, if not downright "un-American," then threateningly non-American. To understand how America came to be as it has been and is, one has to begin with what "worked" for Englishmen of the sixteenth and seventeenth centuries.

1. David T. Wellman, *Portraits of White Racism* (Cambridge: Cambridge University Press, 1977), 220, 235.

Two

In the Times of English Exploration and Colonization

Before Spain ended its long domination by the Moors in 1492, Henry the Navigator of Portugal had taken the lead in European exploration of West Africa. The Catholic powers dominated sea lanes in that part of the world until after the English defeat of the Armada in 1588, which ended Spain's *Siglo de Oro,* "Century of Gold." Both Spain and Portugal developed trade in slaves some time before Englishmen experienced significant contact with Africans. During the seventeenth century, Europe was still convulsed by religious conflict, especially in the Thirty Years' War, 1618 to 1648. Catholic France emerged as the dominant power on the Continent. England was also torn apart by the aftermath of the Reformation, culminating in the Puritan Civil War from 1641 to 1649, the Cromwell Protectorate to 1660, and the Restoration ending with the Glorious Revolution of 1688-1689. These episodes foreshadowed the shaping of America.

Despite the internal upheavals of seventeenth-century England, and also because of them, England's exploration and quest for colonies accelerated. Economic conditions prompted the government to encourage probes for colonies, in the hope of enriching the national treasury. The rising mercantile constituency, plagued by religious turmoil and by the political uncertainty resulting from both economic and religious tensions, pressed for official endorsement of "adventures," the use of private venture capital in hopes of enrichment from abroad. Even as English colonization took root in America (plantations, as colonies were called), England also probed

into new territory elsewhere. But in the American colonies, contact
with Africans first occurred through Dutch trade. Holland, finally safe
from Spain after 1588, and also free of religious struggles because of the
tolerance it was first to cultivate, rapidly emerged as a dominant sea-
power. Dutch traders brought Africans to Virginia in 1619, the year
before the *Mayflower* carried Bradford and the Pilgrims to the region
John Smith would distinguish from Virginia with the name New
England.

How did it happen that Africans were gradually enslaved,
regarded and treated so differently from other "slaves" or servants?
Englishmen in the seventeenth century used the term slave for a non-
English servant, and sometimes they used it in a rather literary way to
refer to a person in any of a number of kinds of bondage. In the first
four decades of African bondage in America, they looked for
differences, and they found them and remarked on them. After about
1660 formal measures were adopted to set apart the Negro from other
servants. "Negro" meant black, related to Niger as in Nigeria.
Negerland is Africa in German, for example.   But the permanent
bondage that developed was not as dramatically different for blacks as it
might now appear.

The only "freedom" for a typical English person on a term of
service was to agree to another term of service. In England, labor was
plentiful and cheap, the cities crowded with unemployed people
dislocated from the countryside by early industrialization. Servitude
was, for all practical purposes, as long as the master wished it to be. In
America it was quite commonly "perpetual," but that meant indefinite,
not necessarily permanent. What happened uniquely to Africans was a
gradual transformation of indefinite servitude into lifetime servitude.
In the 1660s this new meaning became quite well established, and
slavery was set on the path it would follow through the seventeenth
and eighteenth and much of the nineteenth centuries. It was
successively regarded by many as an exceptional arrangement, a
curiosity, an embarrassment, an outrage, and a disgrace; and the more
it came under attack, the more vigorously its practitioners and
beneficiaries defended it.

Again, how did it develop that Africans were treated differently?
Various justifications mounted in proportion as criticism mounted,
from the seventeenth century to the adamant nineteenth. The more
challenges were advanced, the more defensive and self-serving and

emphatic grew the responses. Racism emerged as justification and rationalization of slavery. Yet there was no effective concept of race in seventeenth-century Europe. Leibniz, for example, flatly rejected the notion of human "races." Both reason and faith required a universal conception of mankind. All men were God's work, all had souls, all shared a common human nature. The idea of science, largely embedded in culture through the nineteenth century, continued the Christian separation of the human and social from the "natural." Unlike physics (including chemistry), biology did not develop general laws during the seventeenth and eighteenth centuries. Organic life was not a part of the mechanistic conception of the universe.

Eighteenth-century biology did distinguish between species and "varieties," with species fixed and varieties within them affected by the conditions of their environment. This distinction was used in speculation about human differences, with Buffon, for example, asserting that white was the norm and that climate accounted for other coloration. Ideas of classification which were later treated as rigidly "true" and unquestionably meaningful actually emerged in casual, careless ways. For example, the word Caucasian, which came to be taken so seriously as a "scientific" designation, arose because a German scientist named Blumenbach had a collection of skulls including one from the Caucasus region. He remarked that this skull was similar to German skulls, and he speculated that the Caucasus area might be the source of white people. "Caucasian" was introduced in an ungrounded conjecture about one skull.[1]

Racism is not, of course, an American phenomenon, but a human phenomenon. It manifests "binary" thinking, the nearly universal proclivity for self-definition by contrast: we-they, us-them, insiders-outsiders, Greeks-barbarians, all perceived more in terms of differences than commonalities. People of the most widely varied cultures practice invidious comparison, finding fault with the ways -- and deficiencies in the traits -- of others. Some American Indians had names for themselves which meant "the human beings" in their languages, suggesting that outsiders were something different, and lesser beings. Self-inflation and self-celebration seem irresistible; and efforts to establish worth and dignity and importance seem invariably to lead to claims of superiority. In itself such a human disposition toward racism might be only a harmless defect of the species, and its comical puffery regarded as an interesting version of "original sin" or "innate depravity," meaning unseemly self-regard and lack of humility. The vitally serious problem with it is that claims of superiority so easily lead to domination strategies, racist habits of thought to justify them, and institutionalized mistreatment of others on the basis of the racist justifications. Attitudes and justifying beliefs come to constitute a *Teufelskreis*, a "devil's circle" of reciprocal reinforcement and intensification.

Racism's mind-set tends in its very nature to be adversarial and combative, always potentially if not openly. It includes a claim which the holder is willing to impose upon others if he can. The harmless observation of differences generates what might be called a "versus mind-set." This involves a tragically common logical error, confusing exclusion with opposition. "A implies Not-A" is true in the sense that when A is defined, there is necessarily further reality which is Not-A, that is to say, not included in the definition of A. But the versus mind-set turns Not-A into *Anti*-A. If we are A, "they" become actual or potential adversaries: not just others who are different in ways that occasion no agitation or apprehension. Racism turns others into objects, different in ways which justify adopting a predatory disposition toward them.

Racism in America is one of mankind's most conspicuous cases, for several reasons. Assumptions and beliefs that would seem to militate against racism were instead made to support it. The Europeans who would dominate the land confronted a very significant and diverse aboriginal population. Ominously, Europeans showed contempt and hostility in their first contact with Indians, five hundred years before Columbus. In *The Vinland Saga*, the Norsemen immediately named the Indians *skraelings* or wretches; and their first idea of appropriate behavior toward the strangers was to kill them. Much has been written about how that idea endured to the later nineteenth-century view of General Phil Sheridan, that "The only good Indian is a dead Indian."

By the time of the first national census, in 1790 (in which the Indians declined to be counted) about one fifth of the new nation's population were Africans or of African descent. As it became clear that these people would not to be treated like everyone else, just how they were to be treated had to be established and justified. And, for the dominant English-Americans, their own incipient racism posed a seemingly insoluble dilemma. Their culture held a Marxian contradiction, in which one indispensable feature is irreconcilable with another indispensable feature. Their faith in one creation and in the universality of Christian truth required a benevolent attitude toward others; but they had a versus mind-set and binary habits of thought which required *gradation*, a hierarchical order of "betters" in moral, intellectual, social, cultural, economic and political terms, or at least some of these in any given setting.

1. See T. F. Gossett, *Race: The History of an Idea* (Dallas: Southern Methodist University Press, 1963), 33-38.

Three

Reconciling Slavery with Christianity

Christians of the colonial era felt a powerful faith in the unity of the human species: a faith which undoubtedly accounted for the fact that efforts to abolish slavery were overwhelmingly led by people of conspicuous religious seriousness. After all, the central thrust of Christian faith was not only individual salvation but the universal brotherhood of man, the concern for universal justice derived from *agape* and *caritas*, love for one's fellows.

At the same time, as Winthrop Jordan describes, Englishmen associated proper Christianity with their own culture and characteristics, to such an extent that religious identification, nationality, and ethnicity became inextricably bound together in their consciousness. Christianity came to suggest, if not actually to entail, an association with light "complexion" by the end of the seventeenth century.[1] Color itself, the most obvious difference between Englishmen and Africans, had something to do with faith, which clearly showed divine favor. By around 1680, ". . . taking the colonies as a whole, a new term appeared -- *white*."[2] Their fairness -- a typically ambiguous term referring to either skin or disposition, or somehow to both -- meant that Englishmen were favored, by God, through Nature; favored with membership in a category or great class of men: membership which was literally conducive to salvation, and to progress. Colonial Englishmen cherished the impression of themselves as chosen people, a conviction which became American, lasting far beyond independence and shaping our national relations with the rest of the world.

Divine favor resulted in an advanced form of Christianity, reasonably enough; and the true faith was thought to be attended by the greatest language on earth, and the highest civilization. Anglo-American culture was the product of favored *nature*, with the superiority of culture manifesting that of nature. By contrast, Africans were obviously *ill-favored* literally, as in the expression referring to appearance. They were out of favor with God, and were widely perceived as incapable of rising from heathenism and barbarism without help. (Some Christians concluded that Christian brotherhood toward them *meant* supervision of them.) Their low condition, lack of English speech and English ways, lack of religious enlightenment or technology, showed their deficient nature as surely as the advanced conditions of Englishmen showed their higher status. If it were God's will that Africans be like Englishmen, obviously they would be better *favored*. Christians, particularly since Pope Urban II at the end of the eleventh century, had commonly perceived infidels, Muslims and Jews, as somehow less completely human than themselves. Of course Indians were also subject to classification as a lower order despite the universality of the faith. As Gunnar Myrdal argued in *An American Dilemma* (1944), Anglo-Americans perceived Africans as *culturally* inferior while also perceiving humans generally in *biological* terms; and so they drew the convenient inference that what they saw as inferiority was *innate*.

The development of racism in America perfectly exemplifies that multiple causation which historians constantly observe. The factor of dark color, associated with night, dirt, evil, ignorance and so forth, easily reinforced the binary tendency to assume superiority of one's own culture and language, to say nothing of religion. The religion of the colonial period made sharp distinctions between the regenerate and the unregenerate, and in strict Puritan practice Saints could not take communion with those less favored. "Winning and losing" were much on colonial minds, both spiritually and materially; and the condition of slavery itself seemed to imply abandonment by the Almighty.

There were no accidents in the intellectual world of the seventeenth century, but reasons or causes for everything. Whatever lacked natural explanation simply had to have supernatural explanation, so that, for example, witches who made covenants with the devil were all too real. Robert Boyle, the great scientist who wrote *The Skeptical Chemist*, interviewed miners about demons and goblins in the mine shafts. Newton himself practiced astrology. John Demos tells the story of an accident in a militia company to illustrate what he calls the "layers of causation" in the reality of colonial New England. A young lad in the militia company discharged his weapon during drill, killing a middle-aged militiaman. Why? Well, who could gain by the man's death? It seemed there was a woman who owed him money, whose debt would now be cancelled. Evidently she had caused the boy to fire. But how could such devilish influence affect a member of a Christian community? The pastor decided that the underlying cause was the sinfulness of the whole congregation. The people had not been sufficiently resolute in virtue to ward off witchcraft.

Why were Africans in such low estate? For Englishmen in the seventeenth century, this also could be no accident. There must be causes, reasons; and likely explanations were not hard to find. "Blaming the victim" has always been easy, but never more persuasive than in early America. Africans did not speak as well, did not "know as much," and so did not seem to think as well or feel with such refinement as Englishmen. They looked different, they acted different, and to most Englishmen it made perfect sense to assume that they *were* fundamentally different. The binary habit of thought flourished in a dualistic world of nature and culture, body and mind, flesh and spirit, organism and soul. All men were alike the products of God's work, but God worked in mysterious ways. Only He knew why some were chosen and others damned; and if that were the case with individuals, why not with categories of men?

In any case, the universalism of Christianity stood in puzzling contradiction to what seemed an inescapable fact of life: gradation. Englishmen, like other Europeans, were long accustomed to class stratification. Material possession had become more and more closely tied to personal identity from the middle ages, with what Robert Heilbroner termed the rise of "economic society." Racism emerged against a cultural backdrop in which invidious comparison was habitual. This was not an "odd way of thinking,"[3] but simply the institutionalization of self-interest as capitalism (or proto-capitalism from the thirteenth century) took shape.[4] Capitalism was well under way by the sixteenth century, when the followers of Calvin observed such "innate depravity"; and in the seventeenth, self-interest was presented as legitimate by Hobbes and Spinoza, awaiting only the beguiling formulation of Adam Smith in the eighteenth.   Social gradation was natural and necessary, and tightly fastened to both property and Christian belief, as in the famous analyses of Max Weber and R. H. Tawney, no matter who is more "correct" about the connection.

But gradation of another sort also rose to the surface, and to dominant influence in English attitudes. The old concept of the Great Chain of Being, subject of A. O. Lovejoy's classic study,[5] rose to unprecedented prominence in the eighteenth century, the age of science as taxonomy or classification. Reason supported faith in dictating the reality of universal values, in the form of natural rights and the entitlements of "all men" who were "created equal." Reason also supported faith in positing the reality of gradation, a hierarchical distribution in which all possible forms of life were ranked, from the simplest toward relative proximity to God. In the age of Linnaeus, and of that astonishing optimism that allowed men to classify themselves as wise (*homo sapiens*), the most favored variations of men became a secular elect, destined for salvation and all its cultural and material counterparts and benefits. But Africans, already enslaved in the American colonies and elsewhere, had uncertain position at best on the Great Chain. As discoveries and studies of the anthropoid apes progressed, and as pre-Darwinian evolutionary thought took vague shape from the mid-eighteenth century, the black African appeared to many as a sort of "missing link" between European man and the apes, just as angels had been presumed as links between man and God when the Chain idea was used by theologians in the fourth century. Gradation was a habit of thought, and a familiar basis of action in various spheres of life.

Africans did not seem to illustrate the behavior associated with C. B. Macpherson's "possessive individualism."[6] They held no philosophy of self-evident truth or natural rights, exhibited no respectable religion or science, and seemed indifferent to the social, cultural, intellectual and moral implications of gradation. Liberty, that great developing concern of the eighteenth century, had been a focus of "interest" among Christians from ancient times. Whoever found himself in the position of a slave seemed a non-person, incomplete, appropriately concerned with *ponos* rather than *ergon*, the menial labor of physical necessities rather than the work of Aristotle's "ethical will," aimed at the greatest self-fulfillment. It was easy to believe that "the reason" for African slavery was that slavery was their appropriate condition.

1. Winthrop Jordan, *White Over Black: American Attitudes Toward the Negro*, 1550-1812 (New York: W. W. Norton and Company, 1977), 94.

2. *Ibid.*, 95.

3. Cf. Joel Kovel, *White Racism: A Psychohistory* (New York: Columbia University Press, 1984), 14.

4. See Alan Macfarlane, *The Origins of English Individualism* (Cambridge: Cambridge University Press, 1979); Richard Schlatter, *Private Property: The History of an Idea* (New Brunswick, N. J.:   Rutgers University Press, 1951); and Walter Ullmann, *The Individual and Society in the Middle Ages* (Baltimore: The Johns Hopkins University Press, 1966) for outstanding analyses.

5. See A. O. Lovejoy, *The Great Chain of Being* (Cambridge, Mass.:   Harvard University Press, 1936).

6. See C. B. Macpherson, *The Political Theory of Possessive Individualism* (Oxford: The Clarendon Press, 1962).

Four

The Enlightenment

People of every culture exhibit marvelous resourcefulness in contriving ways to believe what they want to believe; and if we confront a conflict or inconsistency, we are most ingenious at having our cake and eating it too. So men of the Enlightenment, that period of exalted reason and extraordinary optimism, managed to resolve the problem of Christian universality as opposed to gradation, at least to the satisfaction of those whose opinions counted most. Belief in universal natural rights inclined Enlightenment thinkers generally to oppose slavery; but they still tended to believe that Africans were inferior. "Ranks" of men were increasingly associated with "physiognomy," which meant overall physical appearance; and qualities of intellect and behavior became increasingly identified with traits of appearance.[1] In the eighteenth century, the language of writers of every sort, from natural history to the widely read poetry of Alexander Pope, shows pervasive acceptance of the Great Chain of Being as a description of reality. Winthrop Jordan writes that ". . . the popularity of the concept of the Chain in the eighteenth century derived in large measure from its capacity to universalize the principle of hierarchy."[2] If gradation seemed to contradict universality, and both were indispensable, what could be better than a conception that would *make gradation a universal principle?*

At the same time, religious and secular thought shifted in tandem, as it were, to beliefs which were still more congenial to proto-racist views. During the first half of the eighteenth century, colonial

Americans very largely rejected what they had come to see as the fatalism and unreasonableness of Puritanism. The covenant of faith, with its insistence upon predestination, made individual salvation entirely a matter of God's mysterious will. A person could not earn salvation under that dispensation, but could only try to maintain eligibility for it by being "prepared" for the infusion of saving faith, in case God should see fit to give it. Control of one's fate was limited to something like the Boy Scout motto, "Be prepared," but more in a spirit of resignation than of hope. As people gradually enjoyed greater control over their circumstances of life, and correspondingly felt more optimistic and confident, they moved away from predestination in two principal directions. One was Arminianism, a view confusing to modern readers because it was reactionary and monarchical in England, but revolutionary and democratic in America.

Arminianism summarized the Enlightenment in religious terms, asserting that one could achieve salvation by force of will. In effect, men like Charles Chauncy, Jonathan Mayhew, and Ebenezer Gay argued that the individual could *deserve* salvation, in flat contradiction to Puritanism, and that a just God would necessarily grant it when it was clearly deserved. Arminian doctrine spread only among a relatively small élite, but its influence was enormous because it became the orientation of influential thinkers and writers, such as John Adams. The idea of deserving, at first slowly and cautiously advanced, gained momentum; and it implied *criteria* of deserving: virtues or capacities easily recognized by their effects upon behavior. American intellectuals of the Enlightenment adopted the most uncompromising notion of individual responsibility anyone could imagine. Since salvation could be brought about by the power of individual will, individuals had the responsibility for bringing about their own salvation or damnation. Deficient or objectionable behavior now became a matter of individual control by will. You could be good if you really wanted to -- so there was no excuse for not being good.

The Enlightenment also brought what we call "secularization" of thought, in which salvation easily translated into success, and damnation into failure. Puritan culture had already developed strong associations between divine favor and material prosperity; and now Arminianism asserted that success or failure was a matter of individual will and its related capacities for industry, perseverance, temperance and the other Puritan virtues. The criteria of success were, of course, culturally defined, as were the kinds of behavior that led to success. Africans lacked appreciation of the criteria, and their behavior was hardly estimable. They also notably lacked success. Nothing could be simpler, in an Arminian context, than to infer that they lacked the will-power, the virtue, to warrant or deserve salvation.

The second form of rejecting Puritanism proceeded less from intellectual reformulation than from the emotional fervor we associate with the Great Awakening of the 1740s. Remarkable numbers of colonial Americans enthusiastically joined in celebrating a religion of feeling, in sharp contrast to the cerebral persuasions and logic-chopping disputes of their forebears. Revivalism made religious experience accessible to everyone, and appealing to most, permanently transforming American religious life. Emotional religion opened a major phase of the American Revolution, as distinct from the actual War for Independence. The powerful implications of equality from the Great Awakening soon found political expression, coalescing with the natural rights philosophy associated with John Locke, and with the moral sense philosophy, perhaps even more persuasive, stemming from Shaftesbury, Francis Hutcheson, and their followers.

Secular moral sense philosophy contradicted Puritanism, arguing that men are fundamentally virtuous, possessing not only a "sentiment of benevolence," as Hume called it, but a moral faculty or sense which enables them -- without instruction or faith -- to discern moral right and wrong. Again, as with Arminianism, moral sense thought unmistakably suggested individual responsibility for choices. Since you had the moral sense, you had the duty to make choices according to its perceptions. And again, Englishmen were much more likely than Africans to make the choices which led to success, whether one construed success as salvation or as prosperity or achievement. Could it be that Africans lacked will and responsibility, awakened religious sentiment, and a fully developed moral sense as well? The main patterns of religious and moral thought in the Enlightenment all seemed perfectly compatible with assumptions later to be termed racism: the assumptions here termed proto-racism.

No other prominent figure of the Enlightenment illustrates as well as Thomas Jefferson the coming together of an Arminian sense of individual responsibility, moral sense thought, natural rights liberalism, and, at important times, acceptance of the Great Chain of Being. The combination was devastating in its effects on attitudes toward, and beliefs about, Africans. Using the language of Great Chain thinking, with such terms as "Nature's great work," "gradation," and "the department of man," Jefferson carefully reasoned in *Notes on the State of Virginia* that blacks were markedly inferior to whites. Jefferson changed his mind later, as some of his private letters show, but the letters were not published or widely read, while *Notes on Virginia* was revived with fateful timing as part of the 1876 centennial celebration. The work provided valuable support for racists in the turbulent period after the Compromise of 1877 ended Reconstruction. The author of the Declaration of Independence worried about miscegenation, or race mixing, and he thought in the 1780s that desirable racial purity required measures to prevent it. Africans were sometimes even portrayed on the Great Chain of Being as sub-human, a lower species, but more typically as the lowest variety of humanity. In either case, intellectual and behavioral differences appeared significant enough to warrant alarm over "staining" the superior "blood" of whites.

Yet such overtly proto-racist views (Jefferson, of course, would not have recognized the term or the idea "racism") are not the most important aspect of Jefferson's thought with regard to the persistence of racism in America. Another orientation to reality that emerged strongly in the eighteenth century is utilitarian thinking: not just Utilitarianism as a body of more or less systematic thought, but the fundamental tendency to assign value on the basis of utility, or usefulness. This is the style of thinking most often associated with Benjamin Franklin: the practical bent, the fixation on expediency, the preoccupation with what "works," which would eventually find expression as pragmatism and instrumentalism. It is a preference and a mind-set as close to the core of American behavior as any intellectual trait one can identify. But Jefferson illustrates this "lower case" or generic utilitarianism in a different way from Franklin.

Utility, as John Dewey would relentlessly demonstrate, is a standard that gives central importance to means. But it assumes ends. We can assess utility, and assign value on the basis of it, only in terms of some sense of purpose, some end which we identify, whether that end seems more to express the means we adopt or to determine those means. For Jefferson, utility meant contribution to safeguarding life and liberty, and advancing the pursuit of happiness. Like religious thinkers earlier, he faced the problem of reconciling universal moral rights with gradations of earning, willing, and deserving happiness. In Jefferson's Enlightenment mind a political philosophy took shape, which worked wonderfully well for many, but worked to the terrible disadvantage of African-Americans.

1. Jordan, 224, 225, e.g.
2. *Ibid.*, 228.

Five

Human Nature in the Enlightenment

In his introduction to Kant's political writings, Hans Reiss observes that "perhaps the dominant feature" of the Enlightenment is the "growth of self-consciousness, an increasing awareness of the power of man's mind to subject himself and the world to rational analysis."[1] The "himself" part is what is new, and also of course the secularization of self-perception. Freedom for Kant is the power to act in accord with universal natural laws. In John Locke's thinking, the will cannot be free because the object of attention determines how it is to be regarded, making the will a matter of attraction to pleasure and aversion to pain. Enlightenment thinkers generally proceeded on the assumption that they could find out what they had to do, and then they would know what they were free to do. Politically, Kant saw freedom as the exercise of independence, so that it had to come from property to some degree -- as with John Locke and Thomas Jefferson.

All rational beings, Kant says, not only *can* have only one purpose in common, but actually *do* have one in common: happiness. Imperatives, for which Kant is so famous, stem from this purpose, because to will an end is to will the means necessary to achieving it. He contributes in such a major way to the development of liberalism, and through it, individualism, partly because he insists on freedom to pursue happiness, and happiness is subject to infinitely varied interpretations. And that is why *duty*, rather than pure reason, is his necessary guide to action. This is a much maligned idea, often associated with German "authoritarianism." But that association is made by people who do not realize that Kant's idea of duty -- the categorical imperative -- is a version of the Golden Rule: essentially, always to act in such a way that you would welcome or approve having everyone act on the same basis. For example, never treat another human being as a means to an end, but always as an end in him or her self. Never use or coerce people or manipulate or exploit them. It would be difficult to find a more humane statement of moral principle from any thinker, secular or religious. Kant's idea of the absolute sanctity of the individual gave tremendous impetus to individualism, liberalism, and ironically, Romanticism, which he despised.

In interesting relation to Montesquieu, Kant saw justice as "the restriction of each individual's freedom so that it harmonises wih the freedom of everyone else in so far as this is possible within the terms of a general law."[2] His definition of freedom is virtually identical with Provision 4 of the *Declaration of the Rights of Man and the Citizen*, written just four years earlier, in 1789. In this sense he is one of the philosophers who justify both the French Revolution and the rise of liberalism in America.

> Man's *freedom* as a human being . . . [he says] can be
> expressed in the following formula. No-one can compel
> me to be happy in accordance with his conception of the
> welfare of others, for each may seek his happiness in
> whatever way he sees fit, so long as he does not infringe
> upon the freedom of others to pursue a similar end which
> can be reconciled with the freedom of everyone else
> within a similar workable general law -- i.e., he must
> accord to others the same rights as he enjoys himself.[3]

These positions of Kant, the moral imperative and the conception of freedom, are principles at the very heart of the Enlightenment in America as well as in Europe. At the same time, Americans more than anyone else committed themselves to individual responsibility as well as freedom. Confidence in the power of reason and will were truly remarkable in the eighteenth century, and scarcely less in the nineteenth. That optimism which we associate with the Enlightenment, the assumption that individuals can make what they will of their lives, has exerted by far its greatest appeal in America, even to the present. Americans traditionally assumed that if one held principles, one would live by them. Nothing prevented those who took seriously the Enlightenment ideals of moral inviolability and integrity and freedom from implementing them; and indeed they were obliged to do so. America perfectly illustrated Kant's belief in the identification of voluntary action with the exercise of moral freedom or agency. Charles Chauncy, for example, would instantly endorse Kant's principle that action must be autonomous to be moral -- as would any Arminian or libertarian. However, the assertion of will and freedom excluded Afro-Americans, who were not "enlightened," liberal, individualistic or autonomous, and who did not choose or control their lives.

The ultimate expression of Enlightenment liberal individualism is the Declaration of Independence, with its stunningly succinct assertion of universal moral equality and individual rights, and its immediate assertion that governments exist "to secure these rights." John Adams elaborated the same conviction, with echoes of Hutcheson and Bentham, in his *Thoughts on Government* in 1776:

> Upon this point all speculative politicians will agree, that the happiness of society is the end of government, as all divines and moral philosophers will agree that the happiness of the individual is the end of man. From this principle it will follow, that the form of government which communicates ease, comfort, security, or, in one word, happiness, to the greatest number of persons, and in the greatest degree, is the best.

In *The Federalist* (14), James Madison asked,

> Is it not the glory of the people of America, that, whilst they have paid a decent regard to the opinions of former times and other nations, *they have not suffered a blind veneration for antiquity, for custom, or for names, to overrule the suggestions of their own good sense,* the knowledge of their own situation, and the lessons of their own experience? To this manly spirit, posterity will be indebted for the possession, and the world for the example, of the numerous innovations displayed on the American theatre, in favor of private rights and public happiness.

In other words, individual freedom and private rights were sacred, but within the framework of consensus on what was best for most people. The "good sense" of the people would express their "manly spirit" of what would serve their own interests, i.e., their pursuit of happiness. The good sense of the people included innate depravity, of course, as in Adams' quotation from *Ecclesiastes*: "The heart is deceitful above all things, and desperately wicked." One had to be always on guard against rationalization; and Madison, himself trained by John Witherspoon, the successor of Jonathan Edwards, never doubted that self-interest would be served. But the "good sense" of the people also included the universal moral sense, which was to Jefferson as much a part of "the general definition of man" as sight or hearing.

What, then, did the moral sense approve "in favor of private rights and public happiness"?   "The moral sense," Hutcheson had written in words that would echo through generations, "is a general approving attitude toward all acts which will probably produce the greatest happiness of the greatest number." In America, Jefferson propounded both the moral sense doctrine and the utilitarian principle of Hutcheson:

> Some have argued against the existence of a moral sense, by saying that if nature had given us such a sense . . . then nature would also have designated . . . the two sets of actions which are, in themselves . . . virtuous and . . . vicious. Whereas, we find, in fact, that the same actions are deemed virtuous in one country and vicious in another. The answer is, that nature has constituted *utility* to man, the standard and test of virtue. Men living in different countries, under different circumstances, different habits and regimens, may have different utilities; the same act . . . may be useful, and *consequently* virtuous in one country which is injurious and vicious in another differently circumstanced.[4]

In its most basic meaning, utility pervades our habits of thought and is perhaps the most central idea in human experience. We constantly judge what affects us as more or less satisfactory. Our implicit criterion is capacity to satisfy our needs as we perceive them, or usefulness toward our contentment, our happiness. The value of anything is routinely construed as its usefulness in producing satisfaction. But satisfaction is a function of purpose, and utility can be judged, as Jefferson saw, in light of any situation or problem. If the greatest happiness of the greatest number is the collective goal, the most obvious way for me to increase it is to increase my own happiness.

In the eighteenth century, goodness was equated with happiness, and rightness with conducing toward happiness. The pursuit of happiness was also the pursuit of virtue, of meaning in life, of a secular "salvation"; and "good" meant good for attaining happiness, a fundamentally utilitarian definition. Since happiness was equated with virtue, its pursuit was both a right and an obligation. From the later seventeenth century, taking for granted a universal, rational human nature led to a growing assumption of a natural, universal right to pursue happiness, and pleasure. Very early in this pattern, Spinoza asserted that "*absolutely*, everyone is allowed by the highest *right* of nature to do that which *he believes* contributes to his own profit." The Enlightenment developed an inspiring, optimistic conception of human nature as free and basically good, rejecting the helplessness and guilt of the Reformation world-view. Everyone had the moral sense to recognize utility, or interest. What individuals were free to do was to pursue happiness; and that pursuit in itself was basically good because everyone who had healthy and sufficient reason and will could reach the universal goal.

1. Hans Reiss, ed., *Kant's Political Writings* (Cambridge: Cambridge University Press, 1970; trans. H. B. Nisbet), 6.
2. Immanuel Kant, *Foundations of the Metaphysics of Morals* (New York: The Liberal Arts Press, 1959; trans. and intro. Lewis White Beck), 73.
3. *Ibid.*, 74.
4. Thomas Jefferson, letter to Thomas Law, June 13, 1814, emphasis added.

Jefferson's most important political document next to the
Declaration and the statement on religious freedom, was his
famous letter to John Adams dated October 28, 1813, in which he
discusses the society open to virtue and talent. In that letter he argued
for a natural aristocracy meaning rule of the "best," not the
richest. The natural aristocracy Jefferson thought, showed itself by
"virtue and talents" or character and abilities. Those who were most
favored, so to speak, should naturally rise to positions of power and
influence through an open society, for the benefit of the public as well
as for their own appropriate fulfillment. By pursuing their own
happiness, they would serve the general

Six

The Pursuit of Happiness: Utilitarian Individualism

For the persistence of racism, Jefferson's ideas on race are not nearly as important as his mainstream political philosophy. In those ideas about liberty and equality, he reflected not only Hutcheson and Locke, but the Western tradition from Plato. Plato identified happiness as the goal of philosophy. Aristotle then reasoned that the pursuit of happiness was the work of the ethical will toward the greatest possible self-fulfillment, the accomplishment of *sophrosyne* or balance, the condition of being rightly satisfied with oneself. Happiness was personal, the situation of being able to ask yourself, "Have I done as well as could be expected in developing my character and abilities?" and being able to answer yourself honestly, "Yes."

Jefferson's most important political document, next to the the Declaration and the statement on religious freedom, may be his famous letter to John Adams dated October 28, 1813, in which he discusses the society open to virtue and talents. In that letter he argued for a natural aristocracy, aristocracy meaning rule of the "best," not the richest. The natural aristocracy, Jefferson thought, showed itself by "virtue and talents" or character and abilities. Those who were most favored, so to speak, should naturally rise to positions of power and influence through an open society, for the benefit of the public as well as for their own appropriate fulfillment. By pursuing their own happiness, they would serve the general interest: a perfect capitalist process in philosophical and political terms.

The "pursuit" of happiness unmistakably entailed the valuation of whatever led to happiness. What was useful to the individual's fulfillment was valuable. In his natural right to "be himself" the individual American was literally sovereign, subject to no higher authority. As Stow Persons said, considering all the supports for this sense of sovereignty, "Never before or since . . . has a more uncompromising individualism been woven into the fabric of thought."[1] Yet raw egoism repelled people in the eighteenth century as it has since, for various reasons. The people of the Enlightenment still held Puritan ideas of virtue, which would continue for many generations. Their Arminian modification of Calvinism gave them more pride in their virtue, not less. They thought and felt themselves responsible for being what they were, and Hobbes's deterministic concept of human nature was no more appealing to them than Calvin's. The egoistic view had in common with Calvinism the fact that it was unflattering and unattractive, in effect insulting to a free people. Far more than any ancient Greeks, these people could engage the question of Socrates, "How should one live?" The very structure of the question assumed individual responsibility as a point of departure.

The claim of responsibility, painfully drawn from religious experience, was what made possible the enlightened sense of freedom; and what made possible the assumption of individual responsibility was the claim of freedom. These attributes reciprocally implied and reinforced each other. The self-evident truth of natural rights implied natural responsibility in like measure: absolutely. Individual worth and dignity, so hard-won, depended upon individual responsibility; and "perfectibility," the universal human capacity for improvement which was the secular version of Arminian will, made that responsibility as heavy as the freedom was exhilarating. You have the ability to fulfill your potentialities, you have the right to do it, and therefore you have the duty to do it. You could feel the duty to follow your conscience, or moral sense. Your conscience was free, to be sure, and so was your will, your power to follow it. Jonathan Mayhew preached in 1754 from Luke, 12:48, "It is an established maxim of God's equal government that 'Unto whomsoever much is given, of him much shall be required.'" That was a typical emphasis of the time; and an emphasis that left out Africans almost completely. They neither had individual responsibility nor appeared to be prepared to assume it.

Africans were never "prepared" by whites for salvation *as success,* but only for better slavery. The freedom to be good, to do God's will, required a material foundation. In the eighteenth century the small likelihood or even impossibility of a propertyless fellow being *properly* his own man was quite clear. According to the conventional wisdom, as propounded by either Adams or Jefferson, for example, someone whose circumstances made him vulnerable to coercion or manipulation obviously could not be free. Yet he had the right to pursue happiness, to acquire property and to live properly, even if he was hopelessly ill-favored in circumstance. Since he had the right, he had the responsibility to use it. The Arminian extension of will did not introduce a new understanding into the relationship of freedom and responsibility; nor did it invert earlier assumptions about the priority of responsibility. Where responsibility had made freedom possible, freedom was now assumed, and it made responsibility inescapable -- even if the freedom was not usable because of circumstance. The ill-favored of America had "progressed" from being unregenerate because God did not select them for salvation to being failures because of their inherent deficiencies of will and virtue. In the secular, enlightened version, all men were self-evidently entitled to rights of life, liberty and the pursuit of happiness; but those rights did not always come to fruition. Having the right to pursue a goal did not necessarily mean that the goal would be attained. The pursuit of happiness meant the utilitarian pursuit of self-interest: not egoism by name, but rightful and right-full individualism.

How should one live? Responsibly, according to conscience, which implied freedom and dignity -- and the pursuit of self-interest. Several lines of thought fatefully converged, to provide relief from the problem of how to be moral and self-interested at the same time: the Arminian will, the moral sense, natural rights, the liberal doctrine of property, democracy and capitalism. By the end of the eighteenth century, Hobbes had won tacit posthumous acceptance, as far as his psychology was concerned. It was good for people to get what they wanted, and individual pursuit of self-interest was clearly the way to see that most people, the majority, achieved their goal. Competition should be institutionalized for the pursuit of the greatest happiness.

The thinker whose work symbolized the problem of how to reconcile self-interest and moral sense philosophy was Adam Smith. In 1759, seventeen years before he explained capitalism in *The Wealth of Nations,* Smith embraced moral sense philosophy in *The Theory of*

Moral Sentiments. Contrary to later hostile characterizations of him, Smith was deeply concerned for the dignity of individuals, and his principal misgiving about capitalism was that its economic effectiveness could be achieved only at the cost of degrading the workers. (Marx would later say "dehumanizing" them.) This problem was even discussed endlessly in Germany as *Das Adam Smith-Problem.* In America, Smith's ideas were not a problem, but a stroke of perfect genius and an inspiration. His synthesis incorporated individualistic competition, tempered by sympathy for the ill-favored, with equality of moral dignity and entitlement. Social utility, in the form of increasing productivity and prosperity for all, justified the "perverse effect" of degrading labor. The ordinary worker benefited materially from competitive enterprise, but paid the price of being treated as a commodity.

Smith had no illusions about sympathy prevailing over self-interest among the manufacturers and merchants: the benevolent effects of their activities did not depend upon their largeness of spirit. Rather, through the operation of the market's "invisible hand," their avaricious endeavors would yield ancillary fruits for the less enterprising or favored. The wealth of the nation would be the wealth of all its members, as opposed to the wealth of the State under mercantilism. Self-interest was confirmed as morally legitimate, because it inadvertently benefited society as a whole, and therefore the greatest number of its members. In fact, "self-interest was itself a moral principle -- not as lofty as altruism, but, in the mundane affairs of life . . . more reliable and effective."[2]

In Smith's synthesis, egoism became respectable. His famous butcher, brewer and baker provided necessities out of self-regard, but their self-regard showed sympathy, not just rapacious cupidity. In practice, the market would ensure that they recognize fair practices in their own interest as well as in that of their customers. Everyone had to be practically concerned with the approval and disapproval of others. Technical economic achievement aside, Smith's resounding impact came from his integrating of insights from Hobbes and Spinoza with those of Hutcheson. Self-interested, individualistic behavior no longer needed to be condemned, or denied, held in check or apologized for, but simply pursued as natural. Institutionalized competition provided very nicely for the pursuit of happiness -- for those who were able to compete.

In the second paragraph of chapter one of *On the Principles of Morals and Legislation* (1789), Jeremy Bentham defined the utility principle as "that principle which approves or disapproves of every action whatsoever, according to the tendency which it appears to have to augment or diminish the happiness of the party whose interest is in question." Utility, first advanced as a standard for assessing societies and governments, became frankly individualist, and implicitly egoistic. The utility of something to the individual "whose interest is in question" eclipsed in importance the idea of general social utility. It became a moral endorsement of pursuing self-interest. Enchanted figures like Condorcet might reason that such egoism proceeds from false understanding of interest, and that it should be *subordinated* to "true" or "general" interest. But in America, scarcely anyone expected individual interest to be subordinated to anything. It might *coincide* with general or public interest; and Hamilton and Madison exemplify the wisdom of seeking that beneficial situation. But "winners and losers" were required from the outset; and Africans' position as losers had to be justified from the outset.

We often say that individual rights are close to the hearts of Americans, but that racism has damaged our reputation as defenders of individual rights.[3] More accurately, *our own* individual rights are close to our hearts. Our version of "equality" tends to mean "I'm at least as entitled as you are," not "Everyone is equally entitled." Our insistence upon individualism in matters of rights and "deserving" militates especially against the collective and compensatory relief sought by African-Americans, just as it always has against any "class" demands.

Collective conceptions of wants and needs have been perceived as "un-American" in the most literal and historical sense. Our forefathers disclaimed hereditary social position or "status." Before Karl Marx sought the classless society, America already claimed to have it. America simply rejected the idea of class altogether. This claim entailed or required institutionalized competition for position, and that competition had little basis on which to proceed except property. Property, ownership, acquisition became the very foundation of American society. Capitalism became, in the most fundamental way, the religion of America. That is to say, it provided the principal criterion of utilitarian value, the frame of reference in which judgments of importance were made. "What was he *worth*?" people

asked when a man died.   "What were his *effects?*" as indicated in the
real estate note in the newspaper?   These notations represented his
success in pursuing happiness, or his secular American salvation.

An American, as Jefferson representatively defined him, had the
right and the responsibility to hold property, starting with himself.   He
had to be autonomous to be free: he had to possess himself and the
means with which he gained material sustenance.   "God-given talents"
and "natural abilities" came to the fore in the pursuit of happiness, and
the free deserved to be free.   "You can't keep a good man down,"
people used to say; but some men have fatal flaws.   Everyone carried
burdens of varying weight; but, circularly, if you were down you must
not be a "good man" in the fullest sense -- not able to gain by force of
will what is needed to pursue happiness effectively.   What could be
expected if whole categories, whole races were "down," showing
inability to control their lives?

1. Stow Persons, *American Minds* (New York: Holt, Rinehart and Winston,
1958), 77.
2. Gertrude Himmelfarb, *The Idea of Poverty: England in the Early Industrial
Age* (New York: Vintage Books, 1985), 48.
3. See M. F. Ashley Montagu, *Man's Most Dangerous Myth: The Fallacy of
Race* (Cleveland: World Publishing Company, 1964).

Seven

Natural Rights and Self-Evident Truth

Locke's conception of truths that were self-evident to "intuitive reason" drew powerful support in the century following his death in 1704. Thomas Reid succinctly defined self-evident principles as "those no sooner understood than they are believed." Summarizing Locke's formulation, Reid said, "There is no searching for evidence, no weighing of arguments; the proposition is not deduced or inferred from another; it has the light of truth in itself, and has no occasion to borrow from another."[1] The meaning of "self-evident" almost seemed self-evident in the period of the Declaration of Independence; but the application of it in that document presented serious problems, to say the least.

The assertion of self-evident equality among men was weak and uncertain from the beginning. Even now Americans act confused and apologetic when its meaning is questioned, and most seem to think of it as justified, if at all, only by a sort of poetic license. It seems to be an ideal or a rhetorical flourish, perhaps more of a pious ejaculation than a logical claim or description of reality. Its air of unreality is increased in secular times by Jefferson's deistic language: ". . . that all men are *created* equal" and endowed by their *Creator* . . . ." But the equality claimed, first and foremost, was an equality of rights, referring only in a very special way to equality of capacity. The old idea of natural law had gained new life in the seventeenth century, and in the eighteenth it was transformed into something unprecedented. The new "natural rights version of Natural Law [valued] individual prerogatives and satisfactions" and amounted to "an exaltation of human *will* for human ends."[2]   The theory of natural law, established and authoritative, actually *became,* in its most significant form, a theory of natural rights.[3] Its focus on the importance of will is obviously related to the rise of Arminianism as the religious version of Enlightenment in America.

The age of reason needed to justify claims by rational argument. In the mid-seventeenth century Hobbes based equal rights on similarities among men, which were more important than any differences: claims of universal competence which would be endlessly debated.

> Nature hath made men so equall, in the faculties of body, and mind; as that though there bee found one man sometimes manifestly stronger in body, or of quicker mind than another; yet when all is reckoned together, the difference between man, and man, is not so considerable, as that one man can thereupon claim to himself any benefit, to which another may not pretend, as well as he .... And as to the faculties of the mind . . . I find yet a greater equality amongst men, than that of strength;

and "From this equality of ability, ariseth equality of hope in the attaining of our ends." The author of *Leviathan* (1651) has generally been associated in America with tyranny and absolutism, because he thought that only a strong state could make men acknowledge one another's fundamental equality and natural rights. In fact Hobbes's analysis, anticipating Locke's fuller doctrine of self-evident truth, set the direction that led to Jefferson's Declaration.

The problem with the Declaration is confusion of intuitive reason with moral sense, or blurring of the difference between them. This kind of confusion, noted by Hume, presents claims of moral rightness as claims of truth. For example, Thomas Skidmore wrote in 1829, "Rights are like moral *truths,* capable of being understood alike by all men; -- as much so, as the demonstrations of Euclid."[4] The first part of the statement may give no trouble: rights may be like self-evident truths *in that* they are as readily understandable. The second part, however, suggests something about *how* rights are understandable, i.e., in the same way that geometry is, by reason. Skidmore's assertion is typical of natural rights claims, following the Declaration. This type of claim appeals to universal reason, saying "It is true that there are rights derived from a common human nature"; and then, "That common human nature includes the capacity to *understand* these rights: i.e., reason." But the kind of reasoning ability involved in geometry is not by any means universally or equally distributed, so it is not a very effective basis for claiming equal rights. Even if it were equally distributed, such reasoning ability does not readily apply to rights.

Even Locke himself, the formulator of intuitive reason, was very close to the moral sense position without stating it: that is, that everyone has a moral faculty or moral sense, a capacity to recognize right and wrong, justice and injustice. The proposition that all men are created equal is a moral proposition. If it is stated that "All men are created equal in their moral entitlements, and this right should be respected," then we clearly have a question of what is right, for the moral sense to assess, and not a question of what is descriptively true, to satisfy a universal reasoning capacity. But such a moral claim can be answered, "Oh, really? Who says so?"; so Jefferson said, "We hold these *truths* . . ." instead of "We advance these claims . . ." *The rights themselves are not "true," but their validity in terms of justice is asserted to be unquestionable*, and *reasons* are marshalled to support this working of the moral sense. As Jonathan Mayhew said in a 1754 sermon, equality has to be construed as fairness if it is to make any sense at all.

Hobbes had gotten himself into the notorious conundrum of trying to infer what ought to be from what is observed to be, and nobody in succeeding centuries would entirely escape it. But the moral sense doctrine seemed to offer a way out of it, in two ways. First, it flatly claimed that all men who are not deranged have the capacity to judge right and wrong -- and are equal in that way. As Reid put it, the "first principles of morals, into which all moral reasoning must be resolved, are perceived intuitively, and in a manner more analogous to the perceptions of sense than to the conclusions of demonstrative reasoning." Second, the moral sense was a way of dealing with moral questions on the basis of observed behavior, in that we can perceive the "self-evident" *rightness* of certain entitlements -- which are also universal, and therefore equal. In sum, all men are equal in possession of the entitlements the moral sense identifies as right and just. We are equal in the active sense of having the capacity to judge, and in the passive sense of having rights revealed by that capacity.

Most arguments for equality have not been very convincing to Americans because they have not been clear as to what they meant.[5] The difficulty in the Declaration lies largely in the word "truths." By this time Locke's intuitive reason had been blurred into moral sense doctrine, which he himself had even used at times. Jefferson firmly held the moral sense position. His case for natural rights to liberty and equality would have been clearer if he had said "We hold these *judgments*"; but of course it was almost irresistible to make the strongest possible case for a deeply felt conviction, by claiming undeniable *truth* for it, by reason. Truth is a much more definite, emphatic word than "judgment." Jefferson himself said repeatedly that the most we can hope for in moral matters is certitude, the feeling of certainty; but he had utmost confidence in the moral sense, and in its judgments sharing the *nature* of truth revealed by reason. The problem is that moral judgments about what men are entitled to are not at all analogous to the demonstrations of geometry, those favorite illustrations of self-evident truth.

The term "self-evident" instantly brings Locke to mind, and one thinks of "intuitive reason," Locke's idea; but the claim of natural rights in 1776, if not in 1690, was not really made as a truth claim to intuitive reason. It was a rightness claim, made to the moral sense, with the compelling appeal of truth. For us, Jefferson used the wrong word, or a confusing word. He had no doubt about what he meant, and the word "truth" came more easily then than it does now. Even when the words are the same, it is not safe to assume that because Jefferson admired Locke and followed his thinking in some ways, that he reasoned in 1776 just as Locke did in 1690 or earlier.

The confusion came about in a way that is easily understood. Both intuitive reason and the moral sense were presented as natural and universal capacities for "direct and immediate perception" of "right" positions: right-as-correct, and right-as-moral, respectively. Truth and morality might not be the same, but they are inextricably bound together, and were then seen as alike in being irrefutable. Both capacities for "knowing" imply both equality and the boundless natural worth and dignity of the individual. In fact, Locke had seen the egalitarian implications of intuitive reason; and the moral sense was even more egalitarian because it was a feeling. It is much easier to claim a universal equality of feeling than of any form of reason.

Gilbert Tennent explained in his preaching, at the outset of the Great Awakening, that education and knowledge gave no authority or right to prescribe in moral matters. David Hume wrote, "It appears evident that the ultimate ends of human actions can never, in any case, be accounted for by <u>reason</u>, but recommend themselves entirely to the sentiments and affections of mankind, without any dependance on the intellectual faculties." Jonathan Edwards advanced the view that an unlettered person could see the loveliness of God more readily than a learned person could. The great colonial legal thinker, James Wilson, agreed that "education plays virtually no part in the development of morality, a powerfully scientific or logical mind" not being necessary to learning the "truths that should guide our behavior . . . ." John Wise argued in his best-selling 1717 tract that man "is a creature of a very noble character"; and moral sense philosophy expressed that good side of our very nature.

When Jefferson's young nephew, Peter Carr, wrote to him in 1787 about what he proposed to study during the coming college year, Jefferson replied:

Moral philosophy. I think it lost time to attend lectures in this branch. He who made us would have been a pitiful bungler if he had made the rules of our moral conduct a matter of science ... [or systematic knowledge arrived at through reason]. For one man of science, there are thousands who are not. What would have become of them? Man was destined for society . . . . He was endowed with a sense of right and wrong merely relative to this. This sense is as much a part of his nature as the sense of hearing, seeing, feeling; it is the true foundation of morality . . . . The moral sense, or conscience, is as much a part of man as his leg or arm. It is given to all human beings in a stronger or weaker degree, as force of members is given them in a greater or less degree. It may be strengthened by exercise, as may any particular limb of the body. This sense is submitted indeed in some degree to the guidance of reason; but it is a small stock [of reason] which is required for this: even a less one than what we call Common Sense. State a moral case to a ploughman and a professor. The former will decide it as well, and often better than the latter, because he has not been led astray by artificial rules.

The moral sense gave to everyone a basis for self-respect, and in America any man could sensibly think he was as "good" as any other, as much entitled to pursue happiness, because he had the same rights and was just as capable of identifying right and wrong. The rights to liberty and the pursuit of self-interest were equal because they were *absolute*: a word Americans are not generally fond of, but which is entailed by the notion of natural rights. Yet the moral sense, like intuitive reason, revealed itself in conduct, and particularly in self-reliance, personal responsibility and material self-sufficiency. The lack of self-reliance was *prima facie* evidence of a lack or weakness of either or both capacities; and if universal human *capacities* were absent, universal human *rights* might be thought not to apply. Ideas of truth and rights that supported the worth and dignity of man in general could be construed as *reasons* for challenging or denying the full humanity of Africans. What worked for the greatest happiness of the greatest number could also be used to assert the innate inferiority of others; and it was.

1. Thomas Reid, *Essay on the Intellectual Powers of Man* (Edinborough: 1785), VI, Chap. IV, 555.
2. Lester G. Crocker, *Nature and Culture: Ethical Thought in the French Enlightenment* (Baltimore: The Johns Hopkins University Press, 1963), 12, 13, emphasis added.
3. *Ibid.*, 15.
4. See J. R. Pole, *The Pursuit of Equality in American History* (Berkeley: University of California Press, 1978), 126.
5. See Henry Alonzo Myers, *Are Men Equal?* (Ithaca: Cornell University Press, 1959), 67, e.g.

Eight

Equality of Opportunity as an Ideal

God's Will became Nature, and America after the Enlightenment would ostensibly have no Elect and no predestination. But natural rights themselves predestined the "election" of white over black. Racism was the most "natural" disposition imaginable. The natural right to the pursuit of happiness was a right to be unequal, to be privileged, to assert and enjoy inequality. Jefferson's idea of the open society hinged upon "equality of opportunity," and that concept has been the mainspring of tremendous competitive achievements. However, it has little to do with equality as that term is customarily used with regard to class -- or to a category like African-Americans. Grammar here becomes all-important. In America we talk about a self-evident *moral right to equal opportunity* and an *equal moral right to* (unspecified) *opportunity* as if they were the same. In one case "equal" modifies "opportunity" and in the other case it modifies "right." What is meant by Jefferson's prototypical American thought is an equal *right* to whatever opportunity you find, not an equal opportunity. Natural rights philosophy merely replaced the "elect" of Puritanism with people who enjoy (divine favor) "natural gifts" of "virtue and talents." Africans were excluded, since they were obviously not virtuous or talented, as measured by success; and an explanation for their exclusion became more and more essential if their profitable exploitation was to continue.

Individual liberty was a primary focus of interest from ancient times, accentuated by German and English ideas of sovereignty and autonomy. The rise of capitalism transformed the mesne, the serf and the peasant into a journeyman, a man who was paid by the *jour* on a contract basis.   European liberalism slowly developed with the throwing off of religious dictatorship, and it developed on the foundation of capitalism: contract labor.   American history is inconceivable without the separation of church and state, and without the assumption that individual liberty is based on property. Jefferson, like Locke, assumed that status meant real estate, what is proper: that what is proper to freedom is property.   Only in economic self-sufficiency or independence could an individual be sure of political freedom to say or do as he wished.   Anyone who owed money or depended upon another for his livelihood was vulnerable to force or manipulation, and was not "his own man" in his opinions or actions. Hence the yeoman farmer was Jefferson's ideal citizen, drawing everything needed by his family from his own land, a "freeholder" in more ways than one.   The idea of the freeholder is very old, captured in the surname "Franklin"; but America launched a special love affair with it.   This love affair with property as a necessary condition for liberty included no regard for the African-American, who was typically propertyless and evidently not free or "equal."

Equality in America meant the equal treatment of natural equals, favored by God or Nature, in the sense that they could use equal opportunity to demonstrate their natural differences of "gifts" or circumstances: in short, equal opportunity to be unequal in condition. This idea of equality made no provision for equal treatment of any group or category less favored than those who framed it, except eventually to assure them that they had an equal *individual right* to compete for advantage.   It has always been the right that is equal, not the opportunity.   Even if that distinction is not recognized, its application has to be rationalized; and the prevailing rationalization is simply that those who succeed are those who deserve to succeed. Those who succeed provide the rationalization that prevails, and it has not been designed to accommodate African-Americans.   The unsuccessful must necessarily be undeserving, for the successful to be deserving; and lack of success became a strong indication of inferiority. Mainstream American political thought practically insisted that racism take shape.

Actually the idea of equality of opportunity implicitly informed Protestant thought, and perhaps Catholic as well, from Melanchthon's work in the sixteenth century. Rich and powerful people have, after all, always sought ways of thinking that justified their positions. Locke gave the idea marvelous endorsement when he argued so skillfully that each individual is entitled to what his industry has created, right at the time when capitalism, albeit still without a name, was burgeoning. Capital was not well understood. The question would persist, as to what property was "created" by individual industry, and what by social circumstances. In any case, property became inseparable from liberty. In the age of individualism, say from the eighteenth century to now, property is generally assumed to be what justice is mainly about.

One can easily imagine a nineteenth-century conversation about equality, with allowances for custom and language, running like this:

Mary: What happened to the natural right to equality that Jefferson wrote about? I don't see much evidence of it.

John: Nothing happened to it. Everyone has an equal natural right to pursue happiness, just as he said.

Mary: But rights seem empty if we lack the possibility of using them.

John: The right is equal, but the happiness isn't. Happiness is obviously not uniformly distributed, but the right to pursue it is, and it *can* be used.

Mary: If liberty depends on property, which is necessary to happiness, doesn't an equal right to pursue happiness require equal property in some sense?

John: No. The entitlement is *an equal moral right to opportunity, not a moral right to equal opportunity.* Circumstances vary.

Mary: I thought we were talking about establishing the right to equality of opportunity.

John: We have established it. It means that everyone has the same right to opportunity, not a right to the *same* opportunity.

Mary: So equal opportunity can be said to exist in even the most unequal circumstances?

John: Not equal opportunity, equality of opportunity: equality of the right to pursue happiness, not equal probability of attaining it.

Mary: I remember the Calvinists, Jonathan Edwards in fact, saying that
we are free to act as we choose, but of course we can't choose
choices that are not possible. For example, what we don't know
about as a possibility is not a possibility for us, because we don't
know about it. In that sense Bacon was right, knowledge is
power. So our choices are determined in advance by what we
know, what we understand to be possible, and what is in fact
possible in our situations. If I have to spend my life over a tub
and a scrub-board, what do I have the opportunity to
understand? The Puritans said men are unequal, some destined
for happy endings, but most not. I thought we got rid of that
kind of inequality, and were really approaching universal
human rights.

John: We did get rid of that kind of inequality, and all the resignation
and despair that went with it. This is the nineteenth century, for
God's sake, and Edwards has been gone for years! If you want to
talk Puritan ideas, look at Chauncy. His way is the way we want
to be equal. We are equal in all having conscience, and you
women have that especially; but what Chauncy shows us is our
equality of opportunity to *will*, to determine our own lives.
That's Puritan teaching a man can live with: no predestination
nonsense, but the power of your will, and your responsibility to
use it. Equality is not uniformity, it's the diversity of Nature
according to God's will. Even Edwards, to say nothing of
Chauncy or Mayhew, said there must be contrast or the world is
meaningless. "It's beautiful that sin exists and sin is punished,"
or something of the sort. A moral universe is a universe of
blind justice, blind to artificial ideas. We live in a world of
novelty, genuine chance. End results are not always destined --
including our success or failure in the pursuit of happiness. All
we know is that we are free to try. We have the equal right to do
the best we can: that's equality of opportunity!

Mary: I'm sure it's a blessing to have *some* kind of equality, but this is
not very comforting.

***

Our "class" differences, like our similarities, were identified by
reason, but they were not essentially differences *of* reason, not

intellectual. Everyone had the intuitive capacity to grasp self-evident truths as well as the moral sense to perceive right and wrong. Some also had virtues of character which, like the divine light or saving faith in earlier times, enabled them to know what was good for them, to know the good, to pursue happiness effectively. What made them different was as mysterious as God's ways had been earlier, but their difference took the shape of will, perseverance in virtue, and a proper sense of direction. Noah Webster summarized in 1793 how Americans were equal in their rights, noting also what would make them unequal in position. "Here every man finds employment, and the road is open for the poorest citizen to amass wealth by labor and economy, and by his talent and virtue to raise himself to the highest office of the State."

This was never a broadly applicable description of reality, obviously, but it has been a description of a real goal and a pervasive American faith: faith in the individualistic equality of opportunity, not in equal opportunity. The opportunity to which African-Americans enjoyed an equal right tended to be minimal opportunity. Their lack of progress was, however, generally attributed to their failure to use something that never existed and was never even widely sought in America: *equal* opportunity. There is a great deal to be said for the contention that the ideal of equality of opportunity is what made America flourish, and enabled most Americans to "get ahead." Again, something useful for most Americans also supported most Americans' racism.

No thoughtful person was ever consistently convinced of free will "as opposed to" determinism, or conversely. This seemed a classic case of false dichotomy or artificially "binary" thinking. The real question was one of emphasis, not exclusion. Jefferson had the characteristic Enlightenment confidence in will, that ebullient optimism about self-determination; but he also flirted with environmental determinism. In fact, Enlightenment thought generally acknowledged the idea of formative influences, as Jefferson's ideas and actions regarding education abundantly demonstrate. If people could not be changed by environment, why should we be concerned at all about education? In an interesting way, Jefferson anticipated Lincoln with regard to African-Americans. Both men thought optimistically about the possibilities of improvement or "perfectibility." But Jefferson, through most of his active life, agreed with his friend Lord Kames, David Hume's cousin, that there might be species or varieties of men analogous with species of dogs, for example.

He was confused, confined like all of us within the understandings of a time.

Jefferson and Kames were proto-scientific racists. They were pre-scientific but attempting a scientific approach. When that scientific approach took more definite shape, it fell far short of modern standards with regard to rigor of thought. Environmental determinism held limited appeal to the mind of the Enlightenment, which was fixed on taxonomy and gradation, and still confronted official social stratification as a fact of life. The limit of its appeal was, in fact, class. Adams could argue effectively that the natural aristocrats were to be found chiefly among the actual plutocrats: Who else had the leisure and resources to establish himself among "the best"? Obviously a man who had to spend his life regarding the rear end of a mule could not reach some elevated Aristotelian *entelechy* or level of becoming. Only those with favored environment could fully realize their potentialities. So environmental determinism was well acknowledged in Enlightenment thought; but not in a way conducive to sympathy for the oppressed.

The question of the day was, "Could the African be a dark-complected Englishman if his environment were improved?" The answer was, "No." Still, Jefferson thought, by his later years, that the situation of blacks was improving rapidly. In fact it was worsening. Environmental determinism did not satisfy America's need for justification of radically different treatment for African-Americans. Their exclusion from even the cruelly deceptive "equality of opportunity" was so drastic that it required a different kind of determinism to explain. The new taxonomic "science" of biology, entirely outside physics, came to the fore in meeting that need.

Nine

Liberal Individualism and Equality

Liberalism's ideology of freedom as the right to act on interest, sanctified by religion, philosophy and economics, provided a matrix for individualism. Individualism itself is implicitly but not explicitly political, in that its concerns with self-realization, self-expression, and "pagan self-assertion," in J. S. Mill's phrase, imply the conception of self as prior to any social arrangements in both time and importance. It assumes that politics begins with the fact of individuated interest. Rational self-interest was the most civic posture liberalism was capable of adopting, the most political goal in terms of which it could take a navigational fix. Liberalism was the logical and ideological expression of that interest, what Clinton Rossiter called "equality of self-reliance."[1]

John Stuart Mill summarized the concatenation when he asserted, "The only freedom which deserves the name is that of pursuing our own good in our own way." This is what Isaiah Berlin called "negative" or "natural" freedom, freedom to do as you wish, insofar as you are able to carry out your wishes. (Inability to do what you want to do is an absence of *freedom* only if you are unable because prevented by human agency.) Berlin suggested that Mill "confuses two distinct notions," and that with "the 'negative' conception of liberty in its classic form" he saw all coercion as bad and non-interference as good.[2] For African-Americans, national "non-interference" *meant* state, local and "private" economic and social coercion.

The idea of negative freedom implies positive freedom, the freedom to act by choice, as opposed to freedom from restraint or constraint. Berlin distills this obverse: "I wish to be the instrument of my own, not other men's, acts of will. I wish to be a subject, not an object; to be moved by reasons, by conscious purposes which are my own, not by causes which affect me, as it were, from the outside."[3] Discreteness and priority of the individual implicitly inform the liberal stance, whether considered as negative or positive. Carl L. Becker, pondering the same approach to individual freedom some years earlier than Berlin, wrote: "The distinction seems to me a superficial one, since any liberty to do anything implies a freedom from interference with that doing, and any freedom from something implies a liberty to do what the doer might otherwise be prevented from doing."[4] But the difference is nonetheless real, between freedom as being left alone, not interfered with, and freedom as being enabled to act, having what William James would call "live options" opened up for choice.

Individualism considered "purely," for the sake of trying to discover its implications in relation to other concepts, implied nothing at all about how the interests of the individual should or could be served. It assumed, first, that one should be let alone, and that that makes acceptable only the inescapable minimum of power over individuals, no matter what agency is exercising power. Realistically, this would seem to suggest the desirability of democracy, since we live in a world of pushing and tugging, and maximum protection of individual rights requires or includes maximum opportunity for individuals to participate in whatever arrangements are made, affecting their lives. Unhappily for minorities, that maximum opportunity was translated into maximum *number* of participants, populism of some sort, and the individual rights protected became identifiable as the rights *perceived and desired by a majority*. In addition to freedom of action the individual needed a share of power to protect freedom of action, and to define what freedom of action would be protected.

Berlin contends that such terms as "economic freedom" and its counterpart, "economic slavery" are misnomers, and they are of dubious utility except for arousing emotions. But they do excite people, because they express actual experiences of aspiration and frustration related to freedom, even by Berlin's criterion, that the word must refer only to human interference, and not to limitations of capacity to fulfill our wishes. After all, our limitations of "capacity" are largely imposed by human agency, generally in some collective, institutionalized form. Our nutrition, health, leisure, education and so on are not set by "Act of God" or "Nature," so much as by human contrivance. Prosperity and poverty are not divinely ordained but provided by the kind of human decision that allocates percentages of resources to military expenditures or health care.

The word individualism, while used by Jefferson in 1814, and in France as early as 1826, arrived to stay with Henry Reeve's translation of de Tocqueville's *Democracy in America* (1840). By that time individualism exemplified the Marxist concept of contradiction: in some ways it required democracy, or political egalitarianism, but was apparently not reconcilable with it; and American society by that time already required individualism of a sort irreconcilable with some of its own principal doctrines of natural rights. The protection of individual liberty required increasingly egalitarian political participation, but that meant that the view of liberty to be protected would increasingly be the view of majorities, the liberties acceptable and useful to the masses, and to the powerful whom they approved or accepted. The nation seemed to have achieved freedom to be conventional; and one of its conventions was insisting upon racial superiority and "free" competition.

The Founding Fathers, even including Jefferson, regarded democracy skeptically, apprehensively, if not with outright hostility. As has often been noted, they feared "tyranny of the majority," that simple interpretation of democracy as majority rule without safeguards for minorities, or for atypical, unpopular interests. Our mountainous literature on the subject is best exemplified in *The Federalist*, and nowhere better than in Number 10, where Madison examines factions or interest groups, including those particularly dangerous ones constituting majorities. Jefferson's fear of propertyless masses of people vulnerable to manipulation, coercion or demagoguery, which he associated with Hamilton's vision of an urban, industrial society, resembled the prevailing British mistrust of those who lacked a "stake in society." To qualify for participation in public affairs, one should have a personal interest in maintaining and defending the system: property, which was proper. Human nature being self-interested, reliable performance in the public interest was assured only when self-interest coincided with the general welfare, as perceived by those with the greatest "stake" in society. The ease of gaining property in America assured a broad base for democracy; and yet liberalism, initially associated with welcoming and advocating change, remained economically and socially conservative, protecting what had been established against mounting pressures toward any egalitarianism more concrete than natural law or the moral sense suggested.

Natural law, moral law, natural rights, moral sense, Arminian will, utilitarian thinking and romanticism, all held ambiguous implications with regard to equality. Abstractly, philosophically, they suggested equality; but politically and practically they supported privilege. Liberalism's inherent individualism militated against the material treatment of all men as equals, because the worth and dignity of the individual, the very foundations of self-respect, depended so strongly upon *deserving*, being virtuous, proper and propertied. In secular America, the reverberations of hierarchical Calvinist ideas, the election of God's chosen, were more audible than their passive Lutheran counterparts, based on the equal value to God of fulfilling even the humblest duties.

Paradoxically, perhaps, the society that set out deliberately to erase and preclude distinctions of caste and class grew as friendly as the traditional cultures of Europe to material inequality, and would become more so than many. The difference and the justification for it were that in America inequality was seen to stem from differences of "merit," "virtue and talents," so that individuals presumably got what they earned and deserved for what they did, rather than what they were born to get. Old Europe had its secular predestination, success and position determined in advance by birth and wealth; and America kept its own version based on the liberal faith in rewarding individual performance, as if the circumstances of life either had nothing to do with the development of individuals, or were themselves somehow deserved. If there were differences of deserving among categories of people, they would show in the performance of individuals.

All these ideas, beliefs and attitudes implied equality in some ways and inequality in others. Individualism gathered together the anti-egalitarian implications and associated them with liberalism in the name of Freedom for Most People to Compete. But much more than political or civil freedom was involved in an orientation to reality that centered on self-direction, self-realization, and self-expression. Isaiah Berlin remarks that the "lack of freedom about which a man . . . complains amounts, as often as not, to the lack of proper recognition."

In other words, when people yearn for freedom they may not be seeking what Mill would assume, namely security from coercion, or space within which they are legally accountable to nobody for their actions. Equally, one may not be seeking a rational plan for social life. What people most seek is to avoid being ignored as individuals. They want recognition of the uniqueness they feel and claim, rather than being treated as members of some featureless amalgam like a "race," or statistical units without identifiable, specific characteristics of their own.

Berlin thinks "freedom" means to most of us not so much equality of legal rights, or even liberty to do as we wish (although we want these also), as a condition in which we can feel that we are responsible agents whose wills are taken into consideration. "This is a . . . desire to be understood and recognized . . . ." What people generally want, he says, is "simply recognition . . . as an independent source of human activity, as an entity with a will of its own . . . and not to be ruled, educated, guided, with however light a hand, as being not quite fully human, and therefore not quite fully free." As Kant maintained, paternalism is "despotic . . . because it is an insult to my conception of myself as a human being, determined to make my own life in accordance with my own (not necessarily rational or benevolent) purposes, and, above all, entitled to be recognized as such by others."[5] And so, Berlin writes, "it is not with liberty in either the 'negative' or the 'positive' senses of the word, that this desire for status and recognition can easily be identified. It is something no less profoundly needed and passionately fought for by human beings -- it is something akin to, but not itself, freedom . . . ."[6] The need for acknowledgement of everyone's identity and worth was fundamental; but its *denial* was precisely what industrialization and the accompanying liberal competitive views exacted as a price for material progress.

In America the desire to be an independent agent met only liberal individualism's version of equality: the equal moral right to unspecified theoretical opportunity. African-Americans, having been treated as a class, needed to be categorically provided concrete equality of treatment before liberal equality of opportunity could be of much use to them. But the culture of liberal individualism included no provision for providing anything categorically, except rewards to categories of winners.

Freedom in the form of being an "independent agent" assumes the atomistic position of Georg Simmel, that ". . . it is certain in the last analysis only individuals exist." As Santayana put it, "Individualism is in a sense the only possible ideal; for whatever social order may be most valuable can be valuable only for its effect upon conscious individuals . . . . It would be a gross and pedantic superstition to venerate any society in itself, apart from the safety, breadth, or sweetness which it lent to individual happiness."[7] *Whose* individual happiness? In America, that of the person who would claim it and take it, in the spirit of Romantic individualism. Emerson could say, "There is properly no history: only biography." The same spirit shows in Whitman:

> *It is not the earth, it is not America, who is so great,*
> *It is I who am great, or to be great -- it is up to you up there*
>   *or anyone;*
> *It is to walk rapidly through civilizations, governments,*
>   *theories,*
> *Through poems, pageants, shows, to form great individuals.*
>
> *Underneath all, individuals!*
> *I swear nothing is good to me now that ignores individuals.*

One aspect of the tragedy of African-American experience is that because they were originally and for a very long time treated collectively, they needed to be treated collectively a step further before they could benefit from such American individualism. But the individualist mainstream culture included little or no possibility for deliberate collective treatment of anybody. Every mind-set of the culture militated against "favoring" any category of people except the successful, who were already favored by God or nature. Liberalism characteristically took the view that the freedom of the individual to pursue his own good in his own way is best secured by a minimum of interference. It assumed as its goal not the good of the entire society, considered whole, but the freedom of the individual -- because the functional individual must be already able and willing to pursue rational interests. Liberalism's distinctive posture took social organization of every kind as a tool or medium for protecting, extending, and expressing individual needs, rights, and desires. The individualist does not define himself as a member of any group or category except voluntarily and provisionally, for advantage or convenience. Hence any sense of duty or obligation to conform can only be utilitarian in the egoistic sense. If individuals were not functional or competitive, there had to be either something deficient about a group or category to which they belonged, or about their own virtues and talents. Either way they were deficient and undeserving.

Nineteenth-century liberals accurately perceived that the "positive" liberty sought by Rousseau, for example, could demolish their most prized "negative" liberties. They pointed out that "The sovereignty of the people could easily destroy that of individuals." In Mill's memorable expression, such "democratic" thinking led, not to government of "each by himself," but of "each by the rest": essentially the same point that Madison and Tocqueville had made. Isaiah Berlin reflects, ". . . it is clear that [individual liberty] has little to hope for from the rule of majorities; democracy as such is logically uncommitted to it, and historically has failed to protect it . . . ."[8] What democracy in America did protect was the kind of "negative" liberty which most people who were satisfied, or who expected to be reasonably satisfied, wanted. The assumptions of liberal individualism coincided neatly with those regarding race.

The central idea of contract (also treated as "compact" and "covenant") gave dignity and importance to the individual capable of responsible action. In that sense contract elevated everyone and lent impetus to the egalitarian current of individualism. But in practice contract was more an economic idea than a political or moral one. Capitalism, after all, long antedated democratic thought as it appeared in America. Ancient Roman law was strongly based on personal property. In the societies of England and America, ever more devoted to private property even as the appeal of natural rights spread and the demand for liberty intensified, the idea of contract welded liberty to private property, and both to anti-egalitarian individualism. Liberalism took the tack of hierarchical, materialistic individualism in America, all the time asserting equal and universal moral rights to "opportunity." Americans sought individual fulfillment through moral improvement, economic progress, national greatness, and racial destiny, putting race, nation, economy and religion at the service of individual interest. They wanted both merit and equality, but they were much more fond of "the deserving individual" than of universal deserving. Liberal individualism's conceptions of equality as responsibility, and of blame for "failure," worked to make racism plausible and defensible as well as practically appealing.

1. Clinton Rossiter, *Conservatism in America* (Cambridge, Mass.:   Harvard University Press, 1982), 133.
2. Isaiah Berlin, *Two Concepts of Liberalism* (London: Oxford University Press, 1958), 7, 11, 12.
3. *Ibid.*, 16.
4. Carl L. Becker, *Freedom and Responsibility in the American Way of Life* (New York: Vintage Books, 1958), 6, 7.
5. Kant, *Political Writings*, 40-41.
6. Berlin, 43.
7. George Santayana, "Reason in Society," *The Life of Reason* (New York: Collier Books, 1962), 53.
8. Berlin, 48-50.

Ten

The Yeoman Ideal and the Frontier

David Potter remarks that "the tendency to place a premium upon individual self-reliance was no doubt well developed long before the cult of the American as an individualist crystallized in a conceptual form. But it did crystallize, and it took on almost its classic formulation in the thought of Thomas Jefferson." Jefferson provided no description of a "national character," Potter says, but he did "erect a model" for one: "and the model ultimately had more influence than a description could ever have exercised. The model American was a plain, straightforward agrarian democrat, an individualist in his desire for freedom for himself, and an idealist in his desire for equality for all men."[1] No doubt Potter is justified in the assumption that individualism "must have gained greater strength . . . from the reflection that if all men were equal, a man might as well form his own convictions as accept the convictions of someone no better than himself":[2] a reflection quite clear in the New England looking glass of the Transcendentalists. But Jefferson also believed in equal moral entitlement to liberty and the pursuit of happiness, an equal right to unequal opportunity, not a right to equal opportunity. He believed in equality of moral sense, that non-reasoning faculty; but certainly not in the equal ability of each man to "form his own convictions" in any way that involved thinking more than sensing.

If there is a characteristic American insistence on equality, it asserts negatively and defensively that I have as much right as any man to form and express opinions and interests; not that all opinions and interests are created equal. It is the right to create them that is equal, not the opinions or interests. This conception of equality implies and conduces toward fragmentation and antagonism more than cooperation and recognition of common interests as goods in themselves. To say that the desire for freedom is coupled with an idealistic desire for equality is misleading, unless we note that the kind of equality implied by individualism is atomistic, an aggressive assertion of self rather than a concession to others because they are right or have rights. Its natural phrasing is "I'm as good as you are," not "You're as good as I am." It implies a certain belligerency, an expectation of legitimate claims denied, or of illegitimate claims advanced by others. Given Jefferson's time and circumstances especially, that is easy enough to understand, but it is also important to note. Jefferson's individualism is overwhelmingly of the "negative" type, and efforts to make of it a primarily social or fraternal disposition yield no better results than they do with John Stuart Mill's.

Jefferson's attitude toward governments makes clear his perception of the roles of institutions and organizations in general: it is pure liberalism, and perfectly utilitarian from the point of view of the separate, autonomous individual. Governments are to be rejected if or when they fail to serve satisfactorily the purposes of free individuals. Their only justification or excuse for being is that they enable and facilitate the exercise of individual rights and wishes. Jefferson was ever so much better suited to writing declarations than constitutions. He had to flog his mind into paying attention to the construction of that necessary evil, and to the very considerable extent that he did so, he was motivated most by concern that government not have any more than the unavoidable minimum of power for encroaching upon individual prerogatives. The nation had to be strong against the Napoleonic and dangerous outside world. It would be an "empire for liberty," but it was most emphatically *for liberty*, and that meant the personal, individual liberty of its citizens to do as they wished, insofar as circumstances permitted.

The prevailing Jeffersonian conception of the individual as separate, unique, and autonomous -- romantic, utilitarian, focusing on will, rights, and personal traits -- simply opposed self-definition as member of society or of any order. It is egoistic and enterprising, and does not easily lend itself to conciliation with the kind of equality implicit in the idea of community. This is not to say that Americans have not generally found it convenient and advantageous to think of themselves as members of society, societies, and communities. Obviously they have: but only on a secondary or superficial level of definition, and for individual, utilitarian ends. The fundamental definition of self is held back, in reserve, and commitment to common denominators does not extend to full self-identification in terms of them. Our commitments are generally instrumental, discrete, provisional and contingent. No idealism has moved us for long or in numbers to define ourselves in terms of any meta-individual Forms, permanent and immutable or otherwise. And there has never been much place in a Jeffersonian scheme of things for people whose circumstances do not permit them to be autonomous and self-reliant. This perception of reality identifies lack of success with deficiency, individually and collectively.

Jefferson's "plain, straightforward democrat" chiefly expresses his version of democracy in resisting representation of collective interests he does not see as coincident with his own wishes. He believes in the right of everyone, but especially himself, to make his wants known and to pursue what he wants, unhindered. His is a competitive society more than a cooperative one, and he cooperates for the sake of competitive advantage. As Bliss Perry puts it, "The religion and philosophy of the Puritans were in this respect at one with the gospel of the frontier. It was the principle of 'every man for himself'; solitary confrontation of his God, solitary struggle with the wilderness . . . . the sternest school of self-reliance, from babyhood to the grave, that human society is ever likely to witness."[3] Those who did not flourish in this stern school had something wrong with them, and racism provided a plausible, convenient explanation of what was wrong with many.

If the rugged characterization exaggerates, it nonetheless presents an image close to the heart of American folklore. The frontier of the New World, gradually receding inward from the Atlantic coast, has seemed to account for an American sense of differentness, identity, as in the powerfully appealing 1893 thesis of Frederick Jackson Turner.

> The American intellect owes its striking characteristics to the frontier. That coarseness and strength, combined with acuteness and acquisitiveness; that practical inventive turn of mind, quick to find expedients; that masterful grasp of material things, lacking in the artistic but

powerful to effect great ends; that restless, nervous energy; that dominant individualism, working for good and evil; and withal, that buoyancy and exuberance which comes from freedom -- these are the traits of the frontier, or traits called out elsewhere because of the existence of the frontier.[4]

Turner, like Rousseau earlier, saw the people as free and equal; but equal meant to him freed from the artificial distinctions of European class structures, not equally worthwhile as individuals. They were not equal in worth or equally estimable, or deserving. The Frontier conceived of individualism as the expression of character: self-reliance, reliability, steadiness, indefatigable industry and perseverance, and above all, strength of will. It held its own rugged version of Arminianism, leading toward the Gospel of Self-Improvement. Such character was the focus of the enormously popular stories of Erastus Beadle, originator of the Dime Novels, and of "the Edwards": Edward S. Ellis, Edward L. Wheeler, Edward Z. C. Judson (Ned Buntline), and eventually the incomparably prolific master of them all, Edward Stratemeyer.

In one view, as Potter suggests, this Frontier imagery lends itself to actual practices qualifying as democratic:

if all men are equal, each ought to think for himself, but on the other hand, no man should consider himself better than his neighbors, and if the majority have adopted an opinion on a matter, how can one man question their opinion, without setting himself up as being better than they? Moreover, it is understood that the majority are pledged not to force him to adopt their opinion. But it is also understood that in return for this immunity he will voluntarily accept the will of the majority in most things.[5]

On grounds of individualism, self-reliance and frontier virtues -- among other grounds -- the opinions of the majority regarding African-Americans were strongly held.

On one hand, the liberal individualist offers only the most tentative and guarded deference to democracy in relation to himself, finding, as Thoreau said, "little virtue in the actions of masses of men."

On the other hand, practicality requires cooperation, even though "A wise man will not leave the right to the mercy of chance, nor wish it to prevail through the power of the majority." Democracy is less objectionable than the alternatives, where collective action is unavoidable; but ". . . any man more right than his neighbors constitutes a majority of one already." John P. Diggins, for one, writes about America's "contrasting images -- the individual as the source of his own being versus politics as a public duty . . ." and of the "characteristic American longing for solitary individualism unrestrained by the demands of politics."[6] Huck Finn on his raft was "opposite" the towns in every sense, like Paul Theroux's protagonist in *The Mosquito Coast*, who takes Daniel Boone's resourcefulness to a lunatic extreme. America has had a long-standing enchantment with the false opposition of individual to society, and of nature to society. Theroux's character finally realizes that nature is irregular, uneven, and that his quest has been for straight lines and right angles. But since he is part of both nature and society, thoroughly irregular and uneven despite his mastery of technology, he still requires society, if only to condemn and reject.

To the extent that the frontier encouraged such assertive individualism, it also "functioned as a catalyst to precipitate such barbaric modes of behavior as highly civilized societies suppress." The "ignorant generality of immigrants . . . had the sense of moving out of a circumscribed life dominated by magistrate and priest into a largely unrestrained condition"; and Turner's statement romantically assumes "that men in a state of nature could somehow create an adequate culture virtually from nothing."[7]

While the Puritan experience stands in sharp contrast to mythic Western non-conformity, emigrants to the frontier often encountered much more pressure to conform than they had anticipated. Material self-sufficiency and resourcefulness had little or nothing to do with "thinking for yourself," and prevailing views from the larger population predictably pervaded the frontier as well. There is little basis for supposing that beliefs and attitudes associated with racism were any less "normal" on the frontier than they were in the population centers of the east. (In fact, in proportion as individualism was extreme or overstated, the opposite might reasonably be suspected.) Primitive conceptions of unbounded freedom for self-expression remain a powerful frontier legacy even in urban, post-industrial

America. Our various "new" frontiers, set by Samuel Lubell, John F. Kennedy and many others, entail the assertion of freedom over changing environments, extensions of the "conquest" of nature from Francis Bacon's time. America presented boundless opportunities to impose collective will for individual rewards, so the organized as well as the unorganized could invoke folkish virtues to enlighten and justify their pursuit of happiness.

The kind of equality most appealing to a frontier mind-set was emotional, and that derived most importantly from religious attitudes traceable to the Great Awakening. Puritanism's cerebral approach to life stifled self-expression, but the evangelical, enthusiastic Baptist and Methodist interpretations gave full vent to self-expression in a way that generated no tension between individualism and equality. Christianity adapted to and survived all mutations of individualism. At the same time, the total disregard of distinctions in common religious enthusiasm cemented together what community was possible for such a folk; and on a basis of equality that worked to the advantage or disadvantage of none, except for race distinctions.

In a sense, we can discuss democracy as a frontier accommodation of individualism. All men were created equal, in that everyone had veto power over the will of others with regard to himself. "Over himself, the individual is sovereign," as John Stuart Mill wrote. The compact theory of government held sway, but part of the compact was the right of the individual to withdraw from it or ignore it, just as Calhoun reasoned out nullification and the right of secession from the state compact conception of Jefferson and Madison in the 1798 Kentucky and Virginia resolutions. Self-government in the pursuit of self-interest offered little to minorities except to rebel if they could. David Noble notes Carl Becker's realization that ". . . the individualism of that [frontier] tradition was completely negative."[8] Like Herbert Croly a generation earlier, Becker saw some central problems of the twentieth century "stemming from the destructive individualism of Jeffersonianism."[9] Among those problems are aspects of continuing racism and "race relations" as we experience them.

1. Don E. Fehrenbacher, ed., *History and American Society: Essays of David M. Potter* (New York: Oxford University Press, 1973), 232-233.

2. *Ibid.*, 252.

3. Bliss Perry, *The American Mind and American Idealism* (Boston: Houghton-Mifflin Company, 1912), 34.

4. Frederick Jackson Turner, *The Frontier in American History* (New York: Henry Holt and Company, 1920), 37.

5. Potter in Fehrenbacher, ed., 254.

6. John P. Diggins, *The Lost Soul of American Politics* (New York: Basic Books, 1984), 118, 119.

7. Arthur K. Moore, *The Frontier Mind: A Cultural Analysis of the Kentucky Frontiersman* (Lexington: University of Kentucky Press, 1957), 193.

8. David W. Noble, *Historians Against History* (Minneapolis: University of Minnesota Press, 1965), 178.

9. See Diggins, 127.

Eleven

Biological Determinism

After the nation took form, the distribution of wealth grew steadily more unequal through succeeding generations. At the same time, Americans *talked* more and more about equality and democracy. They generally convinced themselves that both were real, and increasing in all ways. This kind of talk, still associated with the Jackson period, naturally generated agitation against slavery; but the more people claimed freedom and equality, the more they needed to justify and defend their behavior, and how they thought and felt toward African-Americans. Especially after Britain ended slavery in all of its territories, in 1833, Americans needed a forceful, compelling explanation or rationalization. They needed a systematic, "scientific" racism.

Discrimination against free blacks began to "set" as institutionalized behavior about a decade after the War for Independence ended, when even the churches began to show incipient systematic racism. The new justification emerging in the early nineteenth century was biological determinism, which, as Condorcet put it, sought to "make nature herself an accomplice in the crime of political inequality." Intellectually, Christianity drew upon Arminian doctrine in varying degrees, insisting that salvation (or success) was within the power of virtually anyone's will, and was therefore a matter of individual responsibility. Rejection of that doctrine took the form of biological determinism, asserting that the will-power needed for virtue, and therefore for salvation or success, was at least largely a genetic trait.

African-Americans either had the capacity of will to compete successfully, and didn't use it, or they lacked it and were "incomplete" or even soul-less. Either way, they were inferior, either unwilling or unable to be as fully human as whites. Some American leaders, like Thomas Jefferson in 1809, suggested that inferior abilities did not imply lesser rights; but that question was largely ignored as the juggernaut of scientific development was employed to meet the practical need for justification of different treatment.

During the early years of the nineteenth century, England produced the most persuasive proponents of a separate kind of humanity for Africans. In the United States, the idea of a separate creation, or multiple creation (polygeny) first found forceful expression in the work of Dr. Samuel George Morton (1799-1851), a famous geologist who shifted his attention to "craniometry" or skull measurement, and concluded that Negroes were a different species. Louis Agassiz, the famed scientist (1807-1873), came to America in 1846, and quickly became a notable proponent of polygeny. Agassiz thought Negroes shared a "human nature," but were the products of a separate creation, and markedly inferior. The more egalitarian ideas were advanced, and the more slavery was called into question, the more vigorously its beneficiaries developed and publicized racial theories to justify themselves. Throughout the century and in the twentieth as well, racist justification and rationalization advanced *pari passu* with exploitation, segregation, and discrimination.

The relative precision and new kind of exactness of experimental science brought increasing public respect for the claims and conclusions of science in general. It soon became evident that the easiest way to get a claim accepted was to call it "scientific." In laymen accustomed to absolutist claims from revelation, habitual deference to religious authority transferred easily to science. Popular respect for science often took the anti-scientific form of unquestioning veneration, and validation by authority. Biological attempts to explain human characteristics and behavior, however shaky as science, got the benefit of every doubt, merely for being labelled scientific. In the age when nationalism burst forth as the dominant political force in the world, science and its applications in technology were building a great nation here. Change, which had been customarily feared and avoided, now appeared differently in the glow of Enlightenment optimism and confidence, Romantic enthusiasm, and material growth. Change was now assumed to be progress, and science was the order and the instrument of progressive change. The truth of scientific assertions seemed manifest in the undeniable progress of America.

Science offered two kinds of explanation of human behavior. Both biological determinism and the environmental determinism of the emerging social science challenged the idea of behavior as "conduct" controlled by will. But the assertions of the environmental determinists found a cool and skeptical reception among a people who saw their lives explained by Arminian and Romantic will-power and by biological determinism. Environmental theories smacked somehow of ideology, and did not share in the authority of science the way genetic theories did. Descriptions of formative influences lacked precision and ease of formulation, and could not convincingly claim to be objective, disinterested, or incontrovertible. Science was presumably above or outside culture in the nineteenth century. Few recognized that it was rooted in the culture, posing itself questions and dealing with answers which were shaped by value assumptions and belief systems.

Biological determinism gave new force to age-old habits of invidious comparison and discrimination against those perceived as significantly different. It posited inherent deficiencies, using the traits of the observer or theorist as standards of acceptability and excellence. Of course real and true patterns of observable difference existed; but the inferences drawn from them, the meanings imputed to them, reflected the interests of those who inferred and imputed. Invidious comparison reified and quantified diverse abilities and qualities, and then applied the principle of gradation, or ranking. Habits of gradation, from the Great Chain and the taxonomy of Linnaeus, were easily applied to ranking people, and to claiming scientific authority for such classification.

Like countless Americans, Agassiz was terrified of miscegenation, or race mixing, and was drawn to polygeny by that fear. Samuel George Morton, the inveterate skull collector and leading proponent of multiple creation, died in 1851, five years after Agassiz lent his authoritative support to the position. Polygeny was then led by Josiah Nott and George R. Gliddon, who co-authored *Types of Mankind*, a work which was very widely read despite its 800-page bulk.

Polygeny remained central to the dominant scientific view, biological determinism, until Darwin's *The Origin of Species* appeared in 1859. By that time polygeny had already generated considerable resistance and opposition, especially in the south, because it contradicted literal belief in the biblical account of creation. From the fundamentalist point of view, there was just one good thing about Darwin's ideas, that they refuted polygeny. As Stephen Jay Gould observes, after the polygenists' debates with biblical literalists, arguments claiming scientific authority became "the first line of defense" for belief in "the unalterable quality of human differences."[1]

To gain scientific authority and public acceptance, pioneering social scientists like the ethnologist Lewis H. Morgan related race to behavior patterns. Different kinds of differences were routinely blurred in both "scientific" and public perceptions. Differences of capacity were almost universally thought to be related to differences of appearance; and differences of moral and political rights were commonly linked to presumptively innate differences of capacity. Racism assumes that performance limitations are related to differences of physiognomy or appearance; and therefore different kinds or levels of deserving are also related to appearance. Nearly everyone who addressed such questions in an influential way seems to have sought evidence to "prove" what was already taken to be self-evident truth. The central question here is, How did Americans develop the mind-set that led them to assume and regard race differences as they did?

Clearly a response explaining the persistence of racism must proceed from the broad utilitarian individualism of the society's formative stages. The emergent culture symbolized by practical men, from John Winthrop to Benjamin Franklin to the pioneers and inventors and entrepreneurs, is full of that utilitarian mind-set, prizing ingenuity, resourcefulness, expediency, practical self-control, industry and perseverance. Americans were understandably disposed from the beginning of colonization to believe in what worked, what got them where they needed and wanted to go. Pragmatism did not spring full-blown from the minds of C. S. Peirce and William James. It was a culmination in the late nineteenth and early twentieth centuries of a long consequentialist tradition personified by Benjamin Franklin. Pragmatism, the "American philosophy," and America's scientific racism were systematically formulated in the same decades.

1. Stephen Jay Gould, *The Mismeasure of Man* (New York: W. W. Norton and Company, 1981), 72. Gould provides a much fuller account of what is summarized here.

Twelve

The Quantification of Difference

From around the middle of the nineteenth century, European race theories buttressed English and American formulations. Gobineau's *The Inequality of Human Races* set out the Aryan, master race theory which would become so notorious later, but which then exerted wide appeal throughout the western world. Houston Stewart Chamberlain popularized the idea of Teutonic superiority, capitalizing on common fears of miscegenation. Sir Francis Galton (1822-1911) drew unwarranted conclusions about racial gradation from his own excellent work in genetics, *Hereditary Genius*, published in 1869, ten years after the epoch-making work of his cousin, Charles Darwin. Gustave Le Bon, best known for his work on "mob psychology," claimed that there are mental differences among races, and that they are impervious to environmental influences.

The study of skull size and configuration, by no means limited to Morton or his fellow polygenists, became particularly fashionable after the appearance of systematic evolutionary science. Darwin himself never studied humans, but his general comments on what he saw as obvious racial differences served to stimulate renewed interest in anthropometry, measuring differences among races. Craniometry created a sensation in America in the form of phrenology, introduced by Dr. Johan Gaspar Spurzheim on an 1832 visit. This was the first, but far from the last attempt to relate behavior to the shape of the skull.[1]

In mid-century a Swedish writer named Anders Retzius contrived what was called the cephalic index (from Greek via late Latin *cephalicus*, head). This was the figure arrived at by dividing the breadth of the skull by its length and multiplying by one hundred. A long-headed or "dolichocephalic" individual was one with an index of 80 or less; a round-headed, short-headed or "brachycephalic" person had an index over 80. Various behavioral traits were associated with the long head, generally characteristic of northern and western Europe, and the round head, associated with the Mediterranean and points south and east. Most influential among the followers of Retzius was Paul Broca (1824-1880), who led a veritable research assault on the human skull, brain, hair, and even body lice in the later nineteenth century.[2]

After 1859 there developed what Gould aptly terms "an unholy alliance" of evolutionary thought and quantification methodology. The age-old magic of numbers worked its spell with renewed impact in the new age of science. Statistics had first exerted beguiling appeal in the later eighteenth century, with the emergence of political economy as a field of study. Condorcet was an Enlightenment pioneer in the field, and Darwin's less famous cousin, Sir Francis Galton was a prominent statistician in the era of scientific racism. The misuse of statistics, which continues to plague us all in reports on every sort of economic and social matter, rapidly accelerated from the time of Franklin. Evidence was adduced to support, but not to challenge, assumptions. A common procedure, more recently made famous by government agencies such as the Department of Defense, was to be very technical and precise, ignoring all questions as to whether your points of departure are sound and complete. Like economic reports now, "scientific" conclusions regarding race were not restricted to the academic world, but were trumpeted far and wide, as warranted by popular interest in the subject. Errors were magnified and compounded as explanations reached the lowest common denominator of understanding, with conclusions readily grasped because they were so thoroughly oversimplified. One thinks of the modern Secretary of State who gave impetus to a regrettable convention, advising the President to explain his military spending requests by telling the public "something clearer than the truth."

There is no way of knowing how conscious or deliberate the distortions of science regarding race have been. Generally, the history of race research to recent times seems to be a classic example of people believing in what they wish to be true. A perfect example is the work of Paul Broca in craniometry, which Gould shows to be a case of simply using the criteria and the methods that get you where you want to be. In America, the whole European effort in scientific racism was summarized by William Z. Ripley, who taught sociology and economics at M.I.T. and published *The Races of Europe*, 1899. Part of any explanation of racism's tremendous appeal on the basis of science is that people could not yet see any "sociology of knowledge," and they naturally posited universal or at least general interpretations of reality, not realizing that these explanations necessarily reflected their own circumstances and vantage points. The realization that we are all prisoners as well as beneficiaries of specific time, place, and culture, was not nearly as strong in the early years of the twentieth century as it would become in another couple of generations.

The nineteenth century's dispositions produced a bewildering variety of scientific and pseudo-scientific "anthropometrics," or human measurements. Some accurate measurements led to drawing unwarranted inferences; and many "reports of findings" were dishonest or simply sloppy. Scientists generally did nothing to challenge or refute craniometry, for example, until the work of Franz Boas in the 1920s. High school biology students in the 1950s were still measuring one another's heads, calculating Retzius's "cephalic index." They insulted classmates with the epithet, "missing link" without ever having heard of the Great Chain of Being, any more than their teachers probably had. Superficially clever, "catchy" simplifications die hard, and they survive far past the time of being discredited in the scientific community. They are "useful," after all: they suit people, please them or satisfy them in some way.

In the late nineteenth century, esteemed scientists and thinkers set the dynamic conception of evolution against the static one of the Great Chain, in whatever ways they found congenial and useful to their world-views. Africans could be a notch down on the Great Chain -- or some distance behind in evolutionary progress. Either way, they were the "missing link" in "God's Great Work." Herbert Spencer, that marvelously appealing interpreter and popularizer of scientific thought, advanced the readily adopted theory that "The intelligence traits of the uncivilized . . . are traits recurring in the children of the civilized." Adults of "lesser" ethnic groupings were comparable in abilities with children of northwest European ancestry and culture, just as everybody who was anybody had believed all along. But now the idea had its scientific *imprimatur* from a great authority.

The catch-phrase of the half-educated classes was "ontogeny recapitulates phylogeny," representing succinctly the late nineteenth century's most persuasive scientific idea about humans. In fact, it was still presented in reputable northern liberal arts colleges as a serious scientific idea in the 1950s, and endlessly repeated by students who were led to believe that education means learning strange terms. The idea of "recapitulation" facilitated ranking of inferior adults, such as the "child-like African." It also led to ranking "superior" children, foreshadowing the "intelligence" obsession of psychologists and others in the twentieth century. G. Stanley Hall, arguably the foremost American psychologist of the early twentieth century, endorsed the recapitulation idea in 1904. Scientists gave it up within two decades after that. But that did not halt its spread, or diminish its popular appeal. People believed what they wanted to believe, which was what they found pleasant and useful to believe. Few knew or cared that "ontogeny recapitulates phylogeny" was nothing more than an odd expression that illustrated popular gullibility for scientific language and had possibly enabled sophomores of an earlier time to impress their dates.

1. See Gossett, 71-72.
2. *Ibid.*, 76, 81.

Thirteen

Social Darwinism and Individualist Competition

After Charles Darwin published *The Origin of Species* in 1859, countless analogies were drawn between the struggle for survival in nature, both within and among species, and human rivalry and competition. These acquired the loose name, Social Darwinism. The ideas of natural selection and the survival of the fittest, in particular, were applied to competition among individuals as well as among races and nationalities. Social Darwinism's individualist version claimed that by a process of natural economic selection, those best equipped for "free" and "open" competition will and do prosper, while the process weeds out those with deficiencies which render them unfit to succeed. As will be seen, this form of materialist or naturalist thought found an especially warm reception in the United States, despite widespread rejection of the religiously troublesome science from which the analogies were drawn. Social Darwinism accommodated those who needed yet another rationale for individualism and invidious comparison, or who did not find traditional explanations satisfying.

In the earlier nineteenth century, while the powerful of Europe fought in various ways against the implications of the French Revolution, and radicals continued to press forward with those implications, America also absorbed the entirely different organicism associated with Edmund Burke and his disciples. This set of beliefs and dispositions is usually called simply "conservatism," a persuasion seemingly in conflict with, but peculiarly complementary to, both political liberalism and Social Darwinism. Conservatism held that society's law and order were ordained by God; and that individuals held rights, and indeed meaning itself, only as members of an organic society. Aristocracy was natural, and difficult to distinguish from plutocracy. Property meant "estate" or (if hereditary) status, position in society. It self-evidently required honor or "worship" (as in "Your Worship"; cf. "Your Honor"), but economic individualism, as in *laissez-faire* capitalism, vulgarly contradicted the natural class order. Conservatism opposed claims of equality, of course, and despised the idea of democracy. It rejected the idea of progress, to say nothing of its alleged inevitability, and prized order, stability and harmony as social and political goals. Intuitive reason remained its favorite faculty, but it found and served individuality in terms of membership in class and nation rather than individualist separateness.

In its worship of private property, conservatism formed a bulwark against socialism, the ideological antithesis of individualism. In its devotion to aristocracy, its anti-egalitarianism, and its opposition to democracy, conservatism stood firm against the universalistic and romantic glorification of *all* individuals; but it elevated individual importance within its version of the social organism, the particular national society. In short, some of its fundamental tenets were easily adapted to the materialist, and at the same time moralistic, world-view of Social Darwinists in America, the paragons of economic individualism -- even though conservatism, taken whole, opposed materialism and its implications of atomistic, selfish competition.

The conservative consecration of property as estate fit perfectly with the liberal Jeffersonian consecration of property as indispensable to liberty. The idea of a natural aristocracy, of an inequality of "virtue and talents," was common to both. So were the conception of society as organism, albeit with different understandings of what that implied; and the acceptance of natural law as self-evident. Both grew out of the Puritan era, taking material fortune as evidence of divine favor in some sense, the reward of God-given abilities. Conservatives thought that those who already enjoyed material fortune were those who deserved it: a static conception of the universe or the social organism as moral. Liberals thought that the social organism needed to be freed from the dead hand of the past to work along natural lines toward the distribution of material fortune in proportion to virtue and talents: a dynamic conception of the universe, or at least society, as progressing toward moral order and social equity. One general ideological orientation favored stability; the other, change through competition.

Both took *deserving* for granted, in a moral universe; and by extension, inequality of deserving except for the liberal claim of universal natural rights to the fundamentals: life, liberty, and pursuing self-interest as one could. The conservative and liberal ideologies merged in America through some sort of syncretism or eclecticism, the nature of which is perceived differently according to how great a role one assigns to the ostensibly conscious choices of those in positions of power and influence.

Since individualism is what has to be conserved, its political expression in liberalism must also be defended, and we have the peculiar spectacle in America of conservatism with regard to liberalism. Individualism is the chief instrument of both, in most contexts. Conservatives resist social reforms, using individualist assumptions upon which no reform can possibly be based. (For example, there can be no real change in the treatment of felons as long as we insist that "It's all up to the individual.") African-Americans, perhaps needless to say, have not been well served by the conservative idea of naturally superior classes, or by the liberal idea of naturally superior virtue and talents (both opposing truly egalitarian democracy) or by the generally held individualist ideas of competition and of individual as opposed to social responsibility.

As Burke is the exemplar of conservatism, so Herbert Spencer is the towering figure in that progressive materialism which brought together conservatism and liberalism in America. All human society was organic to Spencer, so he was on the American universalistic wave-length from the outset. Society evolved, which meant that it necessarily progressed. But it progressed without its minority groups, through universal competition rather than common effort.

Spencer's most central point with regard to individuals is that progress comes through voluntary cooperation only, never through government or other coercion: the point that endeared him to political liberals of the type that advocated permitting "maximum room for self-provision." He went back to Locke, the patron saint of "equality of opportunity," the American creed. Spencer said, in effect, I cannot be sure that the happiness of others does not differ from mine in countless ways and degrees. The only happiness to which I can testify with confidence is my own. Therefore the surest way in which I can add to the aggregate happiness of society is to add to my own. This seemed a reasonable extension of Adam Smith and of the whole utilitarian caste of thought.

There is no denying the reality and necessity of egoism, Spencer said. "Ethics has to recognize the truth, recognized in unethical thought, that egoism comes before altruism." Since our first concern must be survival, we can even go so far as to assume "permanent supremacy of egoism over altruism." In fact we have to pursue our own welfare first if we are to be able to pursue anyone else's welfare, or the greatest happiness of the greatest number. It is, Spencer wrote, "amazing that both the world at large and writers who make conduct their study, should ignore the terrible evils which disregard of personal well-being inflict on the unborn, and the incalculable good laid up for the unborn by attention to personal well-being." Those who are self-destructive visit their sins upon their successors, and just as surely, those who are self-regarding build up assets for future use; so "if egoism is unduly subordinated, there is a decrease of general happiness."[1] Self-regard became not only appropriate and acceptable, but positively saintly, long before the "me generation" of the late twentieth century.

What is the practical meaning of this? The "adequately egoistic individual" keeps or develops the capacity for altruistic action. "The individual who is inadequately egoistic," by contrast, "loses more or less of his ability to be altruistic. The truth of the one proposition is self-evident; and the truth of the other is daily forced on us by examples."[2] Further, excessive altruism can have the effect of *increasing egoism in others*, building dependency and selfishness, as in the spoiled child, or African-American or Indian.

But Spencer was equally persuaded along the lines of moral sense philosophy, with its sentiment of benevolence. He was morally idealistic, and accordingly uneasy about accepting an implicit endorsement of egoism, under whatever name or dispensation. He said that happiness, the "end of action" for all hedonism, *attends* moral success. It is impossible to realize as a proximate goal, or sole, direct goal. Therefore, the method of hedonism, the *conscious* pursuit of happiness, is wrong, because it is selfish, and not progressive. Progress can come only through the voluntary acts of individuals, whose behavior evolves in relation to progressive understanding of utility, as in the thought of Chauncy Wright, Lester Frank Ward, and John

Dewey. But those voluntary acts cannot be merely egoistic if they are progressive. Spencer required individualism in the sense of initiative, self-reliance, and voluntary action; but an individualism which is unselfish and altruistic in *motivation*. Americans were happily informed that in doing well they also did good, as long as that's what they *intended*; and Social Darwinism reinforced their sense of justified disdain or contempt toward those who did neither well nor good.

Spencer thought that it is just as natural for men to act for the benefit of others as for self-regard -- given prior consideration for survival -- but such altruism was instrumental and practical. We all recognize "the identification of personal advantage with the advantage of fellow citizens" and the fact that in "various ways the well-being of each rises and falls with the well-being of all." Hence voluntary association is the rational choice of individuals; but the question of motivation remains. After all, the "egoistic aspect of altruistic pleasure" is undeniable: "whether knowingly or unknowingly gained, the state of mind accompanying altruistic action, being a pleasurable state, is to be counted in the sum of pleasures which the individual can receive; and in this sense cannot be other than egoistic."[3] Or can it? Jefferson had explained how action could be appealing to the actor on the basis of gratification, without being egoistic or selfish. The fact that I act for the benefit of others because it pleases me does not mean that I am egoistic, because one must ask *why* it pleases me; and the answer is that I am the kind of being who is naturally pleased by my own altruism -- not a bad fellow at all! One could be quite comfortable morally while acting altruistically only when literally pleased to do so.

Spencer's later reasoning is of course different from Jefferson's. He finds the greatest happiness principle inadequate as a standard, because he persists in "either-or" reasoning, and "Live for others" is, he says, just as unsatisfactory as "Live only for yourself." We have to reach some sort of "compromise." In each sphere of activity, the greatest egoistic reward attends the most enlightened and effective altruism. On the other hand, self-regarding effort as opposed to other-regarding effort (assuming opposition) is literally self-defeating or self-depriving. Spencer's reasoning is that "general happiness is to be achieved mainly through the adequate pursuit of their own happiness by individuals; while, reciprocally, the happinesses of individuals are to be achieved in part by their pursuit of the general happiness."[4] Spencer developed a truly inspired, even utopian progressive vision of how conduct would evolve, and his extraordinary impact on America undoubtedly rested in large part on his ideals.

People should reach a point where they would compete with one another at being good, by providing one another equitable opportunities to be good, with everyone seeking and gaining the self-satisfaction of altruism without seeking it for self-enhancement. Here was no ruthless, competitive "nature, red in tooth and claw," like that so often associated with Spencer. His vision of society is organicist, materialistic -- and moral to the core. The morality of his social science undoubtedly accounts in very large measure for his appeal in our moralistic society. When Richard Hofstadter wrote that "the United States during the last three decades of the nineteenth and at the beginning of the twentieth century was *the* Darwinian country," it was a Spencerian society he described. Spencer not only wrote evolutionary explanations some time before Darwin (like Lyell and others in various fields), but even used the term "survival of the fittest" seven years before *The Origin of Species* appeared.

Darwin's work verified hypotheses which had long been discussed, and his name therefore attached to patterns of thought with which he had very little to do. Most conspicuous among them was Social Darwinism, in which success was both material and moral, because competitive success satisfied the demands of altruism and Christian charity. The obvious corollary was that the unsuccessful were unfit, deficient, somehow inferior morally.

It was Spencer's thought, as Hofstadter remarks, that made evolution synonymous with progress "toward some very remote but altogether glorious consummation," confirming American optimism and confidence in the society's future. Spencer's evolutionism was teleological and moral, a religion, "a kind of naturalistic Calvinism"[5] which endorsed at once the association of success with virtue and talents, the natural aristocracy as Elect, Jeffersonian equality of opportunity as equal justice according to deserving, and even a push toward pragmatism. A most important implication of Spencer's thought was its "role in turning religion away from metaphysics and toward its roots in experience. Darwinism weakened the dominant apologetic of physical proofs for the existence of God and encouraged recourse to other sources of belief -- the experience of God in the individual conscience or in the historic moral sense of mankind."[6]

The individual was forced to rely on individual capacities, and at the same time fully licensed to do so. Philosophically, this constituted a mere reinforcement of the American individual responsibility and freedom posited in a Puritan, Arminian, and liberal past. It gave powerful impetus to individualism -- and a crushing burden to minorities outside the tradition.

Static conservatism, liberalism, and progressive, dynamic Spencerism merged in capitalist ideology. Economic individualism incorporated property worship, social inequality based on virtue and talent as defined by those who were satisfied, natural law in the form of evolutionary doctrine, and moral justice. As Thomas Nixon Carver put it, "The naturally selected are the children of God." (Jerry Falwell would say in the 1980s that money is God's instrument for expressing approval.) The society was "open to virtue and talents," so everybody was responsible for his or her own social position. It was literally a logical resurgence of Calvinism. We do not choose the qualities we have, the abilities we have, but we are responsible for our salvation-success or damnation-failure on the basis of them, even though it is predestined or determined how effective we can be in the situations wherein we must struggle. The natural aristocracy and the Burkean elite are both interchangeable with the Elect and the fittest. In idealist and materialist views alike, it is the individual as individual who is chosen and who is responsible. At least this was the dominant American extrapolation from Spencer. Nature means competition, which yields progress. Evolution means greater differentiation, diversity and heterogeneity -- implying individualism with the endorsement of natural law, and gradation. Material progress also means moral progress, as with Adam Smith: growth brings greater security and comfort, greater opportunity for self-development, satisfaction, and general happiness.

An alternative, non-Calvinist avenue to the same social views was, appropriately enough, parallel to Arminianism. The Elect or fittest are not predestined or determined to succeed, but choose their own success by force of will. In either case, what was chiefly retained of Spencer in American conviction, aside from progressive faith in evolutionary change, was insistence on individual deserving: nothing new, to be sure, but powerful reinforcement of something central and traditional. In American capitalist thought, we recognize determinism, but what is determined is individualism. We can even be fatalistic, but what is fated is voluntarism. Our *destiny* is to make choices, according to how fit we are: whether we have God-given ability, natural ability, virtue and talent, saving faith, amazing grace, or the Divine Light. The fittest fitted themselves out for evolutionary naturalism as readily as their forebears found assurance of salvation under revelatory supernaturalism.

The most remarkable aspect of America adopting Spencer is one pondered by the Israeli scholar of American thought, Yehoshua Arieli: that this competitive "individualism was not only the ideology of the intellectual elite of the country, but a living faith for most Americans." He says that "the most peculiar aspect of Spencer's vogue in America [was] . . . his conquest of the Protestant church." Spencer's influence united "Malthusianism with the laissez-faire ideology of the Manchester School, and created a formula of individualism which legitimatized American capitalism," according to Beard, for example.[7]

And if it was accurate to say, as Chauncy Wright did, that evolutionary thought involved no more concern for individual happiness than Calvinism did, it is evidently also accurate to say that people did not expect either Nature or God to be solicitous of individuals.   That was not the kind of individual attention or recognition they wished for or required. They just wanted reality described and explained in a way that would permit them their optimism about the efficacy of individual will, choice, and effort. They wanted assurance that things still revealed the gratifying order that John Winthrop had described in 1630: there were rich and poor, successful and unsuccessful, and everybody was as he was supposed to be and pretty much deserved to be.   This country had been immeasurably kinder to slaves *as slaves* than any other slave-holding society, but its traditions did not lead to much sympathy for free people who were "failing."   In a sense, racism was just a general way of explaining "failure," which was about the extent of many Americans' interest in the subject. The Protestant churches, necessarily reflecting the views of their congregations, mainly offered a religious version of popular attitudes.

Spencer insisted on individual liberty as an absolute, and yet envisioned progress through voluntary cooperative effort. His chief American supporter and celebrant, William Graham Sumner (1840-1910), used his Yale professorship to expound the synthesis of religion, economics, sociology and biology. Sumner "brought together three great traditions of western capitalist culture: the Protestant ethic, the doctrines of classical economics, and Darwinian natural selection."[8] And, one might add, the political philosophy of Thomas Jefferson and the American Enlightenment, with the explosive concept of equality harnessed and defined to fit our Puritan-Arminian legacy, as equality of opportunity. While expounding a dynamic, progressive Nature, diametrically opposed to the static world of conservatism, Sumner gave, from Spencer, a formal scientific rationale for what conservatives did and wanted to do, namely, to block reforms, and to block them in the name of progress. Progress demanded that individual freedom and voluntary effort not be interfered with, because progress came about only by letting nature, including human nature, take its course. Hofstadter muses about "whether, in the entire history of thought, there was ever a conservatism so utterly progressive as this"! Or, others would ask, a theory of progress so utterly regressive. As Richard Sennett and Jonathan Cobb put it, "Equality of opportunity would make everyone responsible for his social position." The strongest convictions and dispositions of American society made it a terribly difficult society in which to be a member of a historically handicapped minority.

Absolute individual freedom was indispensable on grounds of utility and in accord with natural law, but it was not mandated as a natural right. Like Burke's conservatism, Sumner's philosophy had no place for universalistic claims of natural rights. "There are no rights," Sumner flatly asserted. However, American conservatism-liberalism, unlike Burke's conservatism, self-consciously strove to be empirical and to draw from experience universalistic inferences.[9] These inferences destroyed claims of equality, as far as Sumner was concerned. "In the cold light of evolutionary realism," he said, "the eighteenth-century idea that men were equal in a state of nature was the opposite of the truth." But in the warm light of history we have to wonder if Sumner believed that *the* eighteenth-century idea of equality was equality of abilities at any particular time. Moral sense philosophy claimed, with varying degrees of confidence, equality of innate ability to perceive right and wrong. Nobody else claimed equal distribution of abilities to nearly the extent that Hobbes had done in 1651. But no; ability is not Sumner's concern. Inequality of abilities is too obvious to require mention. He rejects also the whole political line of reasoning that assumes equal deserving, or entitlement to consideration, as attending human life.

Like Helvétius in the eighteenth century, Sumner assumed immutable selfishness at the center of human nature. Virtue was fidelity to one's self, and it always brought success. He thought it wrong to try to compensate for the lack of virtue, much less to reward its lack. Like Spencer, he says we must cooperate voluntarily out of self-interest, on the basis of utility both individual and aggregate. We live in a determined universe, but what is determined in the universe is free choice, and the problem of poverty is attributable to the fact that not enough people choose to be as comfortable as Sumner.

Sumner could be absurdly binary and dogmatic in his thinking: for example, "Let it be understood that we cannot go outside this alternative: liberty, inequality, survival of the fittest; non-liberty, equality, survival of the unfittest." A writer who asserts that whatever is not X is the contradiction of X does not inspire confidence as a rule; and yet Sumner was astonishingly persuasive with his relentless insistence on a "natural antagonism between liberty and democracy."

Here is Sumner addressing the question, "What is Civil Liberty?":

> The modern jural state, at least of the Anglo-Saxon type,
> by its hostility to privileges and servitudes, aims to realize
> . . . liberty . . . . If all privileges and all servitudes are
> abolished, the individual finds that there are no
> prescriptions left either to lift him up or hold him down.
> He simply has all his chances left open that he may make
> out of himself all there is in him. This is individualism
> and atomism. There is absolutely no escape from it except
> back into a system of privileges and servitudes.

How does this analysis move us beyond Hobbes, two centuries earlier? It only makes the counter-assertion that individualism is progressive rather than destructive, because human nature will lead to voluntary cooperation along lines that recognize fitness and deserving.

Sumner said that there are no more prescriptions for the individual, that his chances are simply left open. Individual purposes are cultivated, elevated, enhanced in a world where there are no *higher* purposes, but rather the concomitant common purposes inferred from each individual's inescapable involvement in society. Americans simply would not have their individual pursuit of happiness discounted, but required, demanded, and got a version of materialism in which their individual differences are claimed, demonstrated to their satisfaction, and taken with utmost seriousness.

A member of his time and culture whether he liked it or not, Spencer even saw "a finer type of man than has hitherto existed" evolving along Aryan racial lines. As Hofstadter writes, biological metaphors abound in history and literature, and Social Darwinism may come to the surface at any time "so long as there is a strong element of predacity in society." In the United States, that element is never far below the surface, because its individualist version is as deeply ingrained with us as the concept of class in European history. No more than anyone before them could Spencer or Sumner reconcile the conception of society as organic with an ethics of individual utility.[10] More of the same individualism was their prescription for any problems associated with individualism. Through its confusions as through its explicit claims, their Social Darwinism supported racism in America, and aggravated its effects.

1. Herbert Spencer, *The Man Versus the State* (Indianapolis: Liberty Classics, 1981; intro. Albert Jay Nock, 1940), 187, 192-193.

2. *Ibid.*, 194.

3. *Ibid.*, 203, 208, 213-214.

4. *Ibid.*, 238.

5. Richard Hofstadter, *Social Darwinism in American Thought* (Boston: The Beacon Press, 1955), 6, 10.

6. Cynthia Eagle Russett, *Darwinism in America: The Intellectual Response, 1865-1912* (San Francisco: W. H. Freeman and Company, 1976), 39.

7. Yehoshua Arieli, *Individualism and Nationalism in American Ideology* (Cambridge, Mass.: Harvard University Press, 1964), 328, 331.

8. Russett, 43.

9. See Ronald Lora, *Conservative Minds in America* (Chicago: Rand-McNally Company, 1971), 222-223.

10. See Hofstadter, 221, n. 33.

Fourteen

Enlightened Self-Interest

The ideas of Hegel generated great academic interest and influence in America, including his proposition that the individual is a social product. But Americans in general tended to see organizations, and society at large, as a set of tools for individual purposes. The individual came first, and the only *fundamental* groupings were "natural," like family and race. Horace Kallen says the "spirit of Individualism and Freedom" was the "spirit that denies" all sorts of rules. It broke bonds, shattered "the regimentations of custom, convention, dogma and prejudice," and frustrated "tyranny and misrule." Individualism offered confidence in progress, in place of stability and order. To do that, it affirmed "the secondary and *utilitarian* nature of all social arrangements -- churches, governments, industrial and financial establishments, schools, every form of association in which individuals come together. They are common *instruments formed to realize individual ends,* and their value is destroyed when their function diminishes or fails."[1] Here is the most central insight into individualism in America, as a national faith and guiding perception of reality and morality. Associations are not only voluntary but *instrumental*: they are means to individual ends. There is no paradox or contradiction, as has so often been puzzled over, in Americans being individualistic and being passionate "joiners" at the same time. They simply use what they join for their own individual purposes.

Darwin evidently got the inspiration for his idea of natural selection through competition from his reading of Thomas Malthus, whose famous analysis (like Franklin's), envisioned people as individually quite helpless in the face of population pressures. Classical economics and utilitarian thought also envisioned the individual as passive, just as Calvinism had done before them, and behaviorism would insist long after them. William Graham Sumner, for example, really was a sort of secular Calvinist, a believer in predestination in the form of luck (as in the Horatio Alger stories), at least with regard to "natural endowments." In their different ways, Alger and F. Scott Fitzgerald harkened back to Thomas Hooker, with his doctrine of *preparation* for salvation. Their versions are readiness for success, as in the motto, "Be prepared." Individuals needed to be ready for what Veblen called the Main Chance, so they could take advantage of it when it appeared. Americans were enormously confident that opportunity would appear. They had to be alert, in order to participate in the inevitable, natural progress. Failure was often acknowledged in the sad expression, "I missed my chance . . . ." or "missed the boat"; and people talked a great deal about their "chances": "You might not get a second chance," "That Big Chance is bound to come . . . ." or ". . . only comes once . . ." or, in the Arminian spirit, "Winners make their own 'breaks' . . ." and so on. The "breaks" might be determined in post-evolutionary America, but it was left to the individual to see them, exploit them, and show the will and "drive" to make the most of them.

Ethical individualism, largely derived from idealism and associated with it in Transcendentalism, was the view that morality was essentially individual, a matter of conscience; but in America it combined (without acknowledgement) psychological egoism, Hobbes's view that men always act in their own interest as they see it, with ethical egoism, which *justified* their always acting in their own interest. When Spencer came along with the doctrine that progress was natural, and evolution was another name for progress, he found an audience which had been made receptive by long experience of improving conditions and was fully convinced that both Enlightenment and Romantic forms of optimism were well founded. The disposition to be optimistic had been evident in Americans since the eclipse of predestination by variations of Arminianism, faith in will; and "enlightened" self-interest was just taken for granted by the early nineteenth century, an approach to life so reasonable as to seem self-evident. We should treat others decently because (or when, or if) it pays. What could be more obvious or enlightened than that?

The dark side of evolution, natural selection over which no individual had any control, sounded like Calvinism, which had never been refuted so much as simply discarded as tiresome and depressing. The bright side, survival of the fittest, powerfully appealed to those who were in fact surviving comfortably; and its version of justice complemented their social, economic and religious understandings of reality as progressive. Visions of progress, convictions of progress, understandably relate progress to the people who hold those visions and convictions. In America, the assumption was that "it's a free country," and anyone who could and would had the chance to share in progress -- to be successful. American faith in progress tended to cast the unsuccessful in the role of spectators, too obtuse or sluggish to find or take their chances: not quite bright or lacking in will. Earlier, they would have been deficient in virtue and talents.

American ideas of progress included chronic tensions, at least until what Leo Marx calls their debasement in the nineteenth century. Not everyone was able to accept the wedding of Christian faith to greed, so that "godliness [was] in league with riches," in Bishop Lawrence's famous turn-of-the-century dictum. Some people were always skeptical about the convenient coincidence of spiritual and material success claimed by beneficiaries of the latter. There were always those who wondered why rewards were so uneven if opportunity was equal, not "catching on" that only the *right* to opportunity was claimed to be equal. Enlightened self-interest took care of all these tensions, to the apparent satisfaction of most Americans. Christian meant some sort of Arminian, devoted to the exercise of will and discipline; and to be one was almost implicitly to be a capitalist in spirit. Individual morality served economic ends, and economic "drive" served moral ends.

Everyone understood the utility of cleverness and resourcefulness, and those who felt manipulated were forewarned by mountains of authoritative literature, plus "common sense," that their enlightened interest lay in cooperating with the progressive efforts of those who were more fit than themselves. The moral right to use one's opportunities was undeniably equal. Freedom required no reconciliation with authority, since authority, properly understood, derived from freedom, and freedom validated authority's legitimacy. Those who were powerful deserved to be. As to collective efforts, civic and even religious efforts were appropriately aimed at the moral progress of the individual. It was a matter of not getting the cart before the horse, but remembering the priority of the individual. Categories of people, like "races," could not deserve anything *as categories*, but only individuals, who would serve others if they helped themselves. Any inconsistency with biological determinism was only a minor inconvenience, if any at all.

Writers often remark that Calvinism dominated American attitudes; but that is accurate only to the extent that determinism dominated perceptions of self-fulfillment, as in luck. What dominated attitudes was concern for readiness to act on opportunities provided by luck, and confidence that (a) automatic progress meant that the odds were in one's favor, and (b) once the luck came, you couldn't "keep a good man down." In the seventeenth century it was desirable to work hard, to work your will on the world, as a form of prayer, or worship. One got ahead materially, but not for his own sake, for Christ's sake. Change was still feared, as almost certain to mean decline -- as it continued to be in England and Europe in the eighteenth century. But in America, Adams and Madison, for example, were confident of progress, with America leading the way. History appeared to be cyclical, with a presumption in favor of the new, the young. That changed in the nineteenth century. The cyclical idea, an ancient one, gave way to linear progress as the very *nature* of change and of history. But it was also clear that not everyone had a "place" in this history.

Science and technology appeared in the eighteenth century to be instruments for overhauling and improving society. Jefferson, the self-proclaimed "meliorist" -- *melior* means better -- wrote that science is progressive. By the middle of the nineteenth century, technology had become virtually synonymous with progress, and innovation was good in and of itself. Science means "knowledge," and knowledge was evolving, which meant progressing. What skepticism found significant expression protested that material progress did not address any "spiritual" needs; but this complaint lacked force in America. Material progress in the nineteenth century complemented the millenialist mood of most popular religion, and the political and social ideas of mobility and opportunity as well.

Hard work brought moral as well as material progress in obvious ways. It kept people out of trouble and on the paths of righteousness, as noted in Henry Ward Beecher's 1844 "Lectures to

Young Men." Guided by the individualist spirit of enlightened self-interest, it also generated what Daniel Callahan now aptly calls a "minimalist" conception of social obligation. A reluctance to set social and political goals for technology pervaded the culture. Technological progress itself became a substitute for politics, as Leo Marx says; and a "mystification" of technology occurred. In an age when progress was assumed to be natural, evolutionary and inevitable, the crucial question was seldom asked, "Progress toward what?" Materialistic meliorism, the creed of "more is better," was assumed, a corollary to the belief that individualism incorporated Natural Law: that the pursuit of self-interest was consecrated if it was clever, affable, and "enlightened."

Like medieval Christians and Calvinists, Americans continued to feel obliged to know and follow the will of God. If individual goals became objects of worship (honor), that could be explained by God willing individuals to follow enlightened self-interest. That's why he enlightened it. As Richard M. Huber says, ". . . the quest for grace became a quest for wealth."[2] One could say that the quest for wealth became a quest for grace, but that would be to impute conscious hypocrisy more generally than is warranted. Van Wyck Brooks made the interesting comment in 1915 that ". . . economic self-assertion still remains to most Americans a sort of moral obligation, while self-fulfillment still looks like a pretty word for selfishness."[3] The success books that poured forth in the 1850s, establishing perhaps the most popular *genre* in American publishing history, truly reflected the experience of many or even most. Kenneth S. Lynn says that success in America was so general and common that these books "were no more than mirrors held up to nature."[4] America was preoccupied with competition long before Spencer came along to provide an explanation for it; and it is small wonder that, as Irving Kristol says, "The history of the United States came to be written as the progressive liberation of the American people from all sorts of prior restraints . . . ."[5]

Timothy Shay Arthur's success of the 1850s, *Where There's a Will There's a Way*, widely read when resolve and perseverance were supposedly the key factors in success, actually showed the desired outcome reached by cleverness and resourcefulness. It celebrated calculating cleverness while purporting to be a paean to determination; or perhaps a strong will makes one more clever. This early example does not show success as coming from character, but rather the hero "hitting upon a plan" that works; and it is not a plan for self-development, but for making profits.[6]   These themes of luck, cleverness, and "singleness of purpose" would of course characterize the work of Horatio Alger, who simply ignited American ambitions and became the most popular author in the world in the last three decades of the nineteenth century: the period when Reconstruction ended, and African-Americans were "free" to try their luck as individuals on their own, to define their interests and advantages, apply their will and determination, seize their opportunities, grasp technology, ride the currents of progress, and to "make the most" of themselves.   They had an equal right to whatever opportunity they could find, in what was really, to an impressive degree, a land of opportunity -- for the majority.

Lynn writes of Alger, "The belief in the potential greatness of the common man, the glorification of individual effort and accomplishment, the equation of the pursuit of money with the pursuit of happiness and of business success with spiritual grace: simply to mention these concepts is to comprehend the brilliance of Alger's synthesis."[7] And synthesis it was, all predicated upon grace, luck, the main chance, and *preparation* for taking advantage of opportunity to overcome adversity and ride the crest of progress. Soon William James would call pragmatism "a new name for some old ways of thinking." The preference for what he called "real winners and real losers" was an ancient one, not just American; but it was also a national disposition in search of a philosophy as the twentieth century approached.

African-Americans, denied mainstream culture and even literacy for so long, clearly did not participate in "the progressive liberation from all sorts of prior restraint"; but prevalent American beliefs and attitudes insisted that it was "up to them." They were not very successful as a rule, and hardly appeared *prepared* for success by any enlightened sense of self-interest or capacity to find and grasp opportunity. Most Americans followed their enlightened sense of self-interest with considerable satisfaction, and responsibility for others who failed to do likewise was no part of their burden in life. What was wrong with the blacks? Their lacks had to be explained; and they were explained in terms of cherished American beliefs, in individual responsibility, individualism, and ability. The conclusion that blacks exhibited common deficiencies as individuals reinforced the conclusion that they were biologically, genetically, innately deficient; and inversely, the assumption of innate deficiency explained their deficiencies as individuals.

1. Horace Kallen, *Individualism: An American Way of Life* (New York: Liveright, Inc., 1933), 235-236, emphasis added.

2. Richard M. Huber, *The American Idea of Success* (New York: McGraw-Hill Book Company, 1971), 107.

3. Van Wyck Brooks, *America's Coming-of-Age* (Garden City: Doubleday Anchor Books, 1958), 17.

4. Kenneth S. Lynn, *The Dream of Success* (Boston: Little Brown Company, 1955), 3.

5. Irving Kristol, "Republican Virtue," *Kettering Review*, Fall 1988, 14.

6. See Huber, 29.

7. Lynn, 7.

Fifteen

Race Ideology and Expansionism

People in Europe had slight difficulty in framing their sense of identity on the basis of the histories of their peoples. In the nineteenth century, the ancient world had not only been glorified during centuries of "renaissance"; it was also newly romanticized in still more extravagant terms. Europeans felt themselves to be heirs to the glories of ancient Athens, the Roman Empire, and all history since remote antiquity. An Italian, a German, a Frenchman or an Englishman could point to centuries of culture as a "national" past in some sense, so there was for most no serious question about what it meant to be a Frenchman, say. Huge tribes, *peoples,* spoke their own languages in more than one way. Even though Italy and Germany had to struggle for political unification (attained in 1859 and 1871, respectively), their ancient cultures gave them a kind of identity that was difficult to generate in response to Crevecoeur's question, "What is an American?" Americans had no such ancient culture, except in the vague sense of being a sort of world-nation, heir to all the cultures from which it drew. In fact, some Europeans still annoy Americans by facetiously dismissing American history as current events -- usually in a restaurant that was serving pretty much the same menu before Columbus sailed.

The United States emerged fairly early in a form that would make it a durable nation-state, and the nation was born yearning for recognition on the basis of its official identity. New nations typically exhibit a powerful thirst for acceptance, the nationalistic feelings of their citizens particularly strong. So the United States embarked upon what has been aptly termed a "search for a usable past": a historical foundation upon which its citizens could claim and feel legitimacy and distinction. Nationalistic consciousness and patriotic fervor mounted through the years when the United States "got no respect" from Britain, France, or any other established power, but was repeatedly and painfully threatened and harassed. From European points of view, the Peace of Utrecht in 1815 was just a sideshow to the Congress of Vienna, but the end of what we call the War of 1812 had tremendous value for Americans in establishing their undeniable independence, sovereignty, and national self-esteem.

The ensuing "Era of Good Feelings" produced a still more satisfying reinforcement of national status: the Monroe Doctrine of 1823. Britain decided that the former Spanish colonies which had recently claimed independence should not become targets for renewed European colonization in the western hemisphere; so George Canning proposed to the American Secretary of State, John Quincy Adams, a joint Anglo-American proclamation warning France and Russia, for example, to stay out of the hemisphere. In a masterly stroke, Adams and Monroe issued such a statement simply as U. S. policy, confident that national interest would ensure British enforcement of the American position. Of course the European powers paid no attention to the U. S. proclamation. Who were the Americans, after all, to be dictating what France and Russia might do? But the greater purpose served was nationalistic self-confidence in the United States. It didn't matter so much how *other* people regarded or disregarded the doctrine of U. S. special interest in the hemisphere. The important thing was that America "laid down the law" to the world: the U. S. was no longer to be trifled with!

Still, such qualified and ambiguous national successes as those of 1815 and after failed to meet the need for a "usable" past. American longing for identity fatefully coincided with Romanticism in a new way, drawing attention beyond the national past (or lack of it) to a *racial* past. General celebration of alleged German traits mounted in the eighteenth century, led by Montesquieu, who discovered foundations of the Enlightenment in German love of freedom, nobility of spirit, chivalry, and genius for instituting just government, for example. These "Germanic" characteristics were found to have long pervaded western Europe, in fact. Frankenland or Franconia is northern

Bavaria, but related to France (*Frankreich*). There was a natural ethnic identity of Enlightened peoples.

Englishmen found identity with Germans to the north and east, and Saxon-worship rose to a crescendo in England even as Americans searched for identity and pride in their past. The rise of American nationalist spirit coincided with the bursting forth of Romanticism, with its strong currents of emotivism and mysticism. Sir Walter Scott became the most widely read author of the western world, and more Americans probably read *Ivanhoe* than any other book but the bible. As Reginald Horsman points out, Romanticism shifted away from the universalism of the Enlightenment in only a few decades. Emphasis on commonality and similarity, as in propositions about "all men," gave way to particularity and emphasis on differences during the first half of the nineteenth century. Uniqueness became the ideal, for both individuals and categories of people. Claims of exclusivity assumed central importance in popular thought and attitudes. Even as ideas of biological determinism gained momentum, people looked for ways in which they were distinctive, distinguished from one another, more than for general traits of "human nature."[1]

What is the seemingly irresistible appeal of claiming distinction for one's nationality or racial group? Prior to or outside individualism, it evidently provides a sense of self-importance, dignity, self-respect, to be a part, a member of a powerful or otherwise distinctive category. But in a culture of individualism, most notably that of America, group distinction supports separate individual self-aggrandizement. The ruling class, the great nation, the high culture or the superior race, all are effective instruments for claiming individual importance above and beyond that conferred by membership itself. Categories serve as launching platforms for individualists. The individualist ideal is distinction among the distinguished; or, to put it another way, it is necessary to establish that one is not merely distinguished among inferiors. Collective superiority undergirds individual distinction, and the two mutually reinforce each other.

Just as competitive economic individualism generated collective instruments -- successive forms of corporate organization -- so it required for its protection and extension the expansionist state, and for its justification the collectivities of race theory. Individualism required and generated the corporation, the corporate government, and the ideology to sustain the depredations of both on grounds of innate superiority or merit.[2] Personal independence in some of its strongest forms was associated with Teutonic, or German, or Anglo-Saxon ethnicity. Frederick Jackson Turner, with his complementary "germ theory" and "frontier thesis," followed the reasoning of Robert Knox's *Races of Men* (1850), picturing the transplanting of superior Anglo-Saxon "germs" or traits from the forests of northwestern Europe into the still more vast forests of North America. Christianity, never long or far away from claims of exclusivity, also found its way into this superior blend by way of writers like Charles Kingsley.

Literature in America through most of the nineteenth century was still largely English literature; and the extreme individualism of American writers like Emerson and Thoreau exuberantly extended the views of English Romantic race theorists like Thomas Carlyle. The American thirst for distinction was even greater than England's, perhaps because insecurity made the need for identity and self-importance stronger. Young nations, whatever the limitations of such an analogy, unmistakably display some of the characteristics we associate with young people. Nobody is more sensitive about being treated as a grown man or woman than an adolescent whose situation and status remain uncertain. Once we know we are adults, no suggestion to the contrary is meaningful. But until we know, the question continues to engage keenest interest and its resolution to warrant great effort. Nations not yet securely recognized tend, like transitional individuals, to exaggerate their claims at times.

Americans appointed themselves the ultimate Anglo-Saxon-and-Teutonic form and branch. At the same time, they set about shaping a satisfying *national* identity on the basis of their putative racial distinction. Since the national past was short (no matter how important the principles of the Revolution and the Constitution), Americans turned to the nation's *future* to support claims of greatness. Of course modesty had been no part of America's colonial background. Our earliest literature resounds with the sense of mission, of special destiny to demonstrate to the rest of the world how a Christian and enlightened society ought to conduct its affairs. Moral superiority was central to American self-perception from the outset, and New England in particular was never bashful about claims of setting an example for the world.

After the War of 1812, hostility between the post-pubescent nation and the overweaning mother country mellowed into ambivalent rivalry. America's uniqueness maintained center stage, but against the backdrop of racial continuity. Special status in the world derived more and more from the conviction of obvious fate or Manifest Destiny to lead the world in progress, under divine favor or natural law or both. What came to be thought of as the Anglo-Saxon race (incorporating "Teuton" if or as convenient) was incomparably well favored; and the natural law that governed its destiny was the law of invincible progress. Such conviction was the principal extension of Enlightenment optimism as it pervaded America in the Romantic nineteenth century.

And how did the Anglo-Saxon-Teuton Americans regard others? Virtually all white Americans from northern and western Europe became "honorary" Englishmen or Anglo-Saxons, or received the benefit of the doubt. Others, in proportion as they were found deserving, would become either the beneficiaries of Anglo-Saxon proximity and tutelage, or the recipients of discipline from the superior majority. Even before the 1780s, American leaders were projecting continental and hemispheric domination, world power, or, in Jefferson's later words, a mighty "empire for liberty." Increasingly, in the next century, these ideas took on racial meaning. The question not much asked about the empire idea was "Whose liberty?" The answer to such a question was implicit, or practically "self-evident": liberty of those who deserved it, whose racial and individual traits alike merited liberty.

The creed of Manifest Destiny eventually wreaked havoc upon all the various groups called Indians. These aboriginal peoples were simply engulfed by numbers and technology, in the name of progress and implicit superiority. If they accepted the Anglo culture, they lost their identity, position, and self-respect -- which Anglos could regard as just what they deserved. If they resisted the onslaught, they were seen as too stupid or perverse to adopt obviously superior ways -- which also showed their inferiority, so that they deserved whatever harsh treatment was required. From the *Requirimiento* of the Spanish in the sixteenth century to the Manifest Destiny of the Anglo-Saxon Americans in the nineteenth, Europeans took their own superiority for granted. The principal grounds for such claims varied from moral to cultural to racial, always with economic underpinnings. In one sense, the story of white destruction of Indian cultures is part of the larger story of European domination of tribal cultures wherever they were encountered, or simply of imperialism.

Racism has not persisted toward American Indians, or even toward later arrivals or "adoptees," in the same sense that it has toward African-Americans. Anti-Indian racism persisted when it was useful, and it recurs only when or if it is useful to whites. Whites depicted Indians as innately inferior when it suited their purposes of expansion and control to do so. By the end of the sixteenth century, the "invisible conquistadores" of European disease had already destroyed as many as seven-eighths of the native population who had been exposed to them. Destruction, both inadvertent and deliberate, continued through most of the nineteenth century. There are so few Indians in recent times, proportionately, that the mainstream culture can "afford" to romanticize or ignore them, or even to indulge them in their efforts to preserve identity and also to participate "successfully" in mainstream society. They hardly pose any threat to major interests, and so there is little "reason" for racism toward them to persist as it does toward African-Americans. This is by no means to make light of the tragic history of American Indians. Many groups were treated with utmost viciousness, and even deliberately exterminated. But the point here is to explain the persistence of white racism, not mistreatment in and of itself. Whites habitually defined Indians in whatever ways suited the whites' advantage, and treated them accordingly.[3] Once Manifest Destiny was fulfilled with regard to the Indians, those who survived seemed no longer important enough to require full-fledged racism, and it began to fade.

Arguments for innate race differences obviously gained momentum long before abolition of slavery became a real issue. As always, people interpreted important ideas to suit their own interests. The idea that "all men are created equal" was an easy target, especially if one insisted that it referred to abilities in a society geared to competition. That all men are in any sense equal was and is held by many to be a "self-evident lie."[4] Imperialist inclinations and racist ideas developed concomitantly for some time, and complemented each other, as conquest required ideological justification and "race purity" justified subjugation. The ideology justified the conquest, and the conquest validated the ideology. Like all Romantics, Americans became preoccupied with what set people apart from one another, more than with what bound them together. But what they perceived as race differences bound *whites* together, loosely if hardly "solidly," and enabled them to hold others in disdain or contempt in the name of progress -- and to celebrate *individual* differences among racial equals.

The static Scale of Being idea remained serviceable long after dynamic evolutionism became a far more persuasive explanation. Instead of the newer understanding replacing the old, the two were combined: an improbable development logically, but "rational" in the usual sense of the term, and not historically unusual. We generally think quite well -- to suit what we want to be true. After World War Two, for example, Americans conveniently and self-righteously associated Germany with unappealing "master race" notions. We tended to "forget" that German training was the training of American scholars for generations, and that both England and America have so much in common with Germany. Germans were, after all, the most numerous immigrants to the United States.

As Horsman says, nothing has served to perpetuate racism more effectively than the "rhetoric of freedom." He writes of the nineteenth century's spectacular adoption of race doctrines: "At the heart of the American and western European consignment of other races to an inferior, lesser human status was the need to justify exploitation and destruction. This need was particularly pressing in countries that prided themselves on their democratic ideals. The rhetoric of freedom could not countenance the mistreatment, exploitation, or destruction of equals."[5]

Contrary to righteous retrospective opinion, which usually finds malice rather than confusion at the heart of things, the thrust of racist influence on national experience shows a more tragic concatenation: a coming together of our most treasured ideals and the thoughts of our most esteemed figures. Racism gained its momentum largely from ideas of freedom and individualism, and from inspiring writers like Jefferson and Emerson. Not that they propounded it consciously, of course: but their splendid appeals dealt with virtue and talent and success and deserving in ways that allowed people to feel comfortable with racism, and even made them need it. The strongest appeals of the Enlightenment and of Romantic individualism, of liberalism and of capitalism, found support in scientific racism. Individualist and racist versions of Social Darwinism likewise reciprocally reinforced each other. The fact that most African-Americans did not prosper as individuals, and were therefore not among "the fittest," suggested that African-Americans were categorically less fit to succeed. If they were unfit categorically, the presumption was justified that any given individual was inferior.

1. Reginald Horsman, *Race and Manifest Destiny* (Cambridge, Mass.: Harvard University Press, 1981), 40-44, 81, 158-159, e.g.

2. See Horsman, 300-301.

3. See esp. Robert F. Berghofer, *The White Man's Indian: Images of the American Indian from Columbus to the Present* (New York: Alfred A. Knopf, 1978); and Ellémire Zolla, *The Writer and the Shaman: A Morphology of the American Indian* (New York: Harcourt Brace Jovanovitch, 1973), trans. Raymond Rosenthal.

4. See Horsman, 275.

5. *Ibid.*, 300.

Sixteen

Intelligence and Eugenics

In the eighteenth century, confidence in the force and "freedom" of will justified strong belief in individual deserving. This confidence and belief grew even stronger in nineteenth century America, but they increasingly prompted the question, "What accounts for the differences among men?" Environmental determinism had, to some degree, already given attention to this question; but its approach found a cold and skeptical reception. The idea that capacities and behavioral traits are shaped by circumstances flew in the face of deep-seated moral and religious beliefs, as well as economic doctrine. Economic success, to be satisfying, had to reflect both moral superiority and intellectual ability, as in Jefferson's "natural aristocracy" formulation. Even if the strength of will itself was largely determined, a more appealing explanation than environment was biological determinism. Ideas of heredity elaborated a massive retreat from evidence of environmental determinism.

Theories of *collective* behavior ironically flourished in a culture of individualism, as biological science remained more taxonomic, more classificatory than experimental. In this vein, supposed ape-like traits were widely attributed to Africans. For example, the supposed sexual "bestiality" of black men called up images of the gorilla for people who did not know that that powerful beast has a remarkably tiny and neglected penis, which it uses for about ten seconds a year to impregnate the astonishingly fertile female gorilla. Any man who wanted to feel superior on the basis of sexual equipment or performance needed only to compare himself with a gorilla.

Anthropometrics also allowed theories like those of Cesare Lombroso to exert wide and even official influence, based on notions of physically identifiable "criminal man." The linked habits of drawing inferences about whole categories of people from measured differences among individuals, and inferences about abilities from differences of controlled performance and of circumstance, seemed irresistible to the "Caucasian" majority. Simple majority-opinion democracy endorsed racism. At the same time, the various forms of anthropometrics, and enchantment with statistics and quantification in general, stimulated both academic and popular curiosity about intelligence, or general mental ability.

Alfred Binet (1857-1911) was the leading pioneer of intelligence studies. Binet sought guidelines for meeting the varying instructional needs of children. He was cautious and restrained regarding the "nature" of intelligence, and always rejected ideas of inherent deficiency, especially by categories. Obviously there are real hereditary differences among people, in mental abilities as in other ways: vision, quickness, capabilities of various kinds. But most people's mental abilities are enormously flexible and malleable, susceptible of dramatic change by appropriate educational treatment. Recognition of this fact underlies the development of Japan's remarkably literate work force, for example. Everyone who is not brain-damaged is presumed to be educable, and something like what we call a self-fulfilling prophecy occurs.

In 1912, the year after Binet died, W. Stern contrived a procedure for measuring performance, establishing statistical norms of performance corresponding to age, and dividing the actual score of an individual by the norm for his or her age. The "intelligence quotient," or IQ swept the educational world, and was soon canonized. In fact, careful testing could establish quite usefully the likelihood of a test-taker's success in systems and other patterns understood by the test-maker. But educators and others less careful than Binet quickly drew disastrous inferences from the scientific fact of hereditary abilities. Every new report was enlisted in the service of beliefs already cherished. Selecting and interpreting as their assumptions inclined them to, Americans widely and tragically concluded that hereditary "levels" of ability were inescapable; and, in an awful corollary, that variations within a group of individuals are related to differences among nationalities and races. Their "norms" were like those of seventeenth-century Englishmen who found the absence of English culture and language evidence of inferiority.

The culture that worshipped ideas of individual will and responsibility more than any other now fell in love with a "scientific" version of innate depravity. Twentieth-century Americans differed from seventeenth-century Englishmen in one important respect above all others: they took inferiority of performance to be not only collective but *innate* by racial category. More than any other people, Americans have been pleased to believe that individuals are what they will to be: that we are very much the authors of our selves, literal "self-made men." How ironic, then, that the rigid hereditarian idea of intelligence and IQ is an American invention and doctrine. Beliefs in individual will and deserving, and in biological determinism of ethnic groups' abilities at the same time, met the needs of North European Americans. They believed the world to be as they wanted it to be, with individualism among the elect and inevitable collective failure or damnation for the rest.

In the 1780s, when the Great Chain of Being dominated thinking, Thomas Jefferson plaintively asked, in *Notes on Virginia*, what he regarded as a rhetorical question: Should not human reproduction be undertaken as carefully as the breeding of horses and dogs, for example? The scientific racism, or biological determinism that arose over the next century brought that question to the forefront of American discussion in a new light, and fears of miscegenation found fresh expression in the sweeping eugenics movement of the early twentieth century. By that time Darwinism had either replaced or been overlaid upon the Great Chain, and natural selection contributed to a national preoccupation with breeding. Between 1907 and 1915, twelve states passed sterilization laws, and a National Conference on Race Betterment was held in 1914. As Richard Hofstadter summarized, eugenicists "were . . . in large part responsible for the emphasis upon preserving the 'racial stock' as a means of national salvation . . ."[1] National salvation, in that age of imperialism, meant national power; and racism assumed the mantle of *patriotism* to complement its scientific endorsement.

In the early twentieth century many Americans saw democracy as threatened by the presence, and the potential participation in public affairs, of ignorant hordes with low "native ability." How could an informed electorate function, with so many who were incapable of informing themselves, or of being informed? The same "scientific" methods that showed white superiority were now used against southern and eastern European immigrants, culminating in the Dillingham Commission report, published by the Congress during World War I, and in the discriminatory immigration acts of 1921 and 1924.[2] In those "national origins" laws, as Gould puts it, "The eugenicists battled and won one of the greatest victories of scientific racism in American history."[3]

World War I provided an opportunity to test enormous numbers of young men, and psychologists soon amassed a vast body of data to validate their assumptions about gradation and heredity. Certain of the innate inferiority of blacks, they administered standardized tests of the cultural resemblance between those who made the tests and those who took them. Very few black recruits bore much resemblance to the psychologists. Black inferiority was "demonstrated" scientifically on a firmer basis than ever. Leading scientists gradually discredited these "findings" during the 1920s, pointing to regional, cultural, health and educational factors as compelling environmental considerations. But, as usual, the simplest explanation remained far and away the most widely accepted. To grasp reality requires more serious attention than most people will give, especially when a simple, flattering explanation is not only available but authoritatively endorsed.

By the 1950s, the Air Force had taken the lead in "personnel processing," including testing. Basic trainees, undergoing the experience of being systematically intimidated and humiliated, were herded together for testing on "stanine" batteries, administered by white, enlisted college graduates with test-taking experience and military power to keep strict order. Anyone who has given or taken a college exam in a large lecture class can testify to the common misunderstandings of instructions, even with a fairly homogeneous, similarly literate population. Testing conditions in the military were not ideal. But test results were carefully examined by special units, such as the Human Resources Research Center at Sampson Air Force Base, New York, handling recruits from the entire northeast.

After a few more days of basic training, assignment clerks called "career counselors" interviewed the trainees and assigned them to further training programs and to on-the-job training on the basis of their qualifications, mainly test scores. Each black recruit's records were marked with a small red X, a simple code identification; and there was a very high positive correlation between "red X" forms (the words black, colored and Negro were never used) and low test scores. The kitchens, motor pools and warehouses of the Air Force filled with blacks. Racism was pervasive, not hostile but simply taken for granted, reflecting the larger society. The triumph of scientific racism in the early twentieth century was so complete that its effects persist long after its dismissal as serious science. Such is the force of inertia, and so strong the appeal of the path of least resistance, that even well-informed white Americans remain "open to the possibility" that biological determinism and scientific racism validly describe reality; and that "intelligence" really is innate, quantifiable, and *collective*. We believe or at least tolerate what we find reasonable: that is, compatible with what we perceive as our interests.

1. Hofstadter, 161, 162.
2. See Oscar Handlin, *Race and Nationality in American Life* (New York: Doubleday Anchor Books, 1957), Chapter V.
3. Gould, 232.

Seventeen

Scholarly and Christian Racism

American social science, developing very fast in the late nineteenth century, was weighed down by the baggage of European racism as well as garden variety assumptions and purposes. In the Progressive period, leading American social scientists, including Lester Frank Ward, Charles Horton Cooley, Edward A. Ross, and John R. Commons, adopted racist assumptions in their opposition to the individualism associated with Herbert Spencer and William Graham Sumner, for example. Ross liked the eugenics idea, and its movement. He and Commons both opposed immigration, Commons the more so because of his pro-union passion. Much racism in the early twentieth century was *liberal and progressive*, with immigration central to the discussion because it was perceived as a principal obstacle to social progress.

Biology, seen as a different kind of science from physics, got blended with cultural studies and political thought, especially in the seemingly endless mutations of Natural Law. The word "law" itself caused no end of misunderstanding, partly through ambiguity and often through contrived equivocation as well. A law of nature, such as the Law of Gravity, *describes* physical reality. It does not *prescribe* what should be. Gravity says thay if you drop something, it will fall; not that it is obligated to fall, or that falling is to be desired. But the idea of natural law, when brought into the analysis of human affairs, has a sneaky way of shifting from description to prescription. It has always presented a strong temptation to identify regularities in our experience (descriptive "laws" of nature), and then to infer what they mean about how we *should* behave (prescriptive "laws" analogous with civil laws). Trouble arises when scientific authority is claimed for prescriptive "laws," and people act on conceptions like a "Law" of Supply and Demand or a "Law" of Survival of the Fittest as if they were truly unexceptionable and inescapable, like the descriptive Law of Gravity. This kind of confusion, both inadvertent and cultivated, pervaded discussion of human groups in the earlier twentieth century, even in the most enlightened circles.

To be anti-racist in the late nineteenth and early twentieth centuries was to risk being regarded as anti-scientific, unpatriotic, and opposed to progress. The scientific racism of the Progressive period was drawn largely from the real progress made in genetics. Evolution as an explanation of reality led to eugenics, which was by no means entirely accepted in the scientific community itself. But eugenics became pervasive in *popular* conceptions of science. Most scientists simply reflected the prevailing assumptions of society, of course. The influence of Franz Boas and his many outstanding students and associates slowly turned the tide against academic racism, beginning with Boas' 1911 landmark study, *The Mind of Primitive Man*. Scientific anthropology hinged upon thinking and feeling oneself into the circumstances of others, rather than simply making invidious comparisons and pronouncing others inferior. But popular attitudes and beliefs are convenient, not scientific. Racism continued to serve the purposes and meet the needs of the many.

A steady river of non-fiction racist writings flowed through even the most respected magazines, to say nothing of books. The central thrust of this writing was more historical than scientific, and it aimed at self-celebration rather than conscious exploitation. I. A. Newby makes the crucial point that Progressive Era historians were not so much concerned to justify discrimination or exploitation as they were to comfort themselves and their readers with accounts of Northwest Europeans' inherent wonderfulness. English and Germanic people in particular were presented as chosen people, "well-favored" in every way, by God or Nature. This "natural selection" held obvious implications for darker skinned people. Racist history reinforced scientific racism, and both gained momentum with systematic segregation in the 1890s. Among the influential popularizers of racist history, Lothrop Stoddard and Madison Grant are most conspicuous; and popularization continued long after the scientists had revised their views. What Ogburn would later call "cultural lag" worked with a vengeance regarding race ideas, with the best scientists far in advance of popular understanding.

Scientists, and scholars in general, tend to assume that when *they* understand or resolve some question, false impressions and solutions are automatically abandoned by the public. Of course nothing could be farther from reality. Ideas like the Missing Link rattle around in the minds of millions long after scholars have given up on them. But in this case, as usual, many factors were at work. Interpretations of Reconstruction played a central role in historical interpretation. These were not so much ideological in nature as sympathetic toward whites in the south. That sympathy predictably expressed the simple, matter-of-fact assumption of white superiority, and took shape in the tacit assumption that whites would and should be dominant. A classic example of its wistful, nostalgic appeal is the 1930 work, *I'll Take My Stand*, by "Twelve Southerners" with impressive literary abilities.

Why did Americans assume that behavior expresses race traits? Enlightenment historians like Gibbon and Hume had rejected the notion, but in the United States it found few critics. Part of the explanation must be the nationalist mood expressed in our historical writing. Americans sought a sense of identity in terms of their nation, and the public embraced the works of historians like Bancroft, Parkman, and Prescott, who accepted prevailing ideas of inherent inclinations as well as influences from collective experience. From the 1850s, the persuasion called Anglo-Saxonism centered on the idea of a genetic trait, a germ, genius, or creative spark found in northwest Europeans, which led to high civilization. (The dark complexion of Egyptians, for example, had to be ignored.) The word "Teutonic" became a dominant concept around the turn of the century, not only in the United States but in Germany and England as well. Herbert Baxter Adams was perhaps most influential in promoting it in historical scholarship, at a time when most American professors still acquired much of their training in Germany. Racist assumptions from the treatment of history found wide audiences through fiction writers like Frank Norris, Jack London, and Owen Wister; while those who expressed serious misgivings, like Mark Twain, Stephen Crane, G. W. Cable and Kate Chopin, seemed merely eccentric on the matter.

The World War I period saw a culmination of racist historical interpretations, building from the appearance of Houston Stewart Chamberlain's work in 1911, and translation of Gobineau in 1912, to Madison Grant's *The Passing of the Great Race*, 1916. With America's entry into the war, ethnic defamation was made systematic by Wilson's propaganda chief, George Creel, adding once again a dimension of outright hostility to popular prejudices. The deliberate inflaming of public opinion against everything German, made difficult by decades of "teutonic" celebration, played upon the most anti-intellectual appeals. It could be no accident that racism reached a crescendo of mindless brutality at war's end, for popular hostility and anger had been fueled by ethnic clichés even as blacks first moved into northern cities in large numbers. The war period encouraged the worst tendencies of invidious comparison and supremacist inclination. In the next decade, the "roaring 20s," the decade of modernism, the Ku Klux Klan enjoyed its greatest popular acceptance.

With historians as with scientists,   anti-African notions gradually lost favor between the two wars; but the earlier racist assumptions still pervaded popular sentiments.   Ideas of innate superiority were congenial to even some of the best informed segments of white opinion. During the 1920s, IQ testing led to conclusions that were devastating for blacks as well as immigrants. But racist literature continued to exert wide appeal, even long after scholars had refuted its assumptions.   Self-improvement and competitiveness flavored the age, emphasizing performance standards which worked to the disadvantage of nearly all African-Americans.

The intellectual history of the 'twenties shows the miscegenation idea in decline and disrepute: but again, for *scientists*. For white people at large, discredited racist science remained valid, and apprehension remained as much alive as ever, alive enough that race-mixing would be the *real* main issue underlying educational desegregation for the rest of the twentieth century. Even if they accepted equality of abilities, white people did not want their children to become accustomed to associating with blacks on a basis of complete social acceptance. Lillian Smith was a notable pioneer in examining the psycho-sexual aspects of racism and education, in *Killers of the Dream*, 1949.[1]

Before the civil rights movement of the 1950s and '60s, opponents of racism found very little comfort or relief. Striking out in anger and frustration (a mistake to be repeated at the end of the '60s, with Black Power), blacks adopted an inverted or retaliatory racism, celebrating themselves and disparaging whites ("honkies," etc.). W. E. B. DuBois, the great scholar and leader of black Americans, may have given unfortunate inspiration in this regard. Black resentment and anger are perfectly understandable, but they led to playing the white racists' own game instead of rejecting it altogether. Despite claims of the importance of self-respect in terms of "black pride," nothing very useful was (or is) served by countering "white is better" with "black is better," no matter how the assertions are phrased.

Naturally enough, blacks always sought and expected support from religious quarters. Offhand, one would think that the Social Gospel, rising from the 1870s to World War I, would have met their expectations. But the Social Gospel movement, focusing on industrial capitalism's effects and involving the Protestant churches in meeting the conditions of this world as well as satisfactorily reaching the next, shared in the fervid nationalism of the period. Reverend Josiah Strong, as outspoken a white supremacist as one would wish to find, was a leader of the Social Gospel. Theodore Munger, Washington Gladden, Lyman Abbott, Walter Rauschenbush, and George T. Herron all shared Strong's Anglo-Saxon racism, albeit without his economic and political aggressiveness. Quite aside from overt religious racism, American churches simply tended to ignore any questions which challenged racist assumptions, as Newby points out. They found it quite comfortable not to consider questions regarding race as moral questions, which was certainly discreet of them, if not valorous. American Protestant churches are, after all, strongly political in their internal affairs, with the material security as well as the moral leverage of ministers tending to be dependent upon the approval by their congregations of the positions they take.

Religious racism, whether active or passive, continued to assume "that racial inequality is the work and the will of God."[2] The "chosen people" idea exerted limitless appeal, with the self-evident special status of Caucasians an obvious manifestation of divine favor. Implications of rightful dominance and exclusivity seemed clear enough. Why did Christian groups generally ignore questions of race? It was unnecessary and uncomfortable to consider them. The question might better be, Why should Christian groups consider such questions when they saw no need to do so? Divine favor was clear, God's will was revealed. Further, in the American Way, success continued to imply deserving; and success was very much a white preserve.

The Roman Catholic Church, being hierarchical and authoritarian rather than congregational or democratic, was more independent of popular acceptance, and might perhaps have been expected to be more morally responsive to race questions. It was not. In fact, W. E. B. DuBois thought that the Catholic Church was the most discriminatory of all. Why would that be? What would make racial discrimination appealing or acceptable to Catholic policy-makers? The Church, while hierarchical, is more political than was often recognized. It too had constituencies to be accommodated, and it has not survived through the centuries by alienating or offending its financial and political supporters. Catholic constituencies have been notably Irish, Italian, and Polish, for example: immigrant groups successively competing with blacks, in relatively low socio-economic positions. Also, the Church has never depended upon reform to maintain the support of its members. It tended strongly to ignore the Social Gospel idea, that seeking social and economic justice would allow spiritual concerns to be more effectively addressed. At the peak of a bitter civil rights housing controversy involving his parishioners, a Catholic pastor in the 1960s could still refuse to mention the matter from the pulpet because "it's too close to Holy Week."[3]

Since religious groups do not share to any great extent the use of information bases from science or from history, they lagged behind even the woefully slight secular recognition of racism's assumptions. Newby summarizes: "The Negro then was virtually friendless. Condemned by science to a subordinate place in nature and disparaged by history for his alleged failure to contribute anything to man's civilization, he now found himself abandoned, ignored, or patronized by Christianity and the nation's religious community."[4]

1. Lillian Smith's *Killers of the Dream* (1949) was reissued shortly before her death, with some new comments: (New York: W. W. Norton and Company, 1961).
2. I. A. Newby, *Jim Crow's Defense* (Baton Rouge: Louisiana State University Press, 1965), 89.
3. Cuyahoga Falls, Ohio, 1965.
4. Newby, 109.

Eighteen

Democratic and Progressive Racism

Utilitarian thinking in the eighteenth century made self-interest legitimate and respectable, and even made egoism broadly acceptable. The individualistic "pursuit of happiness" version of utilitarian thought gave philosophical substance to capitalism. At that time, democracy was regarded with great suspicion and apprehension by almost all who held positions of power and influence. But utilitarian ideas, in a different and less individualistic form, also irresistibly pressed forward the cause of equality and democracy. Utilitarian egoism supported competition and economic inequality, while utilitarian universalism, or socialism, undergirded collective goals and political equality.

The "utility principle," articulated early by Joseph Priestley and later chiefly associated with Jeremy Bentham, was perhaps best and most originally exemplified by Francis Hutcheson, the great moral sense philosopher. Hutcheson deduced from the moral sense an overriding social goal. He wrote, "In comparing the moral qualities of actions," so that we can choose among alternatives, "we are led by our Moral Sense of Virtue" to the conclusion that *"That action is best which procures the greatest HAPPINESS of the greatest numbers: and that worst, which in like manner occasions misery."*[1] In short, what makes an action good is that it intentionally promotes the general welfare, or tends in that direction. As far as Hutcheson was concerned, this is the end of the quest for "justifying reasons" on which action is based. What the moral sense perceives as benevolent is most broadly utilitarian, and good.   And so, in the political sphere, "that *nation* is best which procures the greatest happiness of the greatest numbers, and that worst which in like manner occasions misery."[2]

In the nineteenth century, as both democracy and racism took shape, utilitarian thinking dominated the English-speaking world. The utility principle became the basis for democratic racism. Its goal became the greatest good of the greatest number of people like me, with habits, manners, attitudes and characteristics like mine. Romanticism accentuated differences, categorical and individual, and glorified the self-reliance and self-assertion that capitalism had already institutionalized.

The universalist version of utilitarian thought never really captured America's allegiance, even at the peak of Utilitarianism as presented by John Stuart Mill.   The idea of the greatest good of the greatest number seemed to require a concession that everyone's good was equivalent to everyone else's, which Americans found difficult to make, to say the least. But an ingenious adaptation of the principle was already available, combining egoistic and universal utilitarianism in capitalist fashion by assuming that to serve oneself is to serve the general welfare. After all, I can't be sure what will add to the aggregate happiness or good of the society in a general way, but I can be sure that if I increase my own happiness and those whose happiness contributes to mine, there is more happiness among the greatest number that includes me.   What had social utility was what worked for the happiness of most people; and most people were white.

Cautioned most notably by James Madison in *The Federalist,* especially number ten, by Alexis de Tocqueville in *Democracy in America,* and by John C. Calhoun in his *Disquisition* and *Discourse,* American leaders generally took measures to prevent "tyranny of the majority." Our best political thinkers always realized that democracy in America meant broadly implementing the will of the majority, while at the same time protecting the rights of those who were not part of the majority. In the matter of race dispositions, however, tyranny of the majority flourished, strengthened by capitalism, utilitarianism, simplistic notions of democracy, and romanticism, all burgeoning in the nineteenth century, even as scientific racism gained momentum.

The divergent and conflicting interests of whites have always determined how blacks were treated, and what rationalizations were needed to justify that treatment. After the Civil War, as constitutional and economic conflicts were agonizingly settled, reconciliation and reunification proceeded on the basis of tacit acceptance of racism.[3] Even before the development of full-blown scientific racism late in the century, the North generally and substantially shared Southern ideas of race. Ralph Waldo Emerson, for example, embraced popular racist views, despite his insistence on thinking for oneself. In fact, Emerson's special eloquence in making popular dispositions sound lofty or profound was devastating. The chief formulator of Transcendentalism, New England's moralistic idealism, was Theodore Parker. He wrote that Anglo-Saxons were the best of the Teutonic race, the best of the best, endowed with an "instinct for progress."

Albeit under tremendous political pressure, Abraham Lincoln made explicitly racist statements in 1858, referring to a *permanent* "physical difference between the white and black races which I believe will for ever forbid the two races living together on terms of social and political equality." In 1861 he was prepared to sacrifice blacks' freedom permanently if that would bring about regional reconciliation. Lincoln's views and dispositions represented quite well those of most Americans in the North. He disliked slavery and found it an embarrassment and a disgrace, particularly since emancipation in the British Empire in 1833. However, his feelings of revulsion toward slavery did not lead him to egalitarian acceptance of its victims.

Toward the end of the nineteenth century, racism derived respectability from legal and Populist-democratic points of view, as well as from scientific arguments and theories of social science. It continued to derive "righteous" feelings from the spirit of Redemption -- redeeming the South from the claimed outrages of Reconstruction and outside interference. Outside the South, racism gathered force from the dispositions associated with immigration restriction, especially "Anglo-Saxonism." By the end of the century, when white supremacists were instituting the most rigid segregation by law, scientific racism was so pervasive that vitriolic racist views found a receptive national audience, through even the most enlightened and liberal periodicals.[4] As Thomas P. Bailey observed, the "Southern Way" was close to being the "American Way."

Racism was democratic in the simplest sense: it had overwhelming popular acceptance and support. Preventing blacks from voting ensured that no white faction or party could use them against its white opposition. Their disfranchisement was progressive, proceeding in the name of liberalism, good government, and reform. White solidarity, sometimes exaggerated, nonetheless underlay much of Southern Progressivism in particular. Later, as blacks moved north in large numbers, the "problem" spread, and racist views intensified in the North (as witness events following World War One). But what underlies such views?

To use Kovel's distinction, modern and particularly non-Southern racism is much more "aversive" than "dominative." In 1835, Tocqueville noted that ". . . the prejudice of race appears to be stronger in the states that have abolished slavery than in those where it still exists; and nowhere is it so intolerant as in those states where servitude has never been known . . . ." Tocqueville was noting mainly the racism of aversion, avoidance of people who were looked down upon: the binary mind-set at work, emphasizing differences of we-they, us-them, and the analogous good-bad. It drew support from belief in superiority of abilities, "demonstrated" through equality of opportunity; from massive indoctrination in the ideology of capitalism; from traditions of individual responsibility, back to Arminianism; from an understanding of equality among equals in "virtue and talents"; from egoistic utilitarianism, from romanticism, and from democracy. In short, racism drew support from America's most cherished values and attitudes.

Contentions like Williamson's, that there has been some sort of "White Soul" movement, a determined twentieth-century effort toward white solidarity,[5] should be regarded skeptically. What whites have solidly endorsed, most conspicuously, is individualistic equality of opportunity as an ideal; and the more firmly that concept is accepted as fundamental equality, the more inviting it is to point to deficient performance of blacks as individuals. Every student of how humans perceive has observed that people tend markedly to perceive what they want to perceive and what they expect to perceive. We interpret to our own comfort and advantage, just as we act so in other ways. If blacks are generally "down," they have been perceived as probably lacking something essential to success. There is an implicit moral dimension to failure, where success is salvation. In this regard, American performance has been and is democratic, if that means proceeding according to majority opinion and serving the greatest happiness, security, comfort, and satisfaction of the greatest number. On that basis, the rise of racism was positively progressive.

1. Francis Hutcheson, *An Enquiry into the Original of Our Ideas of Beauty and Virtue*, 1725, III, 180-181.
2. *Ibid.*, II, 3.

3. See C. Vann Woodward, *The Strange Career of Jim Crow* (New York: Oxford University Press, 2d rev. ed., 1966), 6, 70; and *Thinking Back* (Baton Rouge: Louisiana State University Press, 1985).

4. See Woodward, *Jim Crow*, 94, 70, e.g.

5. Joel Williamson, *The Crucible of Race: Black-White Relations in the American South Since Emancipation* (New York: Oxford University Press, 1984).

Nineteen

Pragmatic Individualism

In the later nineteenth century, as biological determinism and racism gained momentum and hardened, the utilitarian core of American culture manifested itself in still more pervasive form. The rise of naturalism, or eclipse of philosophical idealism by scientific materialism, set the stage for "the American philosophy," as pragmatism came to be known. In "The Fixation of Belief," 1877, Charles Sanders Peirce wrote about establishing beliefs by desire -- something like exercising what James would call the Will To Believe, in a set of essays dedicated to Peirce ten years later. Peirce also wrote about fixing belief by tenacity: stubbornness, inertia, or attachment to what one has already hit upon; and by authority, conferring the *a priori* endorsement of self-evident truth on what has been adopted. He said that "the very essence of [the *a priori* method] is to think as one is inclined to think." Such an approach was "distinguished for its comfortable conclusions." It was also very conducive to strength of conviction, or dogmatism.

Peirce did not perceive his own philosophy as utilitarian, which was a major reason for his dissociating himself from the term "pragmatism" after William James adopted it. Peirce agreed with Chauncy Wright that scientific method offered the only path to knowledge (anticipating Rudolf Carnap, for example), but he was skeptical about its applicability to human concerns. In fact, he was convinced that in matters of "values and beliefs . . . philosophy could offer no guidance," and that "feeling or instinct is a more important source." Like Wright's philosophy, Peirce's pragmaticism was purely intellectual, unconcerned with behavior. At the same time, he found the "heart" perceptive in some fashion, recalling moral sense philosophy, and setting a stage for James.

Perhaps like Peirce, William James found troubling the bleakness of a naturalistic world; but unlike Peirce, James showed an intense interest in conduct, and spoke of "truth as something that could vary from individual to individual." Pragmatism would blur the distinction between objective and subjective knowing, undermining empiricism as dogma even while defending it as an indispensable guide to action. Pragmatic philosophy cannot insist that propositions are true, either about relations or about facts of existence. It offers no guarantees of consistency, but simply says "Try this if you think it might do." James saw the world of Royce's idealism on one hand and that of Wright's naturalism on the other as too rigid for comfort. What was needed was a human environment that takes into account and accommodates both the head and the heart, intellect and sentiment: the whole being so staunchly represented by Emerson, for example. As Morton White says, James was a late and great Romantic: he attached as great importance as any thinker to the feelings and personal experience of the individual. Scientific method and logic alone were too constricting and limiting for him. James embraced evolutionary reality, but he emphasized that what was determined by it was chance. He accepted and advocated rigorous epistemology and methodology, but assumed in human affairs a sort of religious individualism which relied more heavily on temperament than intellect. He also shared the intellectual libertarianism of his utilitarian model, John Stuart Mill.

In *Pragmatism*, 1907, James set out the characteristic orientations of his famous "block universes," between which he wished to mediate rather than simply to *choose*, as their respective proponents tended to demand. Idealism, with its corollaries of rationalism, intellectualism, epistemological monism, dogmatism, religiousness, and faith in free will, faced the age-old challenge of materialism, attended by the dispositions of empiricism, positivism, pluralism, skepticism, and determinism. Both persuasions were traditionally dualistic in ontology, claiming, respectively, the priority of the ideal and its imperfect expression in the material world; and inversely, the seminal role of physical reality, from which the ideal is derived. By the first decade of the twentieth century, the "eclipse" of supernaturalism by naturalism was sufficiently advanced that the presumption among intellectuals would be in favor of the more "scientific" explanation of reality.

But the seemingly contradictory block universes were both incomplete from a scientific point of view. Idealism, by this time, was chiefly a devotion to logic and generalization: the "regularities running through experience" (James's expression), statistics, probability, formulation of hypotheses and theories. Materialism implied empiricism, and corresponding attention to specificity, singularity, individuation, particularity, sensory perception, and "experience" as opposed to formal logic and theory. Which was the more "scientific"? There could be no science at all without both aspects. Idealism was indispensable to traditional religion; but that did not mean that religion could not survive with science. James insisted that a "conflict" between science and religion could not, properly speaking, occur, since they did not address the same kinds of questions. Nature is indifferent to individuals, and science can deal with them only as members or specimens; and yet no two of us are precisely the same. "Religion," in whatever sense, accommodates individuals in their subjective selves.

Logical thought had been for decades much under the spell of Hegel: the familiar thesis-antithesis-synthesis-new thesis etc. of the "dialectic" (Cf. "empiric"). The thinking was binary, but it was not just a matter of false dichotomy. It showed the versus mind-set at work, the assumption that negation must be contradiction rather than mere exclusion or separation. If A is defined, runs the example, Not-A is necessarily implied (since A is not "everything" or it would not have to be and could not be defined, except perhaps as "the case.") Does this mean that A implies the reality of Anti-A? No, just Not-A, something other than A. Defining "dinner" does not entail "anti-dinner," but the reality of something other than dinner. With the block universes, or the aspects of science, we confront a pragmatic question of *emphasis* on one aspect: *defining* by exclusion, but not necessarily implying contradiction. Science is simply different from religion, as inference is different from hypothesis or theory. Both are needed. Pragmatism avoids contradiction in the interest of the widest latitude for meeting individual needs.

In 1875 James had posited the pragmatic axiom that "the knower is part of the known," with supremely individualistic implications; and he developed the idea that the real world is the world as known. That year James also asserted the validity of choice, suggesting that the choice of cosmic pessimism is only defensible on the basis of dogmatic commitment to a static universe. Optimism, conversely, is the justifiable choice of those who have faith in a universe potentially good and becoming, rather than statically imperfect. A correspondence appears between James's views and the optimism of post-Darwinian America's popular culture. It is more or less analogous to the coincidence that made Emerson a popular lecturer to crowds whose notion of individual self-reliance was very different from his, and who heard what they found congenial. But James's implication in 1875 is clear: the known world as *the* world implies that the individual can deal with and only with what he is aware of. In other words, the possibility of individual freedom is universal, but the "genuine option" of freedom is not. The successful and the unsuccessful have identical responsibilities in James's world, since their freedom is at least coextensive with what is possible for them. A man may lose happiness whether or not he understands it, because the failure to choose work toward knowing what is knowable is equivalent to the choice of not knowing. The failure to choose moral freedom, however it comes about, is forfeit of one's right to choose conscious responsibility and identity, or full personhood. By its own functional criterion, pragmatism at times recalled none other than Jonathan Edwards.

"The Will to Believe" was originally entitled "The Right to Believe." James's pragmatism reaffirmed and extended the central utilitarian thrust of the culture, but it also emphasized the individualist and subjectivist inclination of that thrust. James did not do much to further either the social consciousness of Mill's utilitarianism or the scientific community sought by Peirce. Why? Individual will remained a powerful article of faith. James felt Arminianism more than Puritanism, in the dogged rejection of determinism and the insistence upon efficacy of choice. There was really no either-or situation in pragmatism, between fatalism and choice, but both at once. In the seventeenth century and even earlier (Calvin lived from 1509 to 1564), fatalism was *combined* with individual responsibility. Human nature was depraved, inescapably self-interested, but men also confronted a positive, constructive equality: equality of opportunity, that abstract natural right to determine their own lives within limits set by circumstance, or "favor": God's will, Divine Light, Knowledge of the Good, or Nature.

By the time James wrote, self-interest had become legitimate and respectable in American life. The prevailing attitude toward democracy in America was as the expression of individual will by equals. Equals in what sense? Equal individuals who knew what was good for themselves, and whose interests were those shared by the greatest number. Individuals with equal rights to pursue their equally valid and defensible interests. Individuals with equal will-power, virtue, and potential for moral self-reliance, regarding both capitalism and democracy. Genius had become the assertion of uniqueness or superiority, the expression of the self as worthwhile. The ideal was not equal opportunity, but equality of opportunity to be unequal, and an equal right to be unequal.

"The knower is part of the known" seems deliberately ambiguous until it is realized that James's intent is to include both the part of man under Emerson's "law for thing," open to scientific study, and the *whole* man, with his moral being that may be considered only under "law for man." In the added dimension, only the knower's own moral self-knowledge is possible. To the extent that the knower is an object, liable to the play of forces as any other object is, he must be known empirically. Beyond that point empiricism *becomes* the intuitive introspection which is Socratic self-realization. It is this dualistic view, the same as Emerson's, that permits James to identify himself as the "complete empiricist" while relying so heavily on intuition. In some dimensions of life, it suggests, the only evidence is intuitive; therefore the empiricist must rely on intuition. Thomas Kuhn makes a similar point when he says that adopting a new scientific paradigm requires an act of faith.

When James elaborated the distinction between scientific questions and human questions, following Peirce, he developed an American intellectual position of first-rank importance: the modern separation of moral philosophy from nature, rather than inferring moral philosophy from Nature. Lester Frank Ward exemplifies the thinkers who were led by evolutionary thought to justify man as subject of his own social experimentation. William James represents those who were led into the same attitude in order to preserve an area of intellectual freedom and individual dignity as traditionally conceived. As Royce said, the Problem of Job can be solved by declining to view the world in teleological terms, as purposeful; and that is just what American social and moral philosophers alike tried to do. They chose a progressive world of choice.

In James's dualism, empirical knowledge is the most useful guide to action *as far as it goes*. It is in assigning limits to ordinary empirical knowledge, a sort of epistemological federalism, that James reaches his points of difference with the positivists who simply exclude from consideration all non-empirical concepts. For James there comes a point where evidence disappears and another kind of knowledge is needed; and it is from this point on that individual intellectual freedom becomes in his thought the most dominant of values.

Needless to say, he had scant regard for those who "live on the idea" of quantification, attempting to quantify what to him was non-quantifiable. It is essential to emphasize that so far as he found empiricism workable James advocated and defended it; but what he called the "real winners" are those who choose truly among the available ideas beyond empiricism, the truly "radical empiricists" who seek and gain moral knowledge. In other words, his thought was interpretive, or hermeneutic, as well as scientific. He viewed all rationalistic schemes of truth as oversimplifications. If James had lived a century later, he would be known as an anti-reductionist, like Clifford Geertz in anthropology, or a deconstructor, dismantling restrictive truth claims.

Late in 1878 or early in 1879 James wrote a note to his wife in which his respect for the importance of temperament in relation to freedom is well intimated. A man's character, he suggested, would be defined by the moment in which his particular mental or moral *attitude* caused him to *feel* "most deeply and intensely active and alive. At such moments there is a voice inside which speaks and says: 'this is the real me!'" Whether such a moment occurred as a condition of maximized freedom and purposeful self-realization would indicate whether that condition would bring happiness or misery; and James would take the degree of inclination toward the condition of moral freedom as an index to the individual's "character." This emphasis on temperament, so largely a function of the biological organism, suggests the proposition that "class" differences are biologically based: a proposition brought from the Puritans to modern American thought by Justice Holmes among many others. Those who are temperamentally drawn to freedom and responsibility are the most fully human and individual. Again, an "elect" is quite possible and even necessary in James's pragmatic world. It did not have to be a northwestern European elect -- but it pretty much happened to be. James's individualistic pragmatism inadvertently complemented the biological determinism or scientific racism of the time. But even more importantly, individualistic pragmatism reinforced the traditions of free will, equality of opportunity, and individual responsibility which made racism so easy to accept that it was practically compelling.

Twenty

Pragmatic Truth and the Concept of Deserving

For James, even as there are physical differences among men, so there are differences in efficacy of imagination, will, and intellect. But the degree of responsibility is the same for all. Moral, intellectual freedom works from unknown possibility rather than the known or knowable possibility to which more mundane kinds of freedom are attached. The validity and efficacy of will is a consistent conception both in James's philosophy and in the individualistic tradition he extends from Emerson. If Van Wyck Brooks had seen James more as an heir of Emerson he might not have been so perplexed by pragmatism's "poetic" aspects, sweeping far beyond its quasi-formal philosophy. But the idea of will in James's thought has to be seen with regard to his idea of truth.

Truth, according to James, is what happens to an idea in the process or event of that idea's successful use. Truth is not "facts": facts merely exist as the given, the raw material of life. The ever-changing sensible reality of facts is linked to ideas through the mind: an arrangement in which mind is the monitor, partly native to one plane, partly to the other, perceiving inuitively the relationships between the two. James attempted to reconcile idealism with naturalism and empiricism by saying that either observable facts or abstract categories might well be realities, as may relations between them. Reality embraces all that is experienced, and it is becoming: for just as facts are changing, so are ideas and the relations of facts to ideas. There is, then, no "Truth," any more than there is Freedom or Equality or any other unqualified designation of what is inherently relative. Only change is constant, only the future can certify present truth, and only belief which is accumulated experience gives useful leads to us.

It is tempting to say that truth is a *condition,* as wetness is, but not physical or factual like wetness. Truth can be enduring and reliable, like the wetness of the ocean, or brief and situational, like the wetness of your coat. Truth reveals itself in action: but the very center of James's philosophy is the conviction that truth is only in the realm of value judgments. Truth is moral, as it is in Plato and in Emerson. It is to thinking what right is to acting. It is what fulfills the individual in terms of his potential freedom and dignity, what brings him the deep, ethical self-approval that is happiness. Far from being advocacy of irresponsible experimentation or systematic support of shallow materialism, the pragmatic view of truth is a concept which brings into the age of science the Arminian version of Puritanism's agonized conscience. The *will* to believe establishes truth.

The components of James's thought come together and mesh in his treatment of choice and will. The known world as *the* world, which is at the same time becoming, suggests that reality somehow assumes the limits the individual wills it to have, as long as that is not demonstrably at odds with the reality of fact. The knower as part of the known must know himself empirically, as an object, and intuitively, as a free and responsible moral subject. If he is to attain happiness, he must know the principles by which he selects and omits the experiences which will establish his reality, his world. His truth will be what is useful to him in light of the purposes he has established for himself; but possibility must be recognized, motivation must be initiated, effort must be sustained, if will is to take effect.

Peirce had written sarcastically that he admired the "method of tenacity" for fixing beliefs. "Men who pursue it are distinguished for their decision of character, which becomes very easy with such a mental rule. They do not waste time in trying to make up their minds to what they want, but, fastening like lightning upon whatever alternative comes first, they hold to it to the end, whatever happens, without an instant's irresolution." Peirce said that these were its "advantages over scientific investigation." Then, in all seriousness, Peirce wrote what he really thought: that ". . . to avoid looking into the support of any belief from a fear that it may turn out rotten is quite as immoral as it is disadvantageous. The person who confesses that there is such a thing as truth . . . and then . . . dares not know the truth and seeks to avoid it, is in a sorry state of mind, indeed."

James gladly took up this challenge. He would confront unflinchingly and tirelessly the nature of truth, no matter how distressing the consequences. In "What Pragmatism Means," 1907, he said "No particular results . . . but only an attitude of orientation, is what the pragmatic method means. *The attitude of looking away from first things, principles, 'categories,' supposed necessities; and looking towards last things, fruits, consequences, facts.*" Pragmatism was a method, then, and "a genetic theory of truth" in which ideas become true "*in so far as they help us to get satisfactory relation with other parts of our experience . . .* " Satisfactory relation with other parts of our experience turned out to be the beliefs that Americans "lived on": choice, will, deserving, individual responsibility, moral equality of opportunity. Ideas became true in proportion as they served the Common Good, the utility principle, the greatest happiness of the greatest number, starting with and including pursuit of happiness by the knower who was speaking.

Nobody could accuse James of not trying to face up to reality; but "the knower as part of the known" held different practical, pragmatic meanings for different Americans. For the intellectual knower, then as now, the known is interpretive and anti-reductionist *as well as* scientific and pragmatic in seeking the common good. For the non-intellectual knower, what is known is foundational, *a priori*, moral, common-sensical, and pragmatic in seeking his own happiness, benefit, satisfaction. Majority and minorities alike, the people know what they want; and it is more gratification, self-esteem, security, comfort, pleasure, or happiness. What is pragmatically true is, then, quite easy to grasp.

James said that each individual must take the risk of error, and "project upon one of the alternatives in his mind, the attribute of *reality for him.*" He further stated that he himself did this for the option of individual freedom. But the fundamental question about freedom remains unanswered, at least explicitly: What freedom will enable one to choose fruitful effort, to choose choice, to know the alternatives, to become self-directed rather than being shuttled around by circumstances? The implied answer is that there is no such freedom: yet James committed himself to it "as if" there were, in the manner of Hans Vaihinger's philosophy. A universe of chance is necessary to the existence of freedom, just as choice of choice was necessary for Charles Chauncy to have a moral universe in the Arminianism of the eighteenth century. But if by freedom we mean a universal condition, if equality is allowed to subsume even this ancient enemy, a guarantee is made; and for James, the possibility of freedom is ruled out for everyone. In this sense, individual freedom entails inequality.

Freedom of choice implies the right to assess values, but it also assumes the ability to choose, so that a distinction between freedom and possibility instantly appears in the concept. We live in a relative world, which enables us to posit absolutes if we wish to or must have them. Descriptively speaking, it is also an aristocratic world, in that we note physiological limitations and chance deprivations of information which inhibit the development of some or most individuals, so that they appear to be altogether determined by forces outside their control. Without somehow discovering the existence of the option, we cannot be free, fulfilled persons; and we may not be temperamentally able to emerge into full humanity even if we become aware of what is, external to ourselves, the possibility of doing so.

The point is that freedom, ordinarily a normative concept, is, when used in a purely descriptive sense, in no way abridged by the limitations of possibility. There are none of James's "real winners and real losers" as far as freedom is concerned, because he makes freedom his highest of normative values, and "democratic" in that it is open to all. Two men have the same freedom to overcome conditioning and handicaps through conscious effort. One is free and able, the other equally free but unable. Both are equally responsible, because each has the same freedom as the other or any other man. Consequences count, and there are definitely real winners and losers in James's universe of *chance possibility coupled with universal freedom*. The natural aristocracy of Jefferson and Adams, the elect of Puritanism, are preserved, because real alternatives are unequally accessible on an individual basis. There is no valid determinism, James says; but temperament, for example, is so close to an unqualified restriction of possibility that accidents of heredity and early environment would seem to predetermine (cf. predestine) the freedom of a given individual to act.

The emphasis of some of James's writing has been attacked as a flight into subjectivism, a retreat from pragmatism and radical empiricism; but in fact it *is* radical empiricism. Radical means at the root (*radix*), and the observable reality at the root of the question is that reason is not sufficient to establish common understandings or convictions or attitudes in all areas of life. James may indeed have given new life or respectability to religious mysticism. He could say: "[Y]ou suspect that I am planning to defend feeling at the expense of reason, to rehabilitate the primitive and unreflective, and to dissuade you from the hope of any Theology worthy of the name. To a certain extent I have to admit that you guess rightly." He meant simply that reason is not very satisfactory for dealing with questions of value and purpose in life, not that feeling is more useful for every sort of consideration. But people are pragmatic when they believe what they find comfortable to believe.

James's philosophy is preeminently a philosophy of individualism, which is no small part of its representative American identification and wide appeal. When he refers to religion as "the great interest of my life," he means something like what the sociologist Elizabeth K. Nottingham defined as religion: whatever value assumptions and attitudes inform one's actions. By that reasoning, a case might readily be made that all persons at all times and places are equally "religious." Apparent differences indicate that many do not know what their religions actually are. This would come as no surprise to William James, any more than to Socrates.

Is it ludicrously obvious to observe that the United States is not an integrated country, not an integer, a "one"? It is a country made up of people mainly devoted to provincial, parochial, and especially personal interests, with little sense of a common good, except implicit agreement on the pursuit of individual happiness. Further, it is a country devoted to competition, and to cooperation primarily for the purpose of furthering competitive interests. We cooperate for our own purposes, and that's how Americans generally understand interest, as individual rather than communitarian. James's pragmatism both acknowledges and promotes that inclination. Happiness is the traditional goal of philosophy, and its pursuit is accepted as an individual right, and even a "natural" right in the given order of things. With ideas of eligibility for happiness, and of preparation for happiness in this world and the next, the idea of *deserving* always advanced, *pari passu*, implying criteria, or virtues. Elitist ideas kept pace with democratic ones. The American Revolution, culminating in the War for Independence, was not a radical egalitarian movement. It posited equality *among equals*. Calhoun, with his belief that only the deserving should have freedom, is just as representative an American as Jefferson is, if not as equivocal and politic.

Deserving also implied more or different individual responsibilities. "Whose fault is it?" and "Who's to blame?" are favorite questions. Presidents, generals and quarterbacks receive grotesquely disproportionate credit and blame. The broader implication is that we all are or should be in control of our lives, and it gradually undermined fatalism in the eighteenth and nineteenth centuries, except for ideas of biological determinism and very selective and limited notions of environmental influence. Individualism worked against equality in many ways. Circumstances were perceived as "destined" as well as chosen, but the most important of those determined by forces other than will were "God-given" talents and opportunities, or "natural" abilities. The dominant American view emphasized will but acknowledged determinants: "You can't keep a good man down," but not everyone can be a good man. Some have fatal flaws, and we all have inherent deficiencies, carrying burdens of varying weights. All problems of "background" are usable to illustrate this.

How about categorical flaws, performance characteristics as evidence of biological as opposed to environmental determinism? The Romantic Age institutionalized invidious comparison as a cultural habit, as well as the accompanying attitudes toward categories of people and individuals alike. Yet the principal thrust was always individualistic. The effect of pragmatism's individualistic force on racial perceptions became much clearer in the later twentieth century than it had been, say, in the 1960s. The legitimacy and respectability of selfishness were renewed in a resurgence of Jamesian pragmatism as national disposition. The pragmatic approval of both individualistic competition and voluntary cooperative competition legitimized egoism and stimulated racism. Carl Rowan exemplifies the distress felt by many over statistics on young black people in particular. Half of black children live in poverty. Only a small percentage of young black men attend college. A ridiculous percentage are "under the supervision of the criminal justice system." Rowan accuses of pandering to white racism those politicians who resist race-conscious compensatory programs. But those politicians are also appealing to what they accurately perceive as fundamental American beliefs, values, and ideals. If this were not the case, racism would be a much weaker force than it is.

Groups seeking redress or compensatory or other special treatment appear to most Americans as literally un-American. The American Way, the pragmatic way of life, is to pursue happiness as an individual. The American Way is individualistic competition, with whatever cooperation serves individual interests. But even groups are supposed to be competitive. Their reason for being is to compete, to serve their members' interests. Never mind, for the moment, whether or not this is the way things are "supposed" to be. It is the way American things are. The idea of the civil rights movement, to which many racists as well as all anti-racists harken back, was fairness. As Charles Chauncy said, justice must mean fairness if it is to mean anything at all. But Americans tend to perceive fairness only as fair treatment *of individuals.* The success of the civil rights movement rested on its contention that race is not supposed to be the basis of advantage or disadvantage. Americans generally accepted that, rejected discrimination, and still do, because they see injustice to groups as unfairness to individuals within those groups.   But the pragmatic perception of truth and virtue and freedom that pervades the society is that equal justice only means identical, impartial treatment of individuals. This postulate will not and cannot be demonstrated by reason or evidence to be valid or true. It is just one important part of the legacy of America's pragmatism.   In breaking away from philosophical traditions, James developed a philosophy based on American experience: but that American experience included the very set of traditions which would make a majority of Americans most resistant to reforms predicated on cumulative or collective grievances.

Twenty-One

Instrumentalism

Of the many lines of thought developed from Peirce and James, the most important are John Dewey's. Dewey struggled valiantly to enlist the epistemology of pragmatism in the service of humanitarianism, democracy, and reform. He sought to make James's individualist pragmatism into a social philosophy, concerned not only with how the individual pursues happiness but still more with how conditions might be ordered to provide everyone the possibility as well as the freedom for self-fulfillment. Dewey's greatest fame justly rests on his philosophical works dealing with education and public affairs, although he also wrote some outstanding systematic philosophy. His adaptation of pragmatism is known as instrumentalism, most commonly associated with his insistence that means determine ends as well as the other way around. (When we arrive at how we will proceed, we shape what kinds of outcomes are possible from our endeavors.)

In relation to this idea, Dewey attempted to bring James's adamant individualism and resistance to determinism into some sort of accommodation with the environmentalist insights of social science. Especially in his educational studies he emphasized the shaping of behavior by shaping the environment, social as well as physical, since the environment determined much of the individual's perceptions and actions. Dewey's thought was closely related to that of early social psychologists and sociologists such as George Herbert Mead and Charles Horton Cooley. Where James emphasized utility for individual purposes, Dewey revived the social utilitarianism of Hutcheson, Bentham and John Stuart Mill, seeking the broadest possible distribution of benefit or happiness. His social philosophy, logically applied, ran counter to the racism of the culture.

Pragmatism is not a social philosophy, and it is not a moral philosophy in the sense of seeking to establish some basis for obligation, duty, or ethical prescription of any sort other than expediency: meeting individual needs or serving individual purposes. It is, as James said, a method of proceeding to make choices, and a theory of truth. Roughly speaking, pragmatism says that what works is true and what is true is what works, and it at least gets past the troublesome question of whether what works works because it is true, or what is true is true because it works. The pragmatist no longer has to be bothered about whether we are discovering or constructing truth, because truth just means what coincides with expediency or practicality.

Like all liberal "social engineers," Dewey thought that the Divine Light was education, and Salvation, its product, was understanding or Intelligence, as he capitalized it. Dewey's version of pragmatism is called instrumentalism. In its social version, education is the *instrument* for validating democracy by empowering people to solve their common problems, and democracy is the the *instrument* of progress. Obviously this is a philosophy of cooperation and egalitarianism rather than divisive individualist competition. Its ends, like those of reformers seeking to repudiate racism, are collective and social rather than individualistic.

Nobody would suggest that individualism in any form was ever intended to support racism. The point is that *it has always been extremely difficult to work against racism without attacking individualism.* The prevalence of individualism means that *individuals generally perceive and define themselves primarily as separate entitities rather than primarily as members of any group or category.* Group identity functions chiefly to reinforce and express individual identity, to serve individual interest. And as long as the dominant pragmatic disposition is construed in terms of *individualist* expediency and competition, social and collective efforts to change treatment of others are reasonably regarded with suspicion and fear, as threats to individual liberty and interest. At the same time, our popular individualism reinforces racist attitudes and contributes to corresponding racist beliefs, because it is competitive and it is conductive to habits of invidious comparison. Individualism draws on the traditions of individual responsibility which constitute the innermost core of both religious and economic doctrines in America. It is immediately threatened by any claim that members of a group, as individuals, are not responsible for their own well-being or their own plight.

John Dewey was not especially interested in racism, but he was passionately interested in using instrumentalism to address social, economic and political matters more effectively. To do that, he needed a different perception of the individual in relation to society, and he formulated it in 1929 and 1930 in a relatively neglected work entitled *Individualism Old and New*. Like Emerson, Ripley, Parker, and the other Transcendentalists a century earlier, many thoughtful Americans of the 1920s worried about soul-deadening conformity, uniformity, and depersonalization. It seemed to them that the world of mass production and material efficiency, the world of Frederick Winslow Taylor and Herbert Hoover, was literally demeaning the individual, as Adam Smith had anticipated, and social critics from Emerson and Karl Marx to Thorstein Veblen had contended. Dewey wrote, "The problem of constructing a new individuality consonant with the objective conditions under which we live is the deepest problem of our times."[1] A prototype like Sinclair Lewis's *Babbitt* offered little help.

The heart of Dewey's analysis is the chapter called, "The Lost Individual," in which he describes how modern individuals are confused and bewildered by their own culture of individualism. The culture seemed to offer nothing to believe in, except competitive self-interest. "It would be difficult to find in history an epoch as lacking in solid and assured objects of belief and approved ends of action as is the present. Stability of individuality is dependent upon stable objects to which allegiance firmly attaches itself."[2] In America, social science made the old individualism bankrupt, and the economic and social environment needed to be structured in such a way as to change "the framework of personal disposition." A broader idea of utility hinged on the realization that it is in everyone's interest for everyone else to be treated with respect, and to be secure, comfortable, and productive.

Utilitarianism initially suggested utility as the universal standard of value, and this was expressed in the Enlightenment fixation on "all men" and what they had in common. The architects of Utilitarianism generally meant by utility what was useful to all and each, not each and therefore all. But the idea had to be adapted to capitalism, and to American social conditions. Universalistic utilitarianism readily became individualistic through the simple argument that nobody agreed on the greatest happiness of the greatest number, except to say that if he himself was happier, then aggregate happiness must be increased. The main concern of each was utility in terms of his own pursuit of happiness. William James observed America's worship of "the bitch-goddess, Success"; and Walter Lippmann lamented that the mentality of business defined the religion of America.

Social philosophers and progressives like Dewey wanted to define individuality as possible only within a meaningful sense of community. They wanted to extend the idea of enlightened self-interest and make of it a unifying social principle, so that the nation would conduct its affairs in a spirit of practical cooperation rather than self-destructive individualistic competition. Dewey wrote that a "new individuality" worth celebrating in a "new individualism" would have to be realistic and practical. Instrumentalism, like pragmatism, succeeded in reaffirming and establishing in more modern form the standard of utility. But the social thinkers could not break the association of utility with personal interest. One reason for that was that they themselves were Americans, shaped by the very culture they sought to enlighten and change.

"If, in the long run, an individual remains lost, it is because he has *chosen* irresponsibility; and if he remains wholly depressed, it is because he has *chosen* the course of easy parasitism."[3] Can this be John Dewey, and not William Graham Sumner? Can such a statement, implying Arminian confidence in will, be reconciled with Dewey's views on individuality through socialization, under social-environmental influences? Yes! The individual who remains lost fails to apply his resources to the practical problems at hand; and so does the one who remains wholly depressed, i.e., in depressed circumstances, the failure. For Dewey, progress can be made, always, through problem-solving. Problem-Solving as Process is the practical equivalent of The Good in Plato; and meaningful individuality attends effort to solve problems, or seek The Good. This is scientific salvation, individualism through doing whatever you can, even like Sisyphus with his rock. If we can choose not to be lost, not to be wholly "depressed," there must be some "assured objects of belief" available after all; and there are! "When the patterns that form individuality of thought and desire are in line with actuating social forces, that individuality will be released for creative effort. Originality and uniqueness are not opposed to social nurture; they are saved by it from eccentricity and escape."[4] In other words, the exercise of individual freedom is (provided the individual is properly socialized) wisely consistent with constructive social aims; and the individual is saved from scientific sin, or antisocial lack of purpose, or lack of conscience, or of meaningful identity.

In 1630 John Winthrop said we have freedom to choose what is Right; in the 1730s Jonathan Edwards said we have free will to choose what is chosen by God's will; in the 1830s Ralph Waldo Emerson said we can choose self-reliance in harmony with Nature; and in 1930 John Dewey said we can choose to bring our patterns of individuality into line with Actuating Social Forces. In the seventeenth century, this individual freedom of choice was determined by God-given faith; in the eighteenth, by either faith or the force of Arminian will; in the nineteenth, by will or "genius" or distinctive force of character; and in the twentieth, by Applied Intelligence. The responsibility of the individual for effective control of life remains an American conviction, in the sense that it is more important in shaping the circumstances of people's lives here than elsewhere: more widely held, and far more strongly asserted.

Yet Dewey's idea of a new individualism departed fundamentally from tradition, because of his pragmatic epistemology. He took James's "knower as part of the known" to an equation of known with knowing, a sort of objectification of process in which a rose, to use Morton White's example, is not the same thing as a rose known or watched by Dewey, or by you -- for a particular time, in a certain light, and so forth. Experience includes relationships, not just entities, as in phenomenology, or in Einstein's description of physical reality. Dewey replaces certainty with exactness, in his rejection of the "spectator theory of knowledge." His admonition is to treat knowledge in the manner of an artist producing a painting rather than a spectator viewing a finished picture. Where an idealist like Royce seeks precision or certainty in the abstractions of logic, Dewey seeks exactness or certitude in the immediacy of sensory experience. An unforeseen effect of Dewey's "new individualism," however, is once again to place tremendous emphasis on individual perspective and individual will.

Since certainty evaporates under the scrutiny of scientific philosophy, to wait for conclusive evidence is, as James said, irrational. One must act "as if" something were the case; and both assumptions and actions affect what comes to be "known." If I am the artist painting the picture, its reality is what I will and expect it to be. Another application is Ibsen's: "I hold that man is in the right who is most closely in league with the future." There is no arguing with anyone about being in league with the future. Pragmatism and instrumentalism set the stage for a radical subjectivism far beyond anything intended by either pragmatist or instrumentalist. If I claim to be clairvoyant, to have mystical insights, what can anyone say scientifically to refute this? Nothing, as James insisted. But the popular extension of the open, pluralistic, exciting universe of the twentieth century was that since nobody knows for sure what it means to be in league with the future, anyone can arrogate to himself as much authority as he wishes to give to his projection, or his claim to rightness. This aspect of early twentieth-century thought led to popular interpretations and attitudes which would dismay the thinkers who made those very interpretations and attitudes appealing.

The same can be said of the emphasis on utility, in its individualistic application. Dewey wrote that "when truth is defined as utility, it is often thought to mean utility for some purely personal end, some profit upon which a particular individual has set his heart. So repulsive is a conception of truth which makes it a mere tool of private ambition and aggrandizement, that the wonder is that critics have attributed such a notion to sane men."[5] Yet of course this is precisely what sane men have done, and there is no wonder why: lacking those precious "assured objects of belief and approved ends of action," they have applied Dewey's ideas to the real world as they perceive it, just as he urged. For all his epistemological and scientific sophistication, it seems that Dewey took it as a self-evident, *a priori* reality -- he would not say "truth" -- that individual interests coincide with cooperative ideals and the common good. Had that been the case, instrumentalism as a social form of pragmatism would have worked powerfully against the attitudes of racism. As it was, social philosophy worked against "scientific" racist beliefs, but instrumentalism provided reinforcement for individualism, stringing intellectual barbed wire around entrenched racist beliefs and attitudes alike.

In the social sciences, Dewey's new individualism, like the related conceptions of Cooley and Mead, prevailed and succeeded. In the society at large, on a popular level, it failed. Instrumentalism was a further reaffirmation of individualistic utilitarianism, a renewal of everyone's license to think and feel that what suits the individual is true. Dewey hoped that people would see how it is in everyone's interest for everyone else to "succeed" by solving practical problems. To the extent that Americans did see that, they saw "everyone else" as a competitive individual, and they correspondingly rejected the idea of "deserving" by groups. In the new individualism, as in the old Christianity, being a person is possible only through community: so everyone's interest is everyone else's. That idea remained unconvincing to the population at large, less true to experience and less satisfying than having winners and losers.

1. John Dewey, *Individualism Old and New* (New York: Capricorn Books, 1962), 32.

2. *Ibid.*, 52.

3. Dewey, *Reconstruction in Philosophy* (Boston: The Beacon Press, 1957), 167, emphasis added.

4. *Ibid.*, 143.

5. *Ibid.*, 157.

Twenty-Two

Ethical Naturalism

In case it needs to be said, John Dewey is presented here as a very influential and representative American thinker, not as an example of racism. But thinkers have no control over the effects of their ideas; and another strain of Dewey's thought lends itself to racist uses, just as individualistic pragmatism and instrumentalism do. That line of thought is ethical naturalism, which applies the pragmatic method to questions which are classified as "moral."

Ethical naturalism does not deal only with what is scientifically or empirically *true*. It concedes that there is no way to establish moral truth by reason or evidence (as G. E. Moore had convincingly argued in *Principia Ethica*, 1903). Instead, it adapts pragmatism by arguing that what works is *good*, in the sense of "moral" and not just in the sense of "valuable." Dewey limits the content of the word "ought," arguing for a non-moral ought of advisability equivalent to any "moral ought" of obligation. What produces the intended outcome is good; and one ought to do it as a simple matter of rationality. There had been some suggestion of this in the work of the great idealist, Josiah Royce, who argued that if you see a divergence or conflict between what you think is practical and what you think is good, you have misunderstood the situation. The two cannot diverge or conflict, fundamentally.

But unlike Royce, Dewey rejected what he called "the quest for certainty," and did not argue that what is moral is therefore practical. Dewey's ethical naturalism developed in the time of burgeoning relativism, and his moral philosophy built upon James's "The knower is part of the known" rather than upon more traditional, rationalistic theory of knowledge.   Morally as well as epistemologically, the perceiver is part of the perceived, and what seems expedient, practical, utilitarian, is relative to the angle of vision, the experience of the subject. Without solving the troublesome question of how what is desirable can be established except on the basis of what is observably desired, the way was opened to moral subjectivism *through pragmatism*. Dewey's own approach to dealing with the implications of this was through improved education, so that people would truly and literally know what was good for them. (The teacher, without benefit of Plato or Dewey, would say, "If you know what's good for you, Young Man, you'll . . . . ")

Like all idealists from Plato onward, Royce thought that the Good would exert an irresistible, magnetic sort of attraction upon anyone who accurately perceived or understood it.   This is the traditional secular form of the Divine Light or saving grace or faith, drawing the true believer toward salvation. Dewey's version of it was an act of faith in human rationality, a hypothesis that if people truly understood what was in their own interest, to their own advantage, they would accept and follow this understanding. He thought that people would act in their own best interests as they saw them, but that they must be educated in ways that would enable them to identify their most inclusive and fundamental interests.

A crucial difference of logic or structure appears between pragmatism and ethical naturalism. Pragmatism avoids the debate between idealism and naturalism, as to whether a belief works because it is true or is true because it works. The overwhelming implication and popular impression is the latter: that if a hypothesis works, that *makes* it true (for as long as it continues to work, in a "becoming universe"). In ethical naturalism the analogous implication is made explicit: if a belief works, that makes it both accurate and good.

Dewey's ethical theory includes no universal valuations, except that Problem-Solving itself is tacitly Good. Valuations are existential guides to action, empirically assessed, and they are arrived at in terms of meeting needs which people feel or otherwise identify. Dewey wrote that "valuation *involves* desiring."[1]   That is, the attachment or imputation of value involves feeling some lack, or some wish for a more advantageous situation. A mere wish, however, is not a desire sufficient to make a valuation, because a wish does not take into account the vital factor of willingness to make the *effort* necessary to effect change. For example, a young person might wish to have a doctor's degree, but not to make the effort to analyze and carry out the *necessary means* entailed by such a goal. Only a person who realistically assesses all the means and costs, such as the years of effort required to earn such a degree, can formulate the serious *desire* to have it (as opposed to the careless wish).

Once the means to satisfy a desire have been acknowledged and accepted, the satisfaction of that desire becomes an "end-in-view"; and a person's ends-in-view then constitute interests. "Ends-in-view are appraised or valued as *good* or *bad* on the ground of their serviceability in the direction of behavior dealing with states of affairs found to be objectionable because of some lack or conflict in them. They are appraised as fit or unfit, proper or improper, *right* or *wrong*, on the ground of their *requiredness* in accomplishing this end."[2] In other words, the value of a belief depends entirely on how essential it is to accomplishing your purpose, meeting your needs. This assessment of value specifically includes moral value.

Whether a belief is "serviceable" or useful to you indicates whether it is good, and "right" as a guide to action. Does this mean right in the sense of a calculation in arithmetic, for example, a correct answer to the perceived lack or problem? Yes, but not only that. It also means right in the sense that you *ought* to follow the belief, because the only standard that determines the meaning of "ought" is "serviceability," expediency, utility. Again, Dewey assumes that what you value as truly good for you, after careful analysis, will also be "moral" by other standards. There is no traditional "moral" obligation to wear a helmet if you ride a motorcycle, or to wear a seatbelt, for example. Thoughtless people argue that you have a "right" to injure yourself. But if you do, you injure others as well, through higher costs of medical insurance, deprivation of others to whom you have made commitments, and so on. It is a *good idea* to use the equipment.[3]

You ought to wear a seatbelt as a matter of common sense, and that satisfies any "moral" requirement as well. It is sensible, practical, and advisable to wear it; it is prudent to wear it; and no meaning is added by saying that it is moral to wear it. There is no more distinction between a "moral ought" of obligation and a "non-moral ought" of advisability: they are the same. If you are doing something that "works for you," you are acting in a moral way as well. This view gained enormous currency and acceptance in the latter twentieth century, obviously. It has momentous implications regarding the persistence of racism.

Ethical naturalism certainly has not in any sense "caused" racism, or caused racism to persist. Rather, the moral legitimacy of whatever appears to an individual to meet his or her needs has made racist beliefs and attitudes more convenient than they might be under moral strictures that based goodness and rightness on some standard other than short-sighted expediency. What lack does everyone desire to meet? Any lack of self-esteem and self-confidence. What problem does everyone need to confront? The problem of identity, establishing a sense of self-worth. What desire does everyone seek to satisfy? The desire for self-respect, for self-enhancement and self-expression among peers, however defined. It is no secret that racist beliefs and attitudes "work" for many people, to meet such needs, solve such problems, and satisfy such desires. They are means to widely adopted "ends-in-view," serving the perceived interests of many. If many misperceive their interests, ethical naturalism has little to say about that: people have a right to adopt what they find useful and to call it good as well as true.

Individualistic or egoistic utilitarianism formalized the value of the useful. Extended to meet new requirements, and renamed pragmatism and instrumentalism, it validates whatever is functional for the individual. It says nothing about "functional for what," beyond individually satisfactory results. It just says to people that that what works is true, and that makes whatever suits your purposes intellectually respectable. Ethical naturalism then confers moral respectability on whatever gets you where you want to go. Both pragmatism and ethical naturalism make a sort of "act of faith" in rational self-interest. Their serious proponents assume that careful consideration and trial-and-error will lead us to enlightened and truly beneficial hypotheses, valuations, and beliefs. Their less thoughtful practitioners are presumably content simply to enjoy the endorsement of self-interest. Dewey clearly hoped that communal responsibility and "social conscience" would derive unprecedented appeal from ethical naturalism. Instead, ethical individualism, earlier associated with Emersonian idealism, got a new and different *imprimatur*. The equation of the moral to the non-moral ought has the practical, popular effect of endorsing whatever beliefs people find comfortable.

---

1. Dewey, *Theory of Valuation* (Chicago: University of Chicago Press, 1939), 15, emphasis in original.
    2. *Ibid.*, 47, emphasis in original.
    3. Cf. Alfred North Whitehead's 1925 assertion that every social action has a moral dimension. The "catch" appears when we try to think of actions, including inaction, that have absolutely no affects on others, i.e., are not at all "social."

Twenty-Three

The Canon of Character

William James said in a letter to H. G. Wells that "The exclusive worship of the bitch-goddess SUCCESS . . . is our national disease." Success meant attaining individual goals; and holding beliefs with which one felt comfortable was an indispensable part of it. Pragmatism, instrumentalism, and ethical naturalism certified people's practical, self-gratifying claims of superiority as true and moral. But ethical naturalism, never widely adopted as an explicit persuasion but pervading ordinary behavior nonetheless, often reinforced the same virtues as traditional morality. It generally endorsed honesty, for example: not because honesty is some sort of virtue in itself, but because it is expedient. "Honesty is the best *policy*," for example, not because it is admirable but if it is generally good for business, or for personal relationships. Traditional virtues remained the elements of enlightened self-interest. Character was an asset, conducive to success.

The absence of character, logically enough, could explain economic and social failure, the lack of success. Early in the twentieth century, Max Weber wrote: "The fortunate [individual] is seldom satisfied with the fact of being fortunate . . . . Beyond this, he needs to know that he has a right to his good fortune . . . that he 'deserves' it, and above all, that he deserves it in comparison with others." Americans wanted success in moral as well as material and social terms, for only moral justification could round out and complete an individualistic perception of self. Ethical individualism in the context of the materialistic success ethic demanded that success arise from moral self-definition, or self-improvement. As Irving Kristol remarks, "The institution of business was thought to make for self-improvement and not simply self-enrichment."[1] America's model in this fortuitous combination was Benjamin Franklin, of course: that legendary practitioner of what Leo Marx calls "a limited and principled self-interest."

Franklin epitomized the canon of character. His utilitarian code glorified the individual will, and his secular Arminianism embraced both moral sense and intuitive reason in its ebullient affirmation of the capacity to be good and to "be somebody." Character development had been both an implicit religious and a secular preoccupation from the beginning of English life in America. When Samuel Smiles wrote in his *Lives of the Engineers* (1862) that the "secret of Anglo-Saxon success" was self-help, he meant not only technological resourcefulness but self-reliance as virtue, just like Emerson. Cultivation of personal virtues led to wealth and position; and the process of cultivating them was individual fulfillment, moral individualism. The idea of character and the study of character assumed steadily greater importance from the seventeenth through the nineteenth centuries, with concomitant popularity of biography, autobiography, the journal and the *Bildungsroman*. By the nineteenth century, character became "a key word" in common parlance.[2]

Warren I. Susman calls nineteenth-century America a "culture of character," with its moutainous literature, both periodicals and books, of edifying and inspiring character studies and models for success. A moral emphasis pervaded these writings, and Susman says the most popular quotation in the country was Emerson's definition of character: "Moral order through the medium of individual nature."[3] Side by side with Social Darwinism, the canon of character produced a Christian road to success which was more attractive to many Americans than the evolutionary version of ruthless competition. Conveniently enough, those with the highest character could achieve individual moral triumph and define themselves as the fittest at the same time, enjoying the best of both worlds, spiritual self-definition and materialistic determinism. One could explicitly reject the atheistic version, rely instead on "Christian" self-help through cultivating character; and still draw private comfort and reassurance from the sense of being naturally selected as superior in ability. Pragmatically, both Social Darwinism and the character canon led to self-satisfaction and self-congratulation for the successful, the former on the basis of natural superiority and the latter on a superior individual effort to build character. Temperament and training presumably inclined people to find one foundation for competitive individualism more attractive than the other; and only a small talent for logic was needed to get the benefits of both.

Yet the pressure to succeed, so much a part of ordinary American life, also brought pressure to conform. "Ambition was laudable, complacency vicious," as Richard Brown writes; but ambition dictated "going along," ingratiating oneself with others, more than intellectual or moral self-reliance. By the turn of the century serious magazines and books featured laments for lost individuality. The depersonalization anticipated by Adam Smith and Emerson, and the dehumanization that appalled Karl Marx, gained new urgency through voices like Herbert Croly's. John Diggins says that

> . . . the idea of authority . . . had become little more than what people thought other people thought . . . . It was this threat of society that tyrannized not man's body but his psyche and 'soul,' for the individual who wanted to think his own thoughts and act on his own convictions risked being abandoned by his peers and shunned by the community. If virtue had anything to do with the demands of conscience, the virtuous man would be forever lonely, regarded as an outcast or, in Tocqueville's chilling phrase, an 'impure being'.[4]

Tocqueville had worried about the danger that individualism would defeat the ideal of commitment to something larger than self, and would at length be "absorbed in downright selfishness."[5] Self-regard dictated the need for social acceptance, which tended to produce conformity in the guise of character. One of the conventions that made up American conformity was racism. But even had that not been the case, the conventions of individualism itself would have made racism an attractive "explanation" regarding success and failure.

T. J. Jackson Lears writes about the common occurrence among middle class people around the turn of the century of neurasthenia, or "nervous prostration." This disorder notably included "paralysis of will" and the sense that "life had somehow become unreal."[6] Lears notes that as commitments were subverted and ethical norms blurred, "Self-control became merely a tool for secular achievement; success began to occur in a moral and spiritual void."[7] Reconciling traditional Christian morality with the demands of personal success presented increasing difficulties, as Americans struggled to maintain identity in a rapidly changing world.   Determinism had to be reckoned with, as people felt that their familiar sense of autonomy was being undermined.   Taylorism, the cult of efficiency, further reduced workers to parts of mechanical processes; and still more, "Fordism" would extend control over their non-working lives, seeking to bring them under the control of a "sociological department" which would penetrate into their domestic, social, and religious activities.   Yet Ralph Waldo Trine, worshipper of Ford, was not unrepresentative in his continued emphasis on progress through self-improvement.   Character development remained deeply ingrained as the key to success of every kind.   And failure of every kind suggested lack of character, for categories of people as for individuals.

1. Kristol in *Kettering Review*, Fall 1988, 15.

2. Warren I. Susman, "Personality and the Making of Twentieth-Century Culture," in John Higham and Paul Conkin, eds., *New Directions in American Intellectual History* (Baltimore: The Johns Hopkins University Press, 1979), 213.

3. *Ibid.*, 214.

4. Diggins, *Lost Soul*, 237, 238.

5. See Diggins, 240.

6. T. J. Jackson Lears, *No Place of Grace: Antimodernism and the Transformation of American Culture* (New York: Pantheon Books, 1981), 7.

7. *Ibid.*, 9, 10.

Twenty-Four

New Thought: From Character to Mind-Set

The turbulent decade of the 1880s brought new immigrant groups in large numbers, unprecedented industrial concentration, bitter labor strife, depression, disease, agrarian protest, distress over alcohol abuse, and pressure for reform (largely led by women). An individualist line of thought that had been building slowly for decades, led by Phineas Parkhurst Quimby (1802-1866), finally "caught fire" in the tinder of the 1880s.[1] A modification of Christian Science, the movement acquired a name in the '90s, New Thought. Through that decade (hardly the "Gay '90s" of nostalgia) and the following one, prices rose twice as fast as income, to the great frustration of middle class expectations regarding success, security and comfort. New Thought gained proportionate momentum. In the two decades bracketing the turn of the century, the canon of character development seemed increasingly inadequate to explain experience.[2] Belief, after all, has to make sense of life; and the character development version of self-improvement left more and more people dissatisfied.

At the same time, evolutionary thought and naturalism in general shook the foundations of traditional religion, challenging the cherished ideas of salvation, immortality, and a transcendent God. The Higher Criticism, like the geological advances begun by Charles Lyell, assailed biblical literalism. If ideal realities were reflective of or derivative from material reality, and material reality was always changing, then ideals, values, moral truths themselves must also be always changing. This implication -- with the attendant loss of soul, self, essence, individuality -- was unacceptable to the public. A new era required a new philosophy, which would "more adequately interpret the facts of experience and at the same time satisfy the deep yearning of the human spirit."[3] New Thought, unlike the canon of character, grew up without support from clergy or established doctrine: an indigenous, popular movement without denominational identity. The movement pervaded popular thinking through a variety of media: periodical literature, self-improvement books, and public lectures as well as sermons under different auspices. It spread both within congregations and outside the pale of religious sponsorship.[4]

New Thought posited an immanent God, the ". . . principle of Pure Spirit. And the essence of spirit is Mind. Therefore the Principle is Universal Mind." Everyone could establish his or her connection with Mind, and express its power through the individual mind. "Since every individual's power is his ability to express this indwelling power of the mind, then what we are is determined by our mental attitudes. Our *character*, . . . our degree of *success* is determined by the thoughts we hold in our minds. Therefore, thinking the proper thoughts . . . will result in the *realization of our desires*."[5] New Thought co-opted character, and by the turn of the century the movement rivalled in popular acceptance the canon of character. Mind-power, not character, was becoming the key to success; but it subsumed character as an effect of mind, rather than eclipsing it. Millions of Americans read New Thought literature without even knowing it had a name, or a base in the religious movement of mental healing originating years earlier with P. T. Quimby. Even in the 1950s and after, readers discovering Norman Vincent Peale in *The Power of Positive Thinking* were generally unaware that they were looking at the latest manifestation of a movement more than half a century old, with millions of volumes of literature claiming and celebrating the power of the individual.[6] Peale stood in a direct line from, say, Ralph Waldo Trine's *In Tune With the Infinite* (1897), a work much favored and endorsed by Henry Ford, for example.

1. See Huber, *The American Idea of Success*, 131.
2. Cf. Huber, 79.
3. Richard Weiss, *The American Dream of Success* (New York: Basic Books, 1969), 12.
4. See Huber, 307.
5. Huber, 135, emphasis added.
6. See Huber, 124-125.

Twenty-Five

New Thought and Psychology

New Thought labelled its idealism pragmatic, and William James said the spread of the movement was "due to its practical fruits." James, famous as the author of America's first psychology textbook, *Principles of Psychology* (1890), as well as for pragmatism, lent enormous impetus to the New Thought movement by his insistence upon the "right to believe": the original title of his famous essay, "The Will to Believe." The individual could respectably believe in anything he or she willed to believe in, wherever that belief did not conflict with empirical evidence. James's "pluralistic universe" was so open and receptive towards diversity, particularly in the area of religious belief (as in the 1901-1902 Gifford Lectures, published as *Varieties of Religious Experience*), that he could be taken to endorse even the most eccentric individualism, provided only that it met the needs of the person who held or practiced it. So New Thought built upon James's foundations, asserting that ". . . achievement [is] in the realm of belief. In effect, they taught that as a person thinks, so he is."[1] The movement incorporated the earlier canon of character. Its conception of character as ". . . the sum of good habits" mirrored current psychological thought, and "references to academic works, particularly to James's *Psychology*, were frequent in inspirational literature."[2]

After his 1911 Clark University lectures, Freud was also adopted by eclectic New Thought writers. For them, as Weiss says, "psychoanalysis was not something new so much as a confirmation of what they already believed."[3] Everything fit together: psychological theory, philosophy, reform enthusiasm, and religion, all committed to the healthy individual. That individual was restored to freedom and dignity, to say nothing of solace and comfort. From the New Thought point of view, science in the early twentieth century took an encouraging turn away from materialism. Adherents to the movement were individualists, and they ". . . rebelled at the separation of individualism from the egalitarian ideal" as they understood it. "Their argument with the Social Darwinists was not that the latter denied individualism," but rather that they were elitist about it, restricting individualism to the fittest.[4] James's universe was democratic in the sense that everybody had a right to believe what suited him or her, and New Thought was downright populist in its complementary doctrine of self-direction.

The will to believe was the will to think for yourself, and what you thought was what you were: so neatly did James's ideas and New Thought converge in reciprocal reinforcement. Together they generated optimism, ebullience, and that resistance to deterministic materialism which they both shared with Royce's idealism. Psychology was still taught in philosophy departments in the Progressive period, and the ". . . kinship between psychologist and moralist" implied that "the healthy life and the good life were virtually identical. Psychotherapy applied the terms health and disease to problems that had conventionally been thought of only in moral terms."[5] As Weiss notes, this union constituted a "new moral creation -- the mind-body-soul complex . . ." Certainly it forcefully restated the continuum of reason-feelings-will. Optimistic agents of New Thought took the new possibility of understanding the subconscious as "further proof that men could remake themselves at will."[6]

Channing Haddock's seven-volume "Power Book Library," led by *The Power of Will* in 1907 (the same year as James's *Pragmatism*), sold about three quarters of a million copies over twenty years. Even John B. Watson's behaviorism was turned to New Thought purposes. Behaviorism was as deterministic as a persuasion could be, but it still allowed for belief that an individual "could be developed in any direction" by the right stimuli.[7] This was the "strenuous age," as Grant C. Knight characterized it in literature: the era whose spirit Theodore Roosevelt personified, when "sin" was not what would later reappear as assertiveness, but rather the failure to assert oneself, passivity. Not that New Thought was brash or offensive: it advocated a calm, cheerful self-confidence not unlike what would ironically come to be known as "coolness." It was a quiet force of mind rather than frantic assertion of the self, but forceful nonetheless, expressing the remarkable capacities of the ordinary individual will.

In the seventeenth century, blacks had been unregenerate, lacking the Divine Light. In eighteenth-century Arminianism, they lacked the effective will for self-direction. In the Enlightenment context, they were deficient in reason, or perhaps simply in entitlement to natural rights. Nineteenth-century Romantic individualism found them "dull and listless," lacking genius. For Social Darwinists, they were clearly not among the fittest. In the twentieth century, the canon of character and New Thought again found them deficient in virtue and will. Pragmatism pronounced the validity of individualistic beliefs, which were predictably conventional, and ethical naturalism conferred moral legitimacy upon prevailing beliefs and attitudes.

1. Weiss, *Dream of Success,* 59.
2. *Ibid.,* 147.
3. *Ibid.,* 211.
4. *Ibid.,* 162.
5. *Ibid.,* 204-205.
6. *Ibid.,* 307.
7. See *ibid.,* 222.

Twenty-Six

New Thought and Success: Mind Over Matter

From Arminianism and from the optimism and self-confidence of the later eighteenth century, the idea that men could make of their lives what they willed became a standard American article. The "real source of power" resided in the will, whether it fulfilled itself in truth, as Royce thought; or, in John Dewey's version, it led to habits, to the cultivation of tropisms or dispositions to react to conditions, which constituted choices of the most advantageous means. Will led reason to success. In *The Book of Business,* Elbert Hubbard informed his readers that "Success is the most natural thing in the world. The man who does not succeed has placed himself in opposition to the laws of the universe." The man who fails has perversely or inexplicably *placed himself,* by act of will, in opposition to reality. He has the same capacity to choose, and therefore the same individual responsibility for his success that Charles Chauncy had for his salvation.

New Thought writers spent little energy on justifying success, but tended simply to insist that it was natural and, like Bolton Hall, who wrote *Thrift,* that it was therefore within the reach of everyone. The person who chose a forward-looking, optimistic frame of mind was already aimed toward success. Richard Weiss says, "This . . . was the core of the new success cult -- states of mind rather than traits of character were the keys to success or failure." Of course will-power and mind-power did not simply eclipse or reject the importance of character. Richard M. Huber lists twenty-seven representative self-improvement works published before 1920, of which seven "reflect a pure character ethic" thirteen reflect "a mixture of the character ethic and New Thought," and seven others are "overwhelmingly New Thought."[1] Such an orchestrator of attitudes as Orison Swett Marden, editor of *Success* magazine, evidently saw these views as compatible, their differences a matter of emphasis. To cultivate will and mind was, after all, to cultivate character. New Thought saw itself as more analytical than the preaching of character, moving back a scientific step or two to how character developed, and through what capacities. It was a "gospel of success" that "gave belief in the individual's power for self direction a new lease on life by providing it with a rationale viable in . . . an industrialized society."[2]

Since New Thought repudiated the materialistic determinism and pessimism that developed in the later nineteenth century, its appeal in the early twentieth was enormous. A loosely defined doctrine, it drew its force from "its confirmation of the individual's power over his destiny, rather than its promise of material goods." Weiss reflects, "So long as the ideal of individualism continues to command devotion, some means of obscuring contradicting realities is likely to remain."[3] New Thought clearly contradicted economic realities, with its buoyant assertion of individual power in a world increasingly dominated by giant organizations; but the force that Weiss identifies was nonetheless real. A "higher" success than material acquisition, the "true" success of realizing one's potentialities as an individual person, remained vitally attractive. Character was in some sense its own reward, and if will and mind produced it and it was not acknowledged or rewarded, other explanations could be sought. Malefactors have often met this need, like witches in the seventeenth century and communists in the twentieth.

Of the many New Thought writers who expressed and inspired popular faith in the individual, Orison Swett Marden was perhaps most conspicuous, with a succession of more than forty-five books, starting in 1894. Marden began as a proponent of the character canon, then gradually and sporadically adopted a New Thought emphasis. His early inspiration, he said, was Samuel Smiles, English author of the best-selling success book, *Self-Help*.[4] But Marden's personal angle of vision reflected an American tradition. His advice to ". . . make yourself a success magnet" brings to mind Benjamin Franklin's self-improvement program. Above all, he rejected determinism and elitism, as found in Social Darwinist thought, for example; just as his eighteenth-century Arminian and Whig forerunners rejected determinism and elitism as found in predestination and hereditary privilege. Even education was rejected, by neglect if not explicitly. Self-education appealed to those who emphasized character development, but even that smacked too much of intellectual pretension for New Thought to endorse.

The egoistic utilitarian view, engagingly veiled in Franklin, has always remained near the surface of individualist attitudes. Radical individualists like Max Stirner (*Ego and His Own*, 1844) dramatically illustrated the rising "pragmatic" spirit of the nineteenth century. The "possessive individualism" of Hobbes and Locke found fullest expression in this view, characterized by William English Walling in 1913: "The individual is to use the world, to use life, and even to use -- himself."[5] New Thought morality sought a humane balance of utilitarian individualism and social concern. Under its aegis, ". . . men were in fact their brothers' keepers . . . . [and] poverty was an unmitigated evil, entirely destructive of moral growth."[6]

The moral mandate of New Thought was to make the most of your own potentialities, to exercise the powers of will and mind and the character they produced; but also to emulate Christ in compassion and mercy toward others. Some writers, like Trine, openly lamented conditions beyond the control of individuals. Individual problems increasingly called for social solutions, as material self-reliance seemed less and less feasible. New Thought blended with social philosophy and anticipated its religious version, the Social Gospel, not repudiating environmental determinism as an aspect of reality, but only fatalism. More and more, individuals seemed capable of fulfillment only through "social organization," the title of Charles Horton Cooley's sociological classic of the Progressive period. Individual will and mind ought to be directed not only toward character but also its expression in cooperative, civic endeavors: in citizenship and public-spirited voluntary associations. By the time of World War One, even *Success* carried articles endorsing social reform, and former apostles of individualism as solitary struggle sought self-realization in concert with others. Society, newly conceived in terms of scientific objectivity, offered new possibilities as an instrument of individual salvation or happiness. But social thought was also guided by the pragmatic principle of utility, whose collective version was the greatest happiness of the majority, not of everyone.

1. Cf. Weiss, 133; 491, n. 32.
2. *Ibid.*, 131.
3. *Ibid.*, 231.
4. See Huber, 145-155.

        5. William English Walling, *The Larger Aspects of Socialism* (New York: The Macmillan Company, 1913), 157.
        6. Weiss, 178-179.

Twenty-Seven

Mind Cure: From Character to Personality

Evolutionary thought, and then Freud in the early twentieth century, undermined the canon of character by challenging ideas of uniqueness and self-control. New Thought responded with a selective adaptation of its own: Mind Cure. Susman describes a change around the turn of the century from "a culture of character to a culture of personality," in which there arose a remarkable interest in personal features of disposition and behavior. "There was fascination with the very peculiarities of the self, especially the sick self."[1] The sick self took the place of the sinful or unregenerate self, or the self deficient in character. It needed treatment, guidance, reorientation.

Mind Cure did not consider "personality," the word suddenly on everyone's lips, as *persona*, mask or projection of inner character.[2] Susman finds the word appearing in the later eighteenth century, and a few instances of its use in the nineteenth, by Emerson, Henry Adams, and Walt Whitman; but early in the twentieth century it quickly became what Raymond Williams calls a "keyword" -- on a list of such words from which "character," formerly so central, is conspicuously absent. Personality was differentiated from character by the former's absence of moral content, or its premise that being appealing or likeable was pragmatically good. So Mind Cure did not extend or defend character, but meant by "personality" an individualism of belonging to some larger understanding. Presented as a form of idealism, it suggested "enjoyment of the capacities of the One . . . . alignment with the universal consciousness." It was close to all forms of salvation, finding meaning in terms of an Oversoul, an Absolute, ". . . rejection of reliance upon the self in favor of reliance upon the super-self . . . "[3] with German resonances and foreshadowings of "Go with the flow."

Meyer says, "No individual was an individual by being unlike other individuals."[4] Mind Cure inverted the Romantic emphasis on differences. Now *alignment* became the crucial consideration, and the individual needed to be *adjusted*, mentally healthy, in order to reach fulfillment or success. "The ideology of success through mind power," Weiss points out, was "intimately bound up with the growth of psychotherapy . . . . Both emerged simultaneously, and the popularizers of the one were often practitioners of the other."[5] Personality emerged as being accepted and recognized within the context of a "set": individualism through conformity! Susman says "personality" came to mean "being somebody." He found this definition in nearly all the self-help and self-development manuals he studied. "The problem is clear," he writes. "We live now constantly in a crowd; how can we distinguish ourselves from others in that crowd?" Where identity had been moral, it now appeared as mere recognition. "Since we live in such a world, it is important to develop one's self -- that is, those traits . . . that will *enable us to think of ourselves* and have others think of us as 'somebodies.'"[6]

Again, character was not abruptly eclipsed. People retained and talked in terms of the earlier canon; but the conception of personality overlaid itself on more traditional ideas, and in some ways subsumed them. To be somebody, one still had to be oneself, as Susman notes. But, he says, "It is an almost too perfect irony that most of the works published and sold in large numbers as self-help in developing an effective personality insist that individuals should be 'themselves' and *not* follow the advice or direction of others. The importance of being different, special, unusual, of standing out in a crowd -- all of this is emphasized at the same time that specific directions are provided for achieving just those ends."[7] Developing an *effective* personality meant presenting oneself in ways that would be acknowledged, accepted, and liked. Children in school, always quick to draw inferences from their elders, began to take frequent popularity polls, surveys on who "has the best personality," indicating or confirming leadership roles among themselves. Mind Cure's version of individualism, condemning integrity while ostensibly advocating it, foreshadowed a time when Americans would be able, apparently without troubling questions, to say that they "like" public figures whom they do not trust.

Contradictions appeared, not only between character and personality, but within each as well. "The older vision of self expressed in the concept of character was founded on an inner contradiction," Susman says. "That vision argued that the highest development of self ended in a version of self-control or self-mastery, which often mean fulfillment through sacrifice in the name of a higher law, ideals of duty, honor, integrity. One came to selfhood through obedience to law and ideals."[8] Such a vision urged in effect a sublimation of self-needs or their redefinition in Arminian terms. Through the powerful exertion of will, one developed character, which was selfhood, individuality; and that exertion *constituted* individualism, as opposed to the pusillanimous seeking of mere approval or seeming expediency. This idealistic and religious vision contradicted the materialistic utilitarian thrust of American success ideas.

The culture struggled incessantly -- and successfully -- to fuse mutually exclusive and contradictory doctrines into a single national faith. When Emerson talked about self-reliance, he became popular because people chose to hear him as urging them to "get ahead" by putting themselves first. When William James explained pragmatism, the meaning that made him uncommonly famous for a philosopher was that the individual is justified in claiming moral truth for whatever he finds profitable in practice. The philosophical heirs of America's Arminian moral individualism, Transcendentalists and Pragmatists alike, preached character; but from Franklin to Dewey and beyond, they *also* preached practicality, and that meant "going along" to "get along." This was the contradiction at the heart of the character canon.

Success and the higher pursuit of happiness as fulfillment or salvation were not always the same, or even reconcilable; but the culture tirelessly, desperately insisted that they were not only compatible but identical. Huber writes, "The scramble for success often collided with the pursuit of happiness."[9] Logically they collided, but consistency ranks low among human concerns. Each was inconsistent within itself, the character canon teaching that integrity led to success, but that one's integrity must be presented in palatable dress; and the Mind Cure personality movement teaching that approval led to success, but that one should always retain integrity in seeking popularity. They were also obviously inconsistent with each other, one claiming ideals and principles to be most valuable, the other deriving and accepting values casuistically from what was admired. But of course people constantly mixed their models, believing what they needed to believe to be comfortable "with themselves."

Both canons were taught, through school, church and press, side by side. American children were chiefly taught in the nineteenth century to be respected and admired by others; and in the twentieth, to be liked and admired. "While both cared deeply what other people thought of them, the modern American must be more attuned to other people in order to get ahead," Huber writes.[10] But this is not a matter of *greater* regard for the opinions of others: it is a different kind of regard. The twentieth-century individual must be more attuned to personality than to character. Mind Cure initially set out a version of personality explicitly rejecting the "mask" or "act" presented by the individual; but that was only a respectful nod to the old canon, a way of gaining acceptance, a mask or act in itself. The new dispensation ingested whatever worked from religion, philosophy, humanistic learning and new science; and the individualism it dispensed was egoistic utilitarianism, pragmatism for a mass culture. It was whatever suited one's purposes, even to the purposes of Mussolini, who enthusiastically embraced it from James's Italian popularizer, Papini.

James wrote a great deal on the will, but his writings "were constantly filtered through the sieve of materialism." Where will had formerly developed and expressed character, it became in Mind Cure a device for reshaping the personality along more "effective" lines. Huber notes that in 1918 one could take for two dollars "The Success Course of Will-Culture and Concentration for Power and Success: I Will Be What I Will to Be."[11] By the early twentieth century, in a society ever more dominated by huge industrial and financial organizations, character seemed increasingly unsatisfactory as a basis for success. Of course the character canon had its calculating, ingratiating "personality" side, going back to Franklin. Lord Chesterfield's letters to his son were full of totally Machiavellian advice, and enormously popular in Franklin's time.[12] But modern circumstances brought out that aspect with unprecedented appeal.

Character was not very effective against industrial depression, even though it was preached, with its New Thought variations, through the 1930s; and, as Huber puts it, "The dam broke in 1936. That year Dale Carnegie published his monumental work in the history of the success idea. *How to Win Friends and Influence People* has sold more copies in America, excluding the Bible, textbooks, and manuals, than any other non-fiction work of the twentieth century."[13] Americans would be what they willed to be, and it now became clear that a great many willed to be successful by being likeable. Carnegie's book sold more than eight million copies. A substantial portion of America's population had long since frankly adopted the strategy of pleasing one another for their own individualistic purposes. They were reading why they were right, while many others prepared to go and do likewise.

Black people, generally very much socially separated from whites, did not tend to develop the traits of "personality" that appealed to whites or made for success through popular esteem. They were not liked or admired by the majority. Most people liked and admired those who "fit in"; and they believed or felt that there was something inferior about those who did not. The mainstream culture had been conditioned by scientific racism and propaganda to disdain the New Immigrants. Second-generation Italian-Americans rejected the "mustache Petes" of their parents' age group, whose agony it had been to watch without objection as their children become unlike them, for the sake of the children's success. African-Americans did not so quickly and visibly become unlike their parents. Nor were they given much more chance to develop popular "personalities" than to demonstrate "character" through success.

1. Susman in Higham and Conkin, *New Directions*, 216.
2. See Donald B. Meyer, *The Positive Thinkers* (Middletown, Ct.: Wesleyan University Press, 1988), 115.
3. *Ibid.*, 116.
4. *Ibid.*
5. Weiss, 105.
6. Susman, 218, emphasis added.
7. *Ibid.*
8. *Ibid.*, 220.
9. Huber, 428.
10. *Ibid.*, 432-433.
11. *Ibid.*, 178.
12. See Huber, 228.
13. *Ibid.*, 231.

Twenty-Eight

Self-Improvement

Beneath all the beguiling theory about "mind," American individualism and success literature never strayed far from the Arminian faith in will. After all, the will determined the mind-set, not the other way around; granted that the mind reciprocally reinforced the will. Determination, perseverance, and control brought success, and these traits depended upon a non-intellectual, non-cerebral capacity, or faculty. When treasured attitudes arise from strong feelings, we seem inevitably to confirm them as rational positions, preferably sealing their validity with cognitive statements or even absolutes. This was what Jefferson and others had done with rights evident to the moral sense, claiming for them the status of truths, and self-evident truths, instead of presenting them as the intuitively appealing standards of justice that they were and are. New Thought and its Mind Cure version similarly tried to make objectives of individual will into axioms of science and intellect in general, much as Locke had struggled to give what he thought to be moral "truths" the status of mathematical certainty. In fact people willed to believe what they wanted to believe, and conferred "truth" upon the results. What they wanted to believe, of course, reflected traditions and customs full of contradiction.

In the later years of the nineteenth century, as New Thought became so important an orientation, sheer strength of will largely eclipsed other aspects of character as the chief factor in success.[1] Perhaps more accurately, will became character. But "character" was a hard master, and Americans spared no effort to ease it into mind-set or personality, something more manageable and less uncompromising. Character was indispensable, since individuals needed to feel virtuous in order to be comfortable; but it needed to be brought under control. That meant it had to be rational, comprehensible and justifiable, but also that it had to fit with other objectives and acceptable conceptions of the self. It had to accommodate ambitions for material success, to enable the successful to feel righteous, and to fit these two services together. Nothing but will could fill the bill. Will served three goals in the service of individualism: to serve and endorse material self-enrichment; to bring about moral self-improvement; and to make the two fit together.

No conflict arose between character and will, perhaps needless to say; but character as strength of determination appeared quite different from character as reliability, trustworthiness, integrity, and moral self-reliance. These aspects of virtue were by no means at odds if the determination in question was resolve to be good, or "sanctified"; but they posed some problems when the chief objective was to get rich. Under the canon of character, virtue was supposed to manifest itself in self-discipline, self-mastery, the control of egoism for the sake of principle. But what if self-discipline and controlled egoism were *equated to virtue and principle?* All that was required was to recognize will itself as character, leading to both moral and material success. Self-improvement virtually entailed self-enrichment, self-enrichment served economic progress, which was good in itself, and the attendant civic improvement promoted self-improvement, Q.E.D.

Will-power as character made material wants acceptable in terms of spiritual needs, made spiritual beliefs endorse material wants, and made the two coincide. One interpretation was that the spiritual needs of individuals diminished or shifted, as in Santayana's conclusion that Americans remained idealists, but they idealized the material. In that case, spiritual beliefs would no longer be useful and no justification for pursuing material success was required. But Americans did not really have to give up spiritual beliefs for the sake of individualism. Pragmatism is the American philosophy, and William James the patron saint, because this approach permitted individuals to hold any comforting spiritual beliefs *as an option* willfully taken. With no requirement of consistency except consistent effectiveness in reaching desired ends, self-enrichment and self-improvement simply coincided and the problem of justifying egoism was solved at last. Two centuries or so of insisting on the efficacy of will put the individual in a position to achieve salvation just by choosing what he wanted to be true, and willing it to be so.

In *Principles of Psychology* James wrote, "Effort is . . . the essential phenomenon of will." Royce commented that the identification of will with personal *energy* was common. John Dewey said that willing is making a personal effort. Will had become both a universal capacity and the supreme arbiter of both truth and virtue. McWilliams summarizes this pragmatic solution, saying that while James "avoided stating . . . that whatever an individual found pleasant was true, there is no doubt that he referred the question of good and bad to the will of the individual, presuming the existence of no other tribunal."[2] The will to believe led to "Believe what you will." Bourke calls this a coalescence of cognition and volition. "As a consequence [of it], many pragmatists make very little difference between a preferential and a volitional decision to act in a certain way. What has happened in pragmatism is not so much that willing has been interpreted as a cognitive function but rather that *knowing has been shifted into the area of volitional activity*."[3] No conflict appears here between reason and feeling; rather, it is reasonable to follow feeling. Will chooses belief; belief endorses will; will expresses feeling. This is hardly new as an individual phenomenon, and in fact brings to mind Voltaire on God, Pascal's Wager and so forth. What is new is such a problem-solving program as a national religion, if religion be the set of assumptions underlying behavior. It is a national religion of subjective individualism.

All this leaves science to be treated in ways that are not troublesome. If it is accurate to say, as Morton White does, that "the story of American philosophy may be told as a tale of radically opposed attitudes toward science," it may also be useful to observe that these reverent and wary approaches have converged regarding belief. Believe what you *feel you must*, on whatever basis compellingly appeals to you -- to get where you want to go, to press your claims and gain your benefits. Perhaps Americans have been ambivalent toward science, but in this century most can evidently afford to venerate it without fear, by willing out of its province any area of concern in which it might prove troubling. For example, scientific racism has been increasingly discredited among scientists themselves since the 1920s, but popular impressions of science allow selective retention of discredited assumptions. It is easy and respectable to adopt a posture of "scientific" skepticism toward recent science when it conflicts with what is desirable to believe; or simply to say that science is unable to answer satisfactorily the questions at hand.

White observes that "James, the Darwinist, the empiricist, the follower of Peirce, spoke up in defense of what he called 'the religious hypothesis.' His first famous attempt in its behalf was his essay, 'The Will to Believe,' which appeared in 1896; the second was his *Pragmatism* of 1907."[4] The religious hypothesis was that the individual is free to choose for him- or herself wherever belief does not conflict with empirical evidence. Science does not debate with religion, any more than it does with poetry. Value judgments received their classification by will, subject to science if that seemed useful, exempted if it did not. Even in the hands of Dewey, who moved easily from pragmatism's implication of "what works is true" to the ethical naturalism of "what works is right," pragmatism produced no systematic ethical position. Ethical naturalism is not characteristic of pragmatism overall: in other words, not a corollary of any theory of truth that is held by all pragmatists. But what pragmatism means regarding individualism is that you can believe what you will (to believe) and reject what you will (to reject), as long as you can satisfy (or disregard) reason and evidence. The egoistic utilitarian implications of pragmatism as philosophy of will were so strong that ethical naturalism seemed inextricably linked with it. Americans have been and still are able to believe what they find comfortable about race, and to believe that they are morally right in doing so.

1. See Theodore P. Greene, *America's Heroes: Changing Models of Success in American Magazines* (New York: Oxford University Press, 1970).

2. W. C. McWilliams *et al.*, *The Idea of Fraternity in America* (Berkeley: University of California Press, 1973), 477-478.

3. Vernon J. Bourke, Jr., *Will in Western Thought: An Historico-Critical Study* (New York: Sheed and Ward, 1964), 42-43, emphasis added.

4. Morton White in Robert E. Spiller and Eric Larrabee, eds., *American Perspectives: The National Image in the Twentieth Century* (Cambridge, Mass.: Harvard University Press, 1961), 21.

Twenty-Nine

The Persistence of Romanticism

In literate circles, the scientific world-view transformed ideas of truth and reality, and expectations with regard to human capacities. Freud thought that men imposed unreasonable expectations upon themselves, in fact, and thereby caused themselves unremitting distress. They tended to forget or deny that life is a "passionate argument," as Hegel said, and to count upon rationality too much. Hans Reichenbach's summary typically characterizes the limits of scientific philosophy. "You want the truth, and nothing but the truth? Then do not ask the philosopher for moral directives . . . . There is no use in asking the impossible." He explains: "The answer to the quest for moral directives is . . . the same as the answer to the quest for certainty: both are demands for unattainable aims . . . . if you want to reach your aims, do not strive for aims that cannot be reached."[1] But this stoical approach only points up what cannot be reached by scientific philosophy. The aim of feeling reasonably certain or quite satisfied suffices pragmatically in the role of certainty; and the very limits of scientific philosophy elevated or confirmed intuition or feeling as the most reliable or only remaining moral guide: the very element so thoroughly discredited *within* the scope of scientific philosophy.

In the twentieth century Romanticism incorporated science, assigning it a dual role, as it were: to provide precision where possible, and elsewhere to follow feeling and justify it. Scientific philosophy, at first antithetical to romantic habits and traditions, got absorbed into a larger romantic scheme of things. As Conal Furay says, "What a people thought and believed in a nation's past has far more compelling power, in the long run, than any preachment of a 'new gospel' for today."[2] Some historians argue persuasively that past attitudes are no longer fundamental; yet there is a sense in which they are exactly that. George Boas remarks that it is even "easy to ridicule" Romanticism; but it is impossible to escape the fact that the Romantics were "our direct ancestors."[3] They made a way of life of individualism, trying to "draw out from within" the individual whatever is noblest, best and most distinctive. Self-development, from Goethe to New Thought, constitutes a positive duty; and self-expression is its attendant and its medium.

What Christopher Lasch calls the "new radicals" participated in a Romantic resurgence of "instinct over intellect," and philosophy gave full moral sway to their preference for feeling as more natural and fundamental than reason. There was nothing to discourage, let alone prevent them from following emotion and will. Like the uncivilized people, the individualists of Homer's *Odyssey*, they could live with "no muster and no meeting," since no group, including the family, exerted authority over them. All the elements of Romanticism persisted into the twentieth century, and found new forms of expression: fascination with the "uncivilized" and with childhood, "natural" and willful. The child intuitively recognized threats to itself from "the family . . . still the transmitter of a sterile and decadent culture, still the agent of 'civilization'; and the child in every man and woman intuitively recognized these things as . . . enemies."[4] Child psychology appeared, notably in the work of G. Stanley Hall, and scholarly attention sought out the "primitive" in both psychoanalysis and the study of cultures. American culture reaffirmed, in new forms, the sentiment of benevolence and the efficacy of will over innate depravity and predestination. New Thought writers "viewed the child from a conviction of man's goodness and divinity."[5]

Work remained the avenue to salvation, but it was a revised work of the ethical, not the ordinary will: *ergon*, not *ponos*. The struggling individual aimed at self-realization and self-expression, and worked to be himself, all that he could be: to "grow" as people would say in the 1960s and '70s. In this process, as E. A. Ross wrote in 1936, feeling eclipsed thought in importance. "Love and hate are the two finest things in life. Strong attractions and strong repulsions, strong loves and strong hates, great successes and great reverses enable one to say at the close, 'I have lived.'"[6] In popular culture the romantic disposition fed upon nostalgia for simple, natural life, self-fulfillment in one or another pastoral Golden Age, but especially that of the frontier. In the Golden West the virtues of Redfield's "folk society" blossomed in child-like simplicity, physically and morally close to nature. Literary romanticism never gave way to deterministic naturalism, but continued side by side to assume the ultimate reality and importance of the separate, discrete individual. Much of psychology followed the same course, with numerous post-Freudians emphasizing "versions of the growing self as indicators of cultural progress."[7]

Arminianism, the religious aspect of the Enlightenment in America, was secularized in turn by the generation of William Ellery Channing. Individual moral agency and responsibility remained central to American thought and passions, with implications always exciting and exhilarating. Optimism reigned, in James's sense of idealistic confidence about the individual's right and power to impress his will on material circumstance, as in Beethoven's supremely romantic dictum, "Seize fate by the throat and make your demands!" Life could be ever better, through the individual's capacity to overcome evil encountered as specific, experienced evils of lack and lure. Self-improvement through free choice, will, perseverance, remained at the center of America's agenda.

This combination of romantic individualism and perfectionism tended toward extremes of various kinds. No area of life more clearly or forcefully illustrates such extremes than the Romantic love "complex," with its absolutes: "happiness is inevitable in true love regardless of problems . . . to be truly in love is to be in love *forever* . . . love is an *all-or-nothing* feeling with no in-betweens . . ." and "when one is in love the beloved becomes his (her) *only* goal in life . . ."[8] No wonder our popular culture is soaked in romantic love along with romantic individualism: it provides the most fundamental, obvious expression of individual need, hope, and will to self-fulfillment. The beloved appears the only goal in life, the "Gnostic mirror" -- the only *means to life*, as opposed to mere existence. Matthew Arnold's romantic speaker in "Dover Beach" proposes lifelong fidelity for personal *reasons* based upon feelings. The feelings rest on observation and inference, after all, not to say calculations of interest. "Better" always carried undertones of utilitarian individualism, "better for me."

To glorify natural, spontaneous, child-like or "primitive" aims is to flirt with raw egoism, for the distinction between self-love and selfishness is often hazy. David Riesman, referring to this distinction in the work of Erich Fromm, says ". . . a 'selfish' person has no real self, and no fondness for the self; *therefore he must continuously seek security in terms of conquests and power* to compensate for his lack of 'self-love.' In other words, the selfish person is not interested in himself, but only in others' evaluation of himself."[9] How could the selfish person be interested in himself, if by definition he "has no real self"? Such a (non-)person lives on reactions, like the solipsistic housecat, which assumes that every move you make is somehow related to it. Peter Clecak says that "most Americans are afflicted with some form of this disease." But the "disease" that is so widespread is persistent romanticism, not selfish absorption. To perceive oneself habitually as a separate entity whose feelings legitimately prevail in guiding one through other considerations is to live in constant temptation to egoism, if not necessarily to adopt it.

Daniel Yankelovitch thinks that we "can't have a society in which people are out only for themselves." Whether we have had one depends upon what one makes of "can't" and "only." We can and actually do have a society in which people tend strongly to be out only for themselves as ends, and "for" all other individuals and groups only as instruments to their individual ends; but perhaps we "can't" survive morally on that basis. Yankelovitch finds the "certain kind of selfishness, a self-seeking Social Darwinism" emphasized in recent American public affairs simply unacceptable. He says it "goes against the grain, against the innate generosity and innate sense of fairness that Americans have imbibed as part of their upbringing and culture."[10] It is tempting to suggest that Americans have imbibed these qualities as a very small part of their upbringing and culture, but it is perhaps as large a part as in any culture. What we have more notably imbibed is the persistent romanticism that has enabled us to keep selfishness "largely concealed in settled social scripts." So far from diminishing, or being eclipsed by an age of naturalism, positivism, and science, romanticism has flourished in America through the twentieth century. Morally speaking, romantics live dangerously; and that ever-present danger of falling into mere meaningless selfishness perhaps accounts for much of romanticism's exhilaration.

Romanticism and idealism came together in the Transcendentalist movement, and they still converge. Santayana said that Americans idealize the material, but the culture idealizes the individual above all. Viewed from an idealist vantage point, as Horace Kallen does, ". . . the Individual comes first, the establishments of society come second; the freedom and fellowship of individuals is the goal, the institutions of government, religion and affairs are but instruments to attain this goal, valid not by what they are but by what they do. This is the whole purport of the idealism which we call American. This is the substance of the philosophy of individualism as a way of life."[11]

A peculiar feature of this American romantic idealism is that in setting the individual above all, it unavoidably constructs an élite, an "elect" of enlightened persons to which the fully realized individual must belong. On a vulgar level this exclusivity, this exclusionist aspect of individualism, ironically found expression in discriminatory emphasis on ethnicity and new conceptions of class. The Enlightenment's universal ideal, Man, as in the Rights of Man, gave way to idealized races, nations, nationalities, kinship groups, a resurgent tribalism on every scale of membership, which brought full circle the Romantic emphasis on the "natural" and primitive. From idealizing the individual as representative of mankind, Romanticism moved to individuals idealizing themselves: an apotheosis of seemingly limitless appeal, and one that can thus be adjusted and carried on as long as will chooses reality.

Difference from one another is a Romantic and an American virtue. "If God made different kinds of things," Boas wrote, it seemed that ". . . He approved of variety; He wished things to be different from one another."[12] Rules and standards generally stood in contradiction to Divine Will, then; and the more so as they claimed universality. Views of the artist as eccentric, not subject to "normal" codes and expectations, continued to exemplify romanticism, generally expressed as healthy pluralism: even "different strokes for different folks," meaning not only for folks of different cultural membership but even more for individuals. Black Americans themselves were not, of course, exempt from the pervasive appeal of Romantic individualism, or of self-enhancement by exclusionist claims.

1. Hans Reichenbach, *The Rise of Scientific Philosophy* (Berkeley: University of California Press, 1951), 323.

2. Conal Furay, *The Grass-Roots Mind in America: The American Sense of Absolutes* (New York: Franklin Watts, 1977), 50.

3. George Boas, ed., *Romanticism in America* (Baltimore: The Johns Hopkins University Press, 1940), xi.

4. Christopher Lasch, *The New Radicalism in America, 1889-1963* (New York: W. W. Norton and Company, 1965), 71.

5. Weiss, 147.

6. E. A. Ross, *Autobiography*, qu. Lasch, *Radicalism*, 172-173.

7. See Peter Clecak, *America's Quest for the Ideal Self: Dissent and Fulfillment in the 1960s and '70s* (New York: Oxford University Press, 1983), 110.

8. Furay, 55, emphasis added.

9. David Riesman, *Individualism Reconsidered* (Glencoe, Ill.: The Free Press, 1954), 40-41.

10. Robert C. Nelson, "An Interview with Daniel Yankelovitch," *Kettering Review*, Fall 1988, 48, 41.

11. Kallen, 241.
12. Boas, vi.

Thirty

Asserting Autonomy: the "Free Agent"

In the twentieth century many people have understandably envied the ebullient, expansive spirit so noticeable in nineteenth-century Americans. We tend to overlook their frequent desperation and to romanticize their courage; but still more to admire their sense of the world offering possibilities for the rational mastery of self and the purposeful control of circumstances. High hopes and expectations seemed to them well founded, their confidence in progress justified by vast possibilities. Their optimism has often inspired and sometimes depressed successive generations looking backward. As a people and as individuals they expressed faith in growth, improvement, and fulfillment. That faith supported both national identity and the most intense anti-social attitudes since the medieval Brethren of the Free Spirit: an individualism far more widespread than any earlier form. A few sets of mystics in past centuries had claimed, like Meister Eckhardt, "I can do all things by my will." Elevation or virtual deification of the self was by no means unheard of; but such views had never approached anything like orthodoxy. In the Romantic garden of nineteenth century America, self-direction and reliance on conscience grew into the right of the individual to invent himself, to create his soul. Anyone could be "in very truth his own God."

Yet a culture so optimistic about the individual choosing himself, willing himself into actuality, perhaps also left the individual without direction and adrift. Where everyone was "created equal" with regard to the pursuit of happiness (i.e., self-assertion), how did the individual learn what constituted happiness -- or what his self meant? If, as Pocock says, ". . . his only means of self-discovery lay in conforming to everybody else's notions of what he ought to be and was . . ." then popular opinion defined what sort of autonomy he could claim and exercise. In a world which, as E. E. Cummings wrote, "is doing its best, night and day, to make you everybody else," the job of establishing a self to be, and being yourself, meant "to fight the hardest battle which any human being can fight, and never stop fighting." The moral individualist who could be his own God might be powerless to create much meaning, confronting as he did the overwhelming Necessity of socialization, acculturation into a conformist web of values and attitudes. He could not even think, after all, about what did not come to his attention, so his "omnipotence" pertained to only a limited range of possibilities. Or did it? American orthodoxy, the conventional life into which people were socialized, "lived on" the assumption of individual uniqueness, as James would say. A conviction of uniqueness *was* orthodox and conventional, commonly taken for granted as a fact of life in America. *To conform was to see yourself as an autonomous individual.*

Mortimer Adler exemplifies a line of thought that finds real moral autonomy subverted by the Romantic assumption of personal, subjective knowledge derived from unique experience. The tremendous influence of John Locke in America included -- regrettably, from Adler's perspective -- the premise that ideas are subjective and ideological. Objecting to William James ("The knower is part of the known") and implicitly to American ethical individualism in general, Adler says that ". . . the knowable exists quite independently of the knower and is whatever it is whether it is known or not, and however it is known." Anything that one person can know, another can know as "genuinely," according to Adler. "Nothing that is knowable by one person alone can have the status of knowledge." This seeming opposition to James is softened considerably by the word, "knowable," as in "capable of being known." Since there is no way of demonstrating what is knowable, we can better describe what is known. That the knowable "is whatever it is" asserts a position related to but not contradicting James's claim about knower and known. James might well find Adler's position here simply irrelevant; but Adler's view aims towards moral individuality as much as James's does.

Whatever cannot be refuted by empirical evidence, rational argument, or a combination of them (such as a unique personal experience) is opinion, "not knowledge." This is a conventional point of departure, but one that inverts the idealist view based on *a priori* knowledge. Adler takes "self-evident" truths to mean assertions we cannot possibly contradict; and for him, transcendental philosophy is simply not to be taken seriously in the twentieth century, whether it is Kant's or Emerson's or Martin Luther King's. Idealism's Knowledge of the Good becomes *useful* when translated into knowing what is good for us, which is what we "ought to desire." We are obliged in some sense to know ourselves, to know our ultimate and proximate interests, and to be rational. This understanding leads to an American liberalism frankly rooted in egoistic utilitarianism. Individual success still appears as a "means" to the common good. As in John Stuart Mill, happiness remains the goal, an inherently individual goal; but we should "also" seek the general welfare. Why? Serving the common good serves the individual end of happiness, since we are interdependent; and cooperation is therefore expedient. Hobbes casts a huge, long shadow, called enlightened self-interest.

From a civic point of view, the problem is that this implicit hypothetical imperative, "If you want to pursue your own happiness effectively, work towards the common good," is not compelling. Hume worried that this reasoning would never be generally appealing, and in fact Americans have not found it very persuasive. Our habit all along has been to talk about deserving more than producing universally desirable results, even though "practical" ranks high in any characterization of Americans by themselves. In this culture, dualistic as it has always been in other ways, the ultimate goal and the proximate goal of most behavior are the same: individual satisfaction, achieved by free and willful acts.

Adler says that ". . . natural freedom is the freedom of the will in its *acts of choice.* Freedom of choice consists in always being able to choose otherwise, no matter what one has chosen in any particular instance. As contrasted with a freedom that consists in being *able to do* as one wishes, it might be described as freedom *to will* as one wishes."[1] The nature of autonomy corresponds to equality of opportunity rather than equal opportunity, and the right to pursue happiness is the right to will it, not to attain it. What we are able to choose as individuals establishes our responsibility, and therein our capacity for moral meaning. We are the products of forces outside our control, perhaps, but we take responsibility for what we *do* as such products of circumstance -- because we make choices as what we are. Our crucial assumption of autonomy is usually but not necessarily that we can do as we choose, as we will. Like Adler, most Americans have insisted upon some kind of "soft" determinism, including freedom of choice, because ". . . the exponents of freedom of choice maintain that such freedom is indispensable to every aspect of moral life." As Charles

Chauncy, the great Arminian, might put it, our choice of choices is necessary to a universe with moral meaning. If we lack such freedom we lack autonomy, and we cannot have meaning.

Adler is representatively optimistic about free choices of habits, for example, and of attitudes, understandings, information, treatment of all kinds. He says "If moral philosophy is to have a sound factual basis, it is to be found in the facts about human nature and nowhere else." However, each human ". . . is to a great extent a self-made creature. Given a range of potentialities at birth, he makes himself what he becomes by how he freely chooses to develop those potentialities by the habits he forms."[2] What about a steadily diminishing range of potentialities after birth, so that he doesn't "freely" choose what he becomes? Autonomy, which is one of the "facts about human nature," requires that one *does* choose freely, but not that the choice be what James would call a "live option." If you choose a self-destructive course of action, or if you choose a kind of habitual life you cannot bring to realization, the *choice* is in any case free, which is all that is required for you to be responsible for how you *act*, no matter what you may be able or unable to do. "There can be no question about the moral responsibility that each of us bears for his or her actions."[3] Without it, there would be no basis for claiming any inherent dignity of the individual *as a unique individual*, which is what Americans have felt, thought, and insisted upon.

Adler says there are different modes of existence for molecules and for humans, and in the latter mode individual identity is quite real. That is, of course, undeniable. The question is, how *meaningful* is the kind of uniqueness we observe? Are we involved in equivocation here, inferring common moral possibilities from our organic regularities (we have a common "human nature" so we must have common moral capacity), and moral identities from our empirical differences (we have different physical codes, so we must be morally unique)? We are choice-making beings "by nature." If all wills are created equal in the sense that they are free, meaning somehow morally entitled to choose what is best, then the individual is an autonomous moral agent when he can *know* what is best. Or, if all wills are presumed to be truly informed of self-interest (what is best), then is every individual an autonomous moral agent only when he can *do* what is best?

The prevailing American view in the twentieth century remained Arminian: individuals can know what to do, and they are responsible for doing or not doing it. Faith in the moral sense remained very much alive, confidence in reason and will provided individual pride of identity, and the ruling self-perception continued to be the individual as autonomous moral agent. The "self-made man" made not only his fortune but his self. Black people generally have not made themselves successful, and the culture has made it convenient to hold them responsible for that.

1. Mortimer Adler, *Ten Philosophical Mistakes* (New York: The Macmillan Company, 1985), 147, emphasis added.

2. *Ibid.*, 157, 163.

3. *Ibid.*, 190.

Thirty-One

Liberal Economic and Political Individualism

Liberalism expressed individualism socially and politically, advancing and elevating conscience and moral sense, natural rights, individual will and responsibility. Liberalism also expressed individualism in economic form, a rationale for industrial capitalism, which adopted the same philosophical, social, political and religious postulates already renowned as the foundation blocks of civil liberty. Authority was grounded in individual purposes, minimally defined, and most characteristically on the basis of contract. John Stuart Mill caught the spirit of an era in his assertion, "Over himself, each individual is sovereign." From its beginnings in the seventeenth century, liberalism confronted the problem of how to prevent a world of sovereign individuals from becoming a war of each against all; and the idea of contract seemed best to serve that common purpose.

Spinoza had shown how to avoid conflict by identifying and pursuing common interests, and by not getting destructively bogged down in irrelevant religious differences. Civilization could genuinely progress on the basis of egoism, because self-interest was rational and therefore predictable and manageable to a considerable degree. Commerce offered orderly management of divergent interests, serving mutual advantage by ignoring conflicting faiths, and often functioning as a substitute for war. True, commercial interests could themselves generate conflicts of interest over territory and so on; but such conflicts were immeasurably more civilized, rational and controllable, more limited in ferocity and scope than the earlier religious wars. Their stakes were not absolute, and rational interest, unlike faith, never required burning anyone at the stake.   National interest in the eighteenth century got redefined as the collective interests at least of those engaged in commerce, and not just the interests of the national treasury.   Capitalism extended mercantilism to include or accommodate liberal individualism.   Civilization profited by the changed perception: as Montesquieu observed, more "tender manners" accompanied the rising power of the mercantile classes. Men could afford to be "gentle men," as conflict became institutionalized into mere fierce competition.

Technological advances, the practical core of industrialization, also facilitated the spread of individualism by extending opportunity to pursue self-interest, or happiness.   D'Alembert reflected that the mechanic arts were more fundamentally human than the liberal arts, because they came closer to being universally accessible. The spread of economic individualism logically accompanied the spread of technology, then.   Defoe had Robinson Crusoe decide that "by making the most rational judgments of things, every man may be in time master of every mechanic art." Carl Mitcham, seeking a philosophy of technology in the late twentieth century, looks back at Timothy Walker in the early nineteenth, with his ". . . prototypical argument that technology is a means for making democratically available the kind of freedom enjoyed by the few in a society based on slavery."[1] Industrialization, economic change, and concomitant social and political change, all added up to progress in America, where William Graham Sumner wanted both "natural" change and a rule of individualism.   But ungoverned change, by the later nineteenth century, brought more organization, and on an ever larger scale, diminishing possibilities for individualism as liberal thought had conceived it.[2]

Individualism had been overwhelmingly conceived as inseparable from property, but important property increasingly meant corporate holdings.   Freedom for self-direction and self-fulfillment came more and more *through* organization, and in America that meant corporate organization. Liberalism had so far literally meant individualism, but individualism anchored in property.   America's legal system carried individualist assumptions to absurdity in an age of dominant economic organizations, by declaring without explanation in 1886 that corporations were persons in the sense of the Fourteenth Amendment, with corresponding privileges, immunities and protection of rights.   Four years later the corporation was found to be not only a legal individual but also individual property (owned by its individual self) with appropriate protection of law. The sanctity of contracts between corporate "individuals" and individual individuals reached its apogee, perhaps, in the *Lochner v. New York* case of 1905; and the axioms of economic individualism remained so sacred, above question and exempt from challenge in popular culture, that its heroes could simply assume the justification of brutal murder over property rights in the 1948 film hit, *Red River*, for example. Economic competition, with absolutely minimal regulation, had the Christian blessings that came with New Thought, and also the secular endorsement of Social Darwinism, disdained or rejected under New Thought morality. Whether according to God's will or Natural Law, competition was the law of the land. When or if it lost the status of Natural Law, the loss set values adrift.[3] James, Croly, Lippmann and Dewey were among the thoughtful writers who pointed out the absence of authority, with nothing in evidence to replace it except power, justified pragmatically.

Reasoned self-interest struggled to maintain the canon of liberal individualism in the age of organizations, informed by the philosophy of pragmatism in several guises. C. S. Peirce had said, "The elements of every concept enter into logical thought at the gate of perception and make their exit at the gate of *purposive action*; and whatever cannot show its passports at both those two gates is to be arrested as unauthorized by reason." Reason, through empirical method, dictated purpose; and purpose implied values. As R. Jeffrey Lustig suggests, Americans continued to think in an "individualist mode" without any longer having a clear sense of what they meant by individualism. "This failure to develop a new theory of individualism" appropriate to changed conditions, "to translate what was valuable in classical liberalism into modern terms . . ." meant profound confusion.[4] Even if liberal individualism could survive economic concentration in the age of organization, it could not survive ethical individualism turning into a parody of itself. The autonomous moral agent, choosing his choices and willing his own identity, became unrecognizable in the corporate spokesman cunningly promoting his interest by claiming a fake individual identity for his organization. Liberal individualism, like the working classes, had indeed come upon hard times.

The rise of the factory system, forming and transforming cities, made anonymous drones of most men, no longer significantly identifiable by their crafts, hereditary homes, or personal characteristics; but those who flourished identified themselves as unique individuals on the basis of their success and the personal qualities they said accounted for it. They asserted themselves and deferred to one another on the basis of this success, constructing a new and simpler counterpart to European class divisions. Yet the outstanding feature of political individualism was always its rejection of class, whether hereditary, plutocratic or Marxist. Political individualism continued to assume rational self-interest, but objected to its widespread frustration. Everyone was self-interested, of course, and rational at least in wanting property, security, and comfort. The question was, with the increasing concentration of wealth and power, how the faceless masses were to pursue their happiness as individuals, as was alleged to be their inalienable right.

Organization offered the only apparent answer. Business and industrial organizations were so successful by the twentieth century that Thorstein Veblen described representative government in America as the representation of organized economic interests. Farmers did their best to emulate the success of other business interests, even seeking for a time to organize a democratic class movement based on seemingly coincident interests of farmers and urban workers. Labor unions themselves fought for recognition, seeking the individual interests of workers through collective power. Despite sometimes desperate efforts, improved conditions came only slowly and haltingly through organized efforts -- except in business itself, where organization was made to complement and express individualism rather than opposing it. The property-owning class was not defined by the culture as a class at all, but as able and deserving *individuals*. Any organized opposition to their interests appeared unfair and opposed to individualism: to initiative, responsibility, and self-reliance.

Complementing capitalist theory, political individualism assumed rational self-interest, which was generally but not necessarily "enlightened." Political individualism asserted that each individual wants his own benefit and has a right to seek it. Second, fairness meant equality of opportunity to seek individual benefit, not equal opportunity as a benefit. Both actual opportunity and actual benefits corresponded at least roughly to the individual's deserving: fitness, character, will-power, personality, or some eclectic conception definable as merit, corresponding to the eighteenth century's "virtue and talents." That is, people tended to get what they deserved, making allowances for God's mysterious ways, or simply for what we don't understand.

Several versions of utilitarianism, including John Stuart Mill's 1863 formulation under that name, tried to reconcile self-interest and concern for the common welfare. Ideally both were the objectives of a civilized individual, and the more enlightened one's self-interest, the more they would be seen to coincide as objectives. In general, however, as Adams, Hamilton, or Madison would quickly have predicted, the common welfare tended to appeal to people in proportion to its utility towards individual goals. Utilitarianism tried to posit both as ends; but enlightened self-interest saw common welfare only as a means to individual ends. Utilitarianism held the universalist principle that "an action is right only if it contributes more to the general happiness than any alternative action open to the agent."[5] Americans' enlightened self-interest tended towards a version which Mill, Godwin and many others had struggled to avoid or refute. An action conducive to the *general* happiness was "right" in proportion as it contributed to *individual* happiness.

All the "social" arguments -- of social philosophy, the Social Gospel, social science, and socialism itself -- would envisage government extending opportunity to pursue happiness, broadening in utilitarian fashion the distribution of material possibilities. These arguments collided head-on with political individualism's dogma of "natural" opportunity, and deserving or merit. American ideas of individual autonomy and responsibility, from the Arminian will to the self-made man, militated against acknowledging any need for "social security" or government extension of opportunity to individuals who might not deserve it. If they deserved greater opportunity, they would earn it. Equality of opportunity meant "liberty and justice for all," and every individual was responsible for what he or she made of it.

Another kind of misgiving or apprehension also supported political individualism against state "intervention" in the distribution of security and opportunity. Tocqueville had dreaded that the government, ". . . acting purely in the interests of the people . . . denatures them, gradually reducing them to sub-human, asocial atoms who are content to glut their lives with petty, materialistic pursuits."[6] The "soft tyranny" of society itself, pressing towards homogeneity, threatened to undermine the inherent worth and dignity of the individual, the uniqueness of the man working as opposed to the worker. Organization, then, was legitimate and desirable only as "private," voluntary association to serve common individual purposes: a position incessantly emphasized, and with enormous appeal, by Herbert Spencer and his American acolytes. Just as Adam Smith and Karl Marx anticipated reduction of individuals to commodities, the "dehumanization" of workers, so American individualists who believed in a "natural aristocracy" and "inherent worth and dignity" also feared "alienation" (Hegel's word), the sacrifice of the moral person to the mere legal individual. Tocqueville and his admirers had recognized ". . . how the energy released by economic self-interest was indeed able to enhance material prosperity, as if the entire society were guided by Adam Smith's 'invisible hand.' But it was nonetheless clear . . . that this 'invisible hand' was not a serviceable bond between the individual and his community."[7]

In the humanistic perspective exemplified by Tocqueville, utilitarian individualism was much preferable to the inherently anti-social Romantic form, tending towards an atomistic society of "infinitely repellent particles." Tocqueville readily acknowledged the social advantages "to be gained from the kinds of relationships described by Smith's famous formula . . . " that we "address ourselves" not to one another's "humanity," but to our unfailing self-regard. But as the nineteenth century passed, industrial society did not take shape just as expected. It was producing goods all right, but not a sense of community. "Instead of this the new industrial world produced an anti-society, whose members met only at points where their humanity was irrelevant . . . cultivating their self-interest while leaving the work of 'community' to some hypothetical, and very distant, 'invisible hand.'"[8] Romantic or expressive individualism offered little social wisdom because it neglected common humanity and left many people without much self to express. Utilitarian individualism, defining the individual so firmly in terms of self-interest, left some with an empty, hollow feeling, because it failed to suggest any substantive sort of self whose utility ought to determine value. Yet the utilitarian form exerted powerful appeal among Americans, insofar as success met the need for distinction and self-expression. Romantic self-expression had utility. People clearly felt a need for communities, but pretty much as contexts in terms of which to posit and support their indispensable sense of individuality.

The progressive efforts toward community by a people who were self-proclaimed individualists involve no contradiction and no paradox. Their motivation evidently remained constant: individual self-fulfillment, or secular salvation. If they were "joiners," they joined for their own reasons, to meet their own needs. The "rivalry" between individual goals and social welfare was not much of a contest in America. Social organization of every kind stood in the relation of necessary means to individual ends. Still awareness grew that "Individualism itself is a social product, like all . . . religions."[9] As a friend and follower of Royce, the psychologist James Mark Baldwin, put it, society needed to discover or construct a "dialectic of personal growth" explaining the individual in society, not "over against" it.

In the 1880s only about six colleges or universities listed courses called sociology, but there were almost two hundred such courses by 1894, doubling again by 1909, and twenty-six textbooks were in use by 1916. The subject was not much related to America in those years, presumably because relatively little social change had occurred here, there being no "old order" or feudal past to overcome.[10] But Americans were after all part of the same philosophical and theoretical traditions, and they found congenial such an emphasis as Durkheim's in "Individualism and the Intellectuals": that the autonomous individual, following his own idea of obligation according to his social and legal rights, is the indispensable basis for discussion of morality. Lester Frank Ward held the first American professorship in sociology, at Brown University in 1906, the same year L. T. Hobhouse accepted a similar appointment at the London School of Economics. American social science focused from the first on the fact that there is no self without social experience. Autonomous man sought membership to fulfill himself, but self-interest was not only selfishness. The natural individual, celebrated through a century of Romanticism, also possessed the sentiment of benevolence and the moral sense, and naturally sought membership for socially beneficial, if ancillary, purposes. Selfhood did indeed emerge through a "dialectic of personal growth," and social science gave its blessing to New Thought and the Gospel of Self-Improvement, whether as character, personality, or willed autonomy.

As George Herbert Mead observed in his foreword to the 1930 edition of *Human Nature and the Social Order* (1902), Charles Horton Cooley followed William James "very closely." The development of a sense of self depended entirely "upon another or others who are necessarily as immediate as the self . . . . The other cannot appear first as an experience of my own self, if my own self appears through the reaction of the individual to others."[11] In the idea of the "looking-glass self," developed in his examination of primary groups in *Social Organization* (1909), Cooley tried "to find the basis of the self in reflexive affective experiences, i.e., experiences involving 'self-feeling' . . ."

Mead, on the other hand, found the "essence of the self . . . cognitive: it lies in the internalized conversation of gestures which constitutes thinking, or in terms of which thought or reflection proceeds. And hence the origin and foundations of the self, like those of thinking, are social."[12] *In either case, the foundations of the self are social.* Philip Rieff points out, in his introduction to Cooley, that for both Cooley and Mead, "Even the body is not a self, *as such*; it becomes a self only when it imagines itself in relation to others . . . . Social communication is thus fundamental to selfhood."[13] But sociology and social psychology did nothing to alter the *motivation* of the utilitarian individualist, or the disposition to approach society -- or community -- as means to fundamentally egoistic ends.   Whether the social foundations of the self are mainly emotive or mainly cognitive, segregated people could hardly develop selves to win esteem from the majority. This could be most readily and satisfactorily explained to the majority as a failure of will and ability.   Again, the culture of individual responsibility, "merit," and "deserving" made racism so congenial as to be widely irresistible, despite the insights of social science.

1. Carl Mitcham, "What is the Philosophy of Technology?", *International Philosophical Quarterly*, 25, 1, March 1985, 73-74.

2. See R. Jeffrey Lustig, *Corporate Liberalism: The Origins of Modern American Political Theory, 1890-1930* (Berkeley: University of California Press, 1982), 31, e.g.

3. See Lustig, 227.

4. Lustig, 257.

5. D. H. Monro, *Dictionary of the History of Ideas*, IV, 445.

6. See William A. Schambra, "Tocqueville and the Dangers of Democracy," *Humanities*, 9, 2, Mar.-Apr. 1988, 14.

7. Paul Zweig, *The Heresy of Self-Love: A Study of Subversive Individualism* (New York: Basic Books, 1968), 250.

8. *Ibid.*, 251.

9. Geoffrey Hawthorn, *Enlightenment and Despair: A History of Sociology* (Cambridge: Cambridge University Press, 1976), 118.

10. See Hawthorn, 191-195.

11. George Herbert Mead, foreword to 1930 edition of Charles Horton Cooley, *Human Nature and the Social Order* (1902) (New York: Schocken Books, 1964, intro. Philip Rieff), xii.

12. Mead, *Mind, Self and Society* (Chicago: University of Chicago Press, 1934), 173.

13. Philip Rieff, introduction to Cooley, *Social Organization* (1909) (New York: Schocken Books, 1962), xix.

Thirty-Two

Modernism Reshapes Liberalism

Twentieth century liberals had to revise their doctrine to reconcile individuality with ideas of community. New models of behavior from the time of Max Weber tended ". . . to fix . . . attention on the more general, environmental factors instead of the unique individual." Liberals faced the challenge of saving as much as possible from the ethical individualism that undergirded moral agency, while recognizing the social origins and meanings of the individual. As Hobhouse put it, "Social well-being cannot be incompatible with individual well-being. But individual well-being has as its foundation the *responsible* life of the rational creature."[1] What was needed was healthy diversity with social identity. Progressives needed to modify sociological and methodological individualism *to save the person by helping the individual.* No actual modern individual still stood solipsistically at the center of his own universe; but the meaning of the individual still stood at the center of the universe of human and particularly moral concerns. Individuals lived only in society, and a new generation of liberals sought to establish what John Dewey called a "new" individualism on that basis. In this endeavor they needed desperately to accommodate the findings and attitudes of science: to recognize Modernism.

Modernism drew out the implications of economic determinism, and of materialistic determinism in general, convincingly demonstrating that individuals are overwhelmingly the products of circumstances outside their control. In addition to economic determinism, which most people associated with socialism, modernism embraced evolutionary naturalism, defining humans as organisms, animals evolving according to the same principles that govern all others, and not the objects of a special creation or of special divine attention. It also incorporated the implications of psychology, Freudian thought in particular, emphasizing the non-rational, visceral springs of human behavior. In the same few decades, modernism drew out meanings of other new scientific understandings: relativity, with suggestions of cultural and moral relativism, and uncertainty, with overtones of subjectivism. All these modernist understandings suggested that individual humans are more passive than romantic or ethical individualists believed: hence the need of modern liberals to redefine the service of persons as serving relatively helpless individuals. The great waves of Enlightenment and Romantic self-confidence, of optimism regarding the individual's capacity to define his moral identity or seize fate by the throat and make his demands, rapidly passed from credibility. An "adolescent" feeling of unbounded possibilities gave way to reluctant awareness of limitations on the individual.

Politically, debate over individualism had focused for more than a century upon equality. Liberalism had viewed it as moral and legal, a natural right to unspecified equality for the most part; where socialism of various kinds had insisted upon material equality as the necessary condition for real moral equality -- the moral right to equal opportunity, as opposed to the equal moral right to opportunity. By the early twentieth century, liberal thinkers who recognized the implications of modernism sought to accommodate both. Libertarian and egalitarian ideology -- the older liberalism of moral philosophy and the new perspective of social philosophy -- both included passive as well as active conceptions of the individual.

Before modernism, liberalism took for granted that the individual's entitlements under natural rights were entitlements to act vigorously on his own behalf, to struggle and compete. He or she was already a free moral agent, and needed only to be recognized as such to exert sovereign will as a full person. Egalitarianism took natural right to be the entitlement of individuals as passive objects confronting massive determining forces; and the freedom sought was freedom to become the subject of one's own life, rather than a helpless object. In short, social philosophy and socialism adopted a modernist mode of thought before liberalism did. Both sought moral agency and dignity for the individual -- the real status of being a person -- but liberals felt obliged to take determinism into account, especially with the rise of modernism in the 1920s. Politically, economically and morally, the question individualists confronted was, How can autonomy, agency, and sovereignty of the self be maintained as intellectually and scientifically respectable claims?

Modernism dealt with the unsettling implications of a universe described by Darwin, Marx, Freud and Einstein, for example; and it also dealt with the Victorian cultural and social world that was so much unsettled by those implications. Daniel J. Singal describes modernism as "a *culture* -- a constellation of related ideas, beliefs, values, and modes of perception" which is comparable with the Enlightenment or Romanticism in that it "supplies nothing less than the basic contours of our current mode of thought."[2] Singal summarized modernism's "signs" in *The War Within* (1982) as a readiness

> . . . to plumb the nether regions of the psyche . . . . the irrational as an integral part of human nature that must never be ignored. Second . . . the universe as turbulent and unpredictable, as opposed to . . . an orderly universe governed by natural law. Third . . . [a] positive view of conflict, whether personal, social, or political. The Victorian objectives of 'bliss' and 'peace' have become unpalatable to twentieth-century thinkers . . . . Fourth . . . an ability to live without certainty, either moral or epistemological . . . [in a world whose] moral standards inevitably fluctuate and must always be considered tentative. Finally . . . . a critical temperament uninhibited by considerations of formal manners: gentility gives way to the necessity of making contact with 'reality,' no matter how ugly or distasteful . . . .[3]

Singal points out that modernism seeks to restore the universalistic disposition of pre-Romantic or pre-Victorian thought: the Enlightenment breadth expressed in claims about "all men" -- but this time with the explicit awareness that, as he quotes William Carlos Williams: "Man is an animal, and if he forgets that, denies that, he is living a big lie, and soon enough other lies get going." This "integrative mode" is perhaps the most distinctive mark of modernism, a reversal of Romanticism's emphasis on differences rather than commonalities, with all the false dichotomies and fragmentations that ensued from that emphasis.[4] Modernism rejects the basic assumptions of the Liberal era: ". . . a predictable universe presided over by a benevolent God and governed by immutable natural laws . . . humankind capable of arriving at a unified and fixed set of truths about all aspects of life . . . moral standards based on a radical dichotomy between . . . 'human' and . . . 'animal.'"[5]   Modernism ushered in, among many other reconsiderations, a radical questioning of gender roles based on assumptions about "what a man is like" and "what a woman is like."   The term itself first gained currency in discussion of religion, more in contrast with fundamentalism than with Victorianism, romanticism, or the presuppositions of nineteenth-century liberalism.   Shailer Matthews, in *The Faith of Modernism* (1924), wrote that ". . . *the use of the methods of modern science to find, state and use the permanent and central values of inherited orthodoxy in meeting the needs of a modern world"* constituted modernism.[6]

While modernism undoubtedly arose in tandem with all forms of naturalism, and is itself an aspect of or another name for naturalism, it can be seen fully and clearly only in light of this "salvage" function which is so central to it.   Modernism is far more than a reversal or rejection or what preceded it.   It is an attempt to incorporate into a scientific world-view perceptions and conceptions of the individual which undergird Western liberalism's claims of inherent worth, dignity, autonomy, and deserving.   To do that, the individual will had to be saved again, just as it had to be saved from earlier kinds of determinism such as predestination.   In the bleak, windy universe of naturalism or modernism, a new "myth," as Mark Pittenger puts it, was needed to replace evolutionary consciousness.   This new myth would have to be "perhaps not more 'true,' but simply more 'useful,' than evolutionary determinism: one that would place human will and desire at the source of thought and action."[7]

The individual will -- albeit determined to be as it was -- weathered the storm of naturalism, maintained legitimacy, and pursued identity along two courses. The will worked through both the collective effort of a new semi-socialist liberalism, and also through subjectivism towards self-referential validation. Modernism itself took its own forms in America, with little in the way of derivative features from Europe; and the "key figures" in launching it were William James and John Dewey, with their pragmatic and instrumental "myths" of truth and pluralism.[8]

David Hollinger describes two modernist types responding to the world of determinism, irrationality, relativism, alienation, and moral confusion.   They employ, respectively, strategies of reference and strategies of artifice: social programs for modifying liberalism and individualism to save what is best in them; and individualist efforts to survive and pursue happiness by inventing a reality that expresses will.   Social reformers offered programs for reordering the national life, "suspicious of moral commitments" perhaps, but nonetheless prepared to regard problem-solving as The Good. The heirs of Hobbes, Hume and Mill, they sought a *science* of morality, while their artistic counterparts flared forth in intuitive, expressionistic freedom. The modernist self could never be established "once and for all" because if it were it could not be authentic. With no closure, modernism introduced an era of the self undergoing lifelong revision, the identity plastic and malleable. But will remained the American key to reality, whether in the path of individualism in community, planned in the manner of science, or in the artificer's path to self-referential validation.

The progressive thinkers wanted to change people's personal views and behavior, in the public interest. Dewey thought that social education could eliminate ". . . the selfish ambitions that presumably generated social conflict."[9] Progressive control of modernism aimed, in William Appleman Williams' words, at a new republic that ". . . will be beautiful instead of ugly" and ". . . will facilitate human relationships instead of driving men into separate functional elements."[10] Individualism would be saved as healthy citizenship, based on recognition of the scientific fact that the self could thrive only through community. Progressive liberalism continued the titanic struggle, since Adam Smith, or Hobbes, or the Puritans, to make egoism respectable. As Lasch points out, this too was indoctrination. What started out as education for reform became education for conformist "citizenship." The middle-class pursuit of material self-interest was supposed to be diverted to civic reform; but education in practice rationalized pursuit of material self-interest *as* progress and civic responsibility. Intelligence manifested itself as adaptatability, and self-seeking was adaptation to the system, to the very culture.

Dewey wrote that democracy was "an absurdity" without faith in the individual; and faith in the individual was ". . . impossible when appetites and desires are conceived to be the dominant factor in the constitution of most men's characters . . . ." The ideal of social progress entailed the attainment of individual freedom "through a fraternally organized society . . . the permanent contribution of the industrial movement to morals -- even though so far it be but the contribution of a problem." The "system of morals which has come nearest to the reflection of the movements of science, democracy, and commerce is doubtless the utilitarian." Its challenge was to present convincingly the utilitarian ethic as individual fulfillment through community rather than through egoistic use of social organization as means to individual ends. Dewey worried that utilitarianism's equation of the good of anyone to that of anyone else was "practically perverted by its excessive interest in the middle and manufacturing classes . . ." through nineteenth-century liberalism.[11]   In other words, utilitarianism had not served democracy, but only the old liberalism. Expediency was good, utility was good, but they had somehow to be made *social* goods if any form of liberal individualism was to survive. Democracy, only recently embraced by the intellectual élite, was the only hope of the future; but it would have to be utilitarian to work, and *universalistic, not egoistic.*

Edward Bellamy had argued that the ". . . primal principle of democracy is the worth and dignity of the individual . . ." not the autonomy of the individual. Louis D. Brandeis, testifying to the U. S. Commission on Industrial Relations in 1915, pointed to the most "fundamental" cause of unrest as "the necessary conflict -- the contrast between our political liberty and our individual absolutism." Political liberty as a general condition required the abandonment of absolute insistence on individual autonomy. Progressive education promised the necessary sense of community, of citizenship, to achieve broad utilitarian consensus. In the early decades of the twentieth century, America's new liberals drew from their own progressive adaptations to modernism "a heady feeling," as Thomas C. Cochrane calls it, "that the evolutionary process could be steered by man. Experiment and measurement could determine social evils, and proper education and legislation could bring them under control."[12] But the social thinkers were far ahead of social realities.

Modernist insights militated against racist beliefs, obviously. Intellectuals and educated people in general tended more and more to abandon, disdain, and denounce racism. Their convictions would make possible great advances in desegregation and increased opportunity for blacks. But the prevailing *attitudes* of Americans, educated and uneducated alike, remained basically unchanged. They held onto traditional beliefs with regard to opportunity. It remained an individual matter, a matter of removing barriers and opening avenues for advancing individual self-interest. Desires were indeed "the dominant factor in the constitution of most men's characters." Most continued to desire and to believe what they found most comfortable or useful to believe, even if it cost them the loss of John Dewey's esteem.

Modern America liked Dewey's utilitarian and pragmatic philosophy all right, but mainly as it could be overlaid on the foundation of individualism. For very good reasons, Americans held an overwhelmingly negative conception of government, seeing its foremost duty as leaving individuals alone. If blacks did not make progress as individuals, they seemed not to grasp reality, or not to take advantage of the opportunities available. And since they did not in general make as much progress as other Americans, it seemed plausible that there was probably something deficient about them in general. In any case, that was the most convenient and gratifying approach for most Americans to take if their attention was drawn to the subject. How they fared might be determined by forces too strong for individuals to control; but maybe how their fate was determined had something to do with how they were. Modern liberalism had not brought American popular culture beyond oversimplifications about will, like "Where there's a will, there's a way" -- especially where someone else's will-power is under consideration.

1. L. T. Hobhouse, *Liberalism* (1911) (London: Oxford University Press, 1964), 60.

2. Daniel J. Singal, in a special issue of *American Quarterly*, "Modernist Culture in America," ed. Singal, 39, 1, Spring 1987, 7-8.

3. Daniel J. Singal, *The War Within: From Victorian to Modernist Thought in the South* (Chapel Hill: University of North Carolina Press, 1982), 8.

4. Singal, *American Quarterly*, 12, 13.

5. *Ibid.*, 9.

6. Shailer Mathews, 1924, qu. David A. Hollinger, "The Knower and the Artificer," *American Quarterly*, 39, 1, Spring 1987, 51, emphasis in original.

7. Mark Pittenger, "Science, Culture, and the New Socialist Intellectuals Before World War I," *American Studies*, 28, 1, Spring 1987, 78.

8. See Singal, *American Quarterly*, 16.

9. See Lasch, *New Radicalism*, 163, 159.

10. See David Noble, *The End of American History* (Minneapolis: The University of Minnesota Press, 1985), 135.

11. John Dewey, "Intelligence and Morals," in, e.g., Perry Miller, ed., *American Thought From the Civil War to World War I* (New York: Holt, Rinehart and Winston, 1954), 232-233, 234-235.

12. Thomas C. Cochrane in Spiller and Larrabee, eds., 95.

Thirty-Three

The Limits of Liberal Reform

The literature of personal inspiration, will-power, and self-help has been by far the most successful category of publication in America. People with the attitudes and beliefs of salvation or success by force of will, of institutionalized competition for prosperity and social position, and of a literature celebrating ambition, resourcefulness, pragmatic efficiency, self-determination, individual responsibility and self-reliance, have welcomed a seemingly endless proliferation of self-help gospels. At the same time, Americans learned in the age of huge corporations that representation and power are the rewards of organization. Goya said that art is self-expression; in America, organization became a kind of self-expression. Every kind of economic interest group demanded to be heard, and struggled to gain recognition for its members: business interests, farm interests, and labor interests. The power achieved by these organizations won grudging acceptance from those outside them. Institutionalized competition dictated the rules, and the organizations that observed those rules attained a kind of respectability because people understood what they sought and were willing to tolerate most of their efforts to manipulate representative government for their own advantage. Individuals complained incessantly about the abuses of organization, but they accepted it as a necessary implement of competition, a tool that is legitimate because it is indispensable for success, shown to be so by the modernist adaptation of liberal values.

Black Americans have never fully shared, for obvious reasons, the mainstream focus on individual life of Arminianism, capitalism, Liberalism, Transcendentalist and Romantic and pragmatic individualism. They began to seek relief, recognition and power in the era of big organizations, when the foundations of American beliefs and attitudes had already been laid, and the traditions of individualism were so intricate, unquestioned and complex as to be virtually unassailable. Recognizing that organization led to power, blacks naturally sought it; but they faced a problem different from those of other identifiable constituencies in the system. Their most obvious problem was poverty. Most poor people have always been white because there are so many white people, but a disporportionate number of black people have always been poor. It can be argued that progress for blacks requires progress against poverty itself: that blacks will be more comfortable only with policies to relieve poverty in general.[1]

But the necessary class consciousness for a serious attack on poverty is simply missing in America. Every effort to mobilize such an effort has failed, because Americans believe in only one class, the middle class. Unlike Germans or Japanese, for example, Americans do not generally believe that it is in their individual interest to have everyone else as comfortable and productive as possible. Americans do not recognize either interdependency or class to the extent that other modern societies do; and they are correspondingly unsympathetic to the poor. They see the middle class as including all those whose circumstances range from reasonably comfortable to quite luxurious. There is no real upper class, but only *individuals* who have benefited enormously from the system. There is no real lower class, but individuals who are ill-favored: who have failed, through some misfortunes or defects, to make use of the system. That is why Americans allow ill and other incapacitated people to live in abject poverty. They tend at least to suspect "deserving," or God's will at work.

Shelby Steele perfectly represents the mainstream, middle-class perspective when he expresses his annoyance at hearing people talk "as though middle-class status was an unearned and essentially passive condition."[2] Precisely that perspective severely limits the usefulness of his "solution," which aims at policies that would eliminate poverty "and that instill those values that make for self-reliance."[3] The values that make for self-reliance *are well instilled*, and they are exactly the values that militate against acceptance of relief for African-Americans or anyone else on a class basis.

Drawing on the examples of economic groups, African-Americans have struggled for progress, recognition and power as a special interest. But the definition of an interest group on a racial basis, rather than an economic or political one, widely appears inappropriate, exclusionist, and undemocratic. Historically, Americans conferred legitimacy on collective economic interests only with considerable reluctance. Ultimately, they recognized the need for collective bargaining, in the interest of fairness. But "collective bargaining" on the basis of race is suspect, alien to tradition. It suggests a different kind of collectivism, separatism rather than acceptance of the society's established beliefs and procedures. The traditional values of American striving for advantage can be described as "in themselves, raceless and even assimilationist."[4] However, those traditional values permit the continuation of racism by blocking anti-racism.

Modernism brought more recognition of determinism, more acceptance of the fact that people do not design or invent themselves, and a great increase in social awareness from the 1920s through the 1960s; but the society is quite evidently unwilling to move away from the self-help doctrines of individual initiative and responsibility. These attributes of individualism may well be the only practical point of departure for individual black people to use the opportunities the society provides;[5] but they also constitute a formidable obstacle to black people without much opportunity, considered collectively. Individualism seems to set severe limits on the kinds and degrees of collective liberal reform the society will accept.

Steele writes, in italics for emphasis: *"The most dangerous threat to the black identity is not the racism of white society (this actually confirms the black identity), but the black who insists on his or her own individuality."*[6] He strongly approves "individuality over group identity."[7] Whether "black identity" is useful to African-Americans, or, as Steele thinks, a sort of handicap, or both, it remains useful in the mainstream culture of individualism. Traditional individualism of the kind espoused by Steele accommodates blacks with opportunity, just as it accommodates anyone else who has real opportunity; but it clearly works against changing whites' beliefs and attitudes regarding blacks. There is good reason to doubt whether comfortable whites -- or blacks like Steele -- *can* change their individualist stance in the foreseeable future. They have been shaped by it, and how they are shaped includes their habits of invidious comparison and pragmatic explanation to suit their own purposes. Individualism certainly does not require racism: but it does perpetuate its own congenial version of "black identity."

1. See Shelby Steele, *The Content of Our Character: A New Vision of Race in America* (New York: St. Martin's Press, 1990), 91.

2. *Ibid.*, 108.

3. *Ibid.*, 91.

4. *Ibid.*, 95.

5. See *ibid.*, 23, 30, 99, *e.g.*

6. *Ibid.*, 72.

7. *Ibid.*, 23.

Thirty-Four

Free Will and Determinism

Arminianism really set the mood of America. It defined what Americans needed to believe about themselves, and provided them a self-perception as satisfying as it was necessary. Each individual took moral responsibility for his or her life, and everyone had the power of will to function as free moral agent. Only such a volitional conception of the individual made possible the sense of oneself as inherently worthwhile, dignified, and in control. Millions of Americans were thrilled to echo W. E. Henley, "I am the master of my fate: I am the captain of my soul." Whatever its philosophical validity or deficiency, a will to believe in will itself simply pervaded American culture: a confidence in self-direction that verged on "self-evident" or revealed truth. The evidence that impressed the faithful was the evidence suggesting that "You can't keep a good man down." "Cream always rises to the top"; and never mind scum.

From the eclipse of Calvinism by Arminian views in the early eighteenth century, the power of free will was set against determinism; and in popular attitudes it posed a simple, straightforward opposition. Either you were in control of yourself or you were a largely helpless product of circumstances beyond your control. Americans bristled at the very thought that they were largely helpless. Their experience seemed to militate against any such idea, and their will was never stronger than in taking responsibility and credit for what they were. Their forebears had explicitly rejected European ideas of status -- hereditary, fixed social position -- and of class. Without established relationships, even a conspicuously successful American might lack the secure sense of identity that an English servant had: that firm, unquestioned sense of self, of who one is and how one fits into the order of the world. Americans collectively sought a sense of identity in their "Manifest Destiny," since they lacked a "usable past" in terms of which to define what it meant to be an American. But as individuals their only hope of a secure sense of identity, of self and of self-respect, required the claim of authoring themselves, inventing their lives or "careers," claiming freedom to be what they would be and taking responsibility for being what they were.

Americans have always been uneasy in the face of one another's "failure," sometimes moved to be compassionate and often to be generous, and yet fearful of treating others as less autonomous agents than they had to believe themselves to be, in order to maintain self-respect. We tend to do penance in impulsive and ritual ways, like lamenting the horrible lives of "New York's hundred neediest families" every Christmas in *The New York Times*: not aiding by policy or law the millions of needy people, the ghastly percentage with blighted lives, but privately giving alms to a symbolic little sample who have been utterly crushed. We sympathize and donate money, returning with a sense of relief to the hundreds of pages of that great newspaper full of hilariously overpriced garments, meals, hotels, and so on. The point is this: Americans are disposed to be kind, large-spirited, and generous; but we are inhibited by the beliefs we need to hold about ourselves, and therefore about others as well. Assuming that there is some mysterious degree of determinism, that some people just have the worst luck imaginable, we tend to think of them with sympathy but also as the "exceptions that prove the rule." The rule is that we are generally in control of our lives, self-determining agents operating through free will, being what we choose to be in setting our goals, disciplining our efforts, seizing fate by the throat and making our perfectly rightful demands.

R. E. Hobart describes how devotees of free will get caught in binary thinking, imagining that they must reject determinism (and by extension, social responsibility) in order to maintain free will and the individual dignity based upon it. Hobart says that ". . . the controversy between the doctrine of free will and determinism . . . is based upon a misapprehension . . ." and that "the two assertions are entirely consistent . . . ." They have been opposed to each other in our minds " . . . because we have not realized that free will can be analysed without being destroyed, and that determinism is merely a feature of the analysis of it."[1] Think, for example, of a conflict situation in which temptation vies with better judgment. "It may . . . happen that the noxiousness of the temptation does not affect [the individual] so powerfully as its allurement, and that he succumbs. It is no whit less true, according to determinism, that he could have willed otherwise. To analyse the fact expressed by 'could' is not to destroy it . . . . Everybody knows that we often will what we do not want to will, what we do not prefer . . ." The argument leads to a conclusion that we do what we like best "on the whole," and that the seeming opposition of determinism to free will is "a question of the meaning of words."[2]

Determinism, seeming to deny free agency, appears as the position of reason and science, while free will seems indispensable to individual morality, because without it there is no basis for responsibility. Hobart says, "The worst waste is the clash of best things. In our subject it is time this waste should end."[3] We do encounter uncontrollable interference with the power to act as we prefer. But the free, responsible part of our actions is the *determined* part, the part that expresses the self. The random part, not determined or willed, is morally meaningless. "The whole alarm is an evil dream, a nightmare due to the indigestion of words. The past has created, and left extant, a free-willed being."[4]

We commonly apologize or attempt to explain, excuse or justify ourselves by saying "I was not myself": and that may well literally have been the case. But it was not determined, it was undetermined and therefore not a free expression or act. It was not characteristic, not expressive of character or identity or self. Hobart writes, "The principle of free will says: '*I* produce my volitions.' Determinism says: 'My volitions are produced by *me*.' Determinism is free will expressed in the passive voice."[5] And what of that most central of American concerns, deserving?

> A man is to be blamed only for what he does *himself*, for that alone tells what he is. He did not make his character; no, but he made his acts. Nobody blames him for making such a character, but only for making such acts. And to blame him for that is simply to say that he is a bad act-maker . . . . To cause his original self a man must have existed before his original self. Is there something humiliating to him in the fact that he is not a contradiction in terms?[6]

Hobart's good thinking persuades us, if we are receptive; but the culture at large clings to simplistic either-or proclamations, like the view of Konrad Lorenz that all determinism has the effect of releasing people from "any responsibility for what happens in the world."[7] Americans have always been terrified of a world without moral meaning: hence the absolute necessity of replacing the failed Puritan determinism with Arminian will, both religious and secular, and with individual responsibility of the most inclusive sort as an axiom. A seemingly "anti-Arminian" thinker like B. F. Skinner frightens and bewilders his readers because he offers no rational alternative to accepting a reality in which collective will affects how individual traits are determined. He presents motivation in traditional American form: enlightened self-interest. But the self who holds the interests is a social invention, not a "natural" free agent. Americans generally find such a self unsatisfactory and repugnant, not surprisingly in light of natural law and Arminian traditions.

Placing free will against determinism, in the interest of individualism, is central to popular assumptions regarding African-Americans. The main objection to determinism is still the same as it was for Charles Chauncy, that determinism removes moral meaning from the individual and from the universe itself. There is a sort of unquestioned presupposition that individual responsibility requires free will that is somehow undetermined. But there is also a political aspect to America's individualistic revulsion towards ideas like Skinner's. Daniel Singal captures the essence of it in a single reference to anti-modernist movements as new forms of "absolutism in the manner of scientism, orthodox Marxism and the behaviorism of B. F. Skinner . . . ."[8] Determinism, in the form of behaviorism, seems to threaten political as well as moral individuality; and of course Skinner delighted in shocking readers, choosing such a deliberately provocative title as *Beyond Freedom and Dignity*, for example.

Can a science of behavior, which would demolish racist beliefs (if not attitudes), also permit something Americans are able to accept as meaningful individualism? Most Americans tend to view blacks *as individuals with regard to opportunity, but categorically with regard to "characteristics."*[9] Why? Individualism, as it is commonly needed and cherished, requires that blacks be held to the same expectations and requirements as whites; and that any deficiencies of performance be matters of *individual* will, character, and ability. It "follows" that "failure" by a conspicuous percentage of blacks must suggest shared individual deficiencies associated with but *not determined by* or excused by race traits. White Americans need this view to support the kind of Individual they need to believe in for their own self-esteem. Hence collective action was suspect from the first, because it attempted to treat what were perceived as widespread deficiencies in the performance of responsible individuals as if they could be corrected by treatment of a category to which those individuals belonged.

1. R. E. Hobart, "Free Will as Involving Determination and Inconceivable Without It," in Bernard Berofsky, ed., *Free Will and Determinism* (New York: Harper and Row, 1966), 63-64.

2. *Ibid.*, 76.

3. *Ibid.*, 95.

4. *Ibid.*, 91.

5. *Ibid.*, 71.

6. *Ibid.*, 83.

7. Konrad Lorenz, *The Waning of Humaneness* (Boston: Little Brown and Company, 1983, trans. Robert W. Kickert), 11.

8. Singal in *American Quarterly*, 20-21.

9. See University of Chicago poll results of three hundred communities, *Newsweek*, Jan. 21, 1991, 57, e.g.

Thirty-Five

Behaviorism and Individualism

The Behaviorism introduced by John B. Watson and others in the late nineteenth century distressed and shocked many Americans because of its radical materialism and mechanistic vision of human activity; but Watson, while he was a forceful and persuasive writer, was vulnerable to criticism for oversimplification and superficiality. B. F. Skinner, the leading behaviorist of the twentieth century, was certainly not simplistic or superficial. His views are therefore all the more distressing and shocking to individualists who require autonomy as a basis for morality and identity. Skinner writes that there has never been a more important subject than how human behavior is controlled, and that scientific progress "has probably never demanded a more sweeping change in a traditional way of thinking . . ." In the world of modern science, he says, "The direction of the controlling relation is reversed: a person does not act upon the world, the world acts upon him."[1]

In short, the Arminian and Romantic and quintessentially American view of the individual imposing his will upon circumstance is flatly discredited and dismissed. Skinner calls traditional views of autonomy unfortunate nostalgia for inherent dignity and spiritual values that never were. "Such fragments of outmoded behavior tend to be 'wistful' -- that is, they have the character of increasingly unsuccessful behavior" because they do not describe reality. He regrets that such "reactions to a scientific conception of man . . . . immobilize men of good will . . ." and suggests that "anyone concerned with the future of his culture will do what he can to correct them."[2] Clearly Skinner's work is a refutation of individualism as traditionally and conventionally conceived; yet it is vitally important to note that he says a *person* does not act upon the world, but is acted upon. Human beings in the aggregate do act upon the world, decisively. The question is whether we act realistically and rationally.

If power resides in "the environment" as opposed to the "autonomous" individual, then responsibility must be radically reconsidered. Does individual responsibility vanish with "free will" in the usual sense? Skinner says that it does not, but that responsibility develops differently than assumed in former times. People have to be conditioned, or educated, or trained, to behave well: usefully, productively, creatively. Individuals then will behave as if they were "moral" or "responsible" in the old meanings. They may not be committed, dedicated, or idealistic, but they can be taught to act as if they were, which is consequentially the same thing: nothing but the social application of pragmatism as a theory of truth. Does this mean that pragmatism implies such a totalitarian revision of individuality that a culture based on will and self-direction might actually be forced back to duty, standards, and a "moral career" for each person? Not necessarily, but it definitely contains that kind of possibility, making many Americans as uneasy about it as Daniel Singal.

Pragmatism appealed just as strongly to Mussolini as it did to Franklin Roosevelt, after all. But if we are not to have purposeful education or conditioning, then what, Skinner would ask, are we to have? He extends the citizenship education concern of many progressives, but most definitely without the "permissiveness" associated with their educational ideas. "Permissiveness," he writes, "is not . . . a policy; it is the abandonment of policy, and its apparent advantages are illusory. To refuse to control is to leave control not to the person himself, but to other parts of the social and nonsocial environments." Subjective individualism in an age of science is simply lazy and irresponsible. "The fundamental mistake made by all those who choose weak methods of control is to assume that the balance of control is left to the individual . . . when in fact it is left to other conditions."[3] As in so many other ways, nature abhorrs a vacuum; and if the formation of behavior patterns is not organized, they will be formed by purposeless or exploitative and malevolent factors.

In a famous line, Skinner says "To be for oneself is to be almost nothing." He argues that "We must all begin as babies, and no degree of self-determination, self-sufficiency, or self-reliance will make us individuals in any sense beyond that of single members of the human species."[4] What we need to do, then, is to use our aggregate will and reason to shape the environment in all ways, toward commonly desirable ends. Valuing autonomy for its own sake at this point is primitive. "Autonomous Man," Skinner's favorite target, serves the same purpose as God in religion, or demons, goblins and witches in the seventeenth century: that is, to explain whatever is not understood. Autonomy, or self-determination, is a construct that accounts for what we can't account for in other ways, just as supernatural explanations in the past sufficed to explain whatever lacked natural explanation.[5]

The early socialists, Robert Owen in particular, first saw that individual behavior is shaped by the environment. Eventually it became clear that "environment" is both inside and outside individuals, so there is no sharp distinction between "nature and nurture." The important point is that environment and behavior interact, reciprocally shaping each other, as John Dewey suggested. The individual is shaped by the environment, but individuals acting in concert shape the environment that shapes them. Our problems stem very largely from the fact that our enlightened self-interest is insufficiently enlightened. We fail to recognize that it is in everyone's best interest for everyone else to be as productive, secure, and "successful" as possible. We still want to deserve and condemn rather than giving up our claims to self-contrived uniqueness and cooperating in the common interest.

A typical American reaction to Skinner is horror at the specter of the "anonymous drones" such a controlled society might produce. Skinner recognizes the power of what he calls "the literature of freedom," as in Leibniz and Voltaire, but he pleads for a realistic settlement, in which the individual retains the ability to do as he wishes, but recognizes that one has to wish within the range of one's possibilities.[6] Like Felix Oppenheim and Erich Fromm he ponders the "feeling of freedom" as opposed to any objective conditions which could be reasonably characterized by the word. He recognizes that ". . . a system of slavery so well designed that it does not breed revolt is the real threat."[7] But such a system can come from various directions. It brings to mind Cook-Taylor's description of the factory system in the 1830s: "The factory combines the perfect despotism with the perfect freedom." The same might be said of systems in general, perhaps: that they obliterate individuality while permitting non-conformity in meaningless ways that satisfy and enchant their subjects. For Skinner, control means setting the range of possibilities from which choices are made; and he undoubtedly intends to extend Kant, that most exquisite of moralists, in the recognition of what it means that freedom comes through order, not chaos; or to extend the best insight of Hobbes, for that matter. He is similar to C. S. Lewis in his conviction that danger lies in "mere Nature," in chance and conflict far more than in any effort to recognize and act upon the ways in which we are the objects of our own powers.

The literature of freedom has vehemently insisted that we are threatened by what Lewis calls "the abolition of man" through determinism, relativism, and behaviorism. Skinner replies that an individual is not "a body with a person inside, but . . . a body which *is* a person in the sense that it displays a complex repertoire of behavior."[8] What this "unfamiliar picture" abolishes is only

> . . . autonomous man -- the inner man, the homunculus, the possessing demon, the man defended by the literature of freedom and dignity. His abolition has been long overdue . . . . He has been constructed from our ignorance, and as our understanding increases, the very stuff of which he is composed vanishes. Science does not dehumanize man, it de-homunculizes him, and it must do so if it is to prevent the abolition of the human species.

Anonymous drones truly belong to the past, not to the scientific society. "The slave in the cotton field, the book-keeper on his high stool, the student being drilled by a teacher -- *these* were the machine-like men."[9]

To those who argue that the inherent worth and dignity of the individual would be destroyed by scientific treatment of behavior, Skinner replies:

> It is only autonomous man who has reached a dead end. Man himself may be controlled by his environment, but it is an environment which is almost wholly of his own making. The physical environment of most people is largely man-made . . . . [and] the social environment is obviously man-made -- it generates the language a person speaks, the customs he follows, and the behavior he exhibits . . . .

Collective self-control is then required for cultural evolution. Skinner readily concedes that human ". . . individuality is unquestioned. Every cell in [a human] body is a unique genetic product, as unique as that classic mark of individuality, the fingerprint. And even within the most regimented culture every personal history is unique. No intentional culture can destroy that uniqueness, and . . . any effort to do so would be bad design." Nevertheless, Skinner fears that "In spite of remarkable advantages, our culture may prove to have a fatal flaw." That flaw is an antique understanding of individualism, unchanged from its Enlightenment and Romantic foundations. He says, for example, "There is a sense in which Dostoyevsky may be right. A literature of freedom may inspire a sufficiently fanatical opposition to controlling practices to generate a neurotic if not psychotic response."[10] For example, an epidemic individualist "neurosis" may support and require its racist corollary.

In less controversial terms, other social scientists reinforce the implications of behaviorism with regard to individualism. The view of William James, that the individual can invent his reality, dominated anthropology in the era of Franz Boas. The next generation argued, like Leslie A. White, that individuals express culture and that the James-Boas conception was a conceit, "an example of crass anthropocentrism . . . . simply deism reduced to human dimensions." This ". . . exaltation of the individual human being . . . is not only prescientific; it is anti-scientific. It is one of the greatest, if not the greatest, obstacle to the achievement of the science of man, cultures and society . . ."[11] In economics, Clarence E. Ayers seized upon the comment of Emerson, "There is properly no history: only biography." He writes:

> With all respect to Emerson . . . exactly the reverse is true, as the biographical dictionary itself attests. It identifies these individuals with their native soil, their parents, their wives and children, with all the schools they have attended, all the positions they have held, the professional associations and private clubs to which they belong, and even, in the end, their churches. This is as it should be, indeed as it must be; for a separate individual is an abstraction unknown to experience. There is properly no biography: only history.[12]

Walker Percy wrote, in *The Message in the Bottle*, about "a secret . . . which every scientist knows and takes as a matter of course, but which the layman does not know . . . . The secret is this: Science cannot utter a single word about an individual molecule, thing, or creature in so far as it is an individual but only in so far as it is like other individuals."[13]   Willard Gaylin says that in our ". . . most individualistic of cultures . . . we are finally beginning to realize . . . the sad but primitive biological fact that there is no such thing as an individual human being . . . . The concept of a biologically complete individual human being is truly the myth of our time."[14]

The twentieth century brought new support for possessive individualism, forcefully and compellingly expressed in the pro-choice movement, and in feminist literature like the celebrated *Our Bodies, Ourselves*.   But in many contexts, the peculiar possibility arises that individualism no longer expresses individuality.   For example, eccentric behavior loses meaning as it becomes acceptable; and it becomes acceptable because nobody cares or pays much attention to it. At the same time, some social analysts notice that there is individualism of an old kind even in the scientific world of B. F. Skinner, or those who still more explicitly deny individuality. Christopher Lasch, for example, thinks that ". . . the morality of enlightened self-interest lives on in behavioral psychology . . ." and he is perfectly correct. "A behaviorist like B. F. Skinner," he says, "stands perfectly in the utilitarian tradition in his quest for a 'better moral order' with 'no need for moral struggle.'"[15]   Whether that is fair to Skinner, it is clear that Skinner is indeed utilitarian, that he assumes self-interested behavior, and that the utilitarianism he describes in American culture is egoistic, individualistic in the extreme.

Lasch says "Skinner scandalizes liberals by carrying their own assumptions and prejudices to unpalatable conclusions. He makes explicit what liberal humanists *prefer to ignore* [i.e., will to ignore]: that the therapeutic morality associated with twentieth-century liberalism destroys the idea of moral responsibility, in which it originates . . . ."[16] Somehow the irony is inescapable, that Puritanism is in such disrepute in America, and has been for so long; and that Skinner's world is so similar to John Winthrop's, with all responsible for each. But the resemblance is accompanied by many differences, inevitably. Skinner's ideas undergird contemporary ethical thought, often unacknowledged but unmistakably present as assumptions. And the American individualist is not so easily backed into a corner either. Biologists, physicists, major novelists, psychologists, philosophers, anthropologists, historians and economists may say only that there is no *scientific* basis for the old individualistic postulates.

The effect of that may be, as Skinner feared, more to discredit science with the public than to discredit what the public wills to believe.   Behaviorism, now unfashionable, and social science in general leave room for some kinds of individualism, but those kinds left available are subtle and difficult. They lack the comforting warmth of myth, just as James's or Royce's logical analyses of immortality lack the warmth of heavenly fantasies; and so they lack the broad appeal of myth. The individual as Autonomous Man retains that appeal. So do racist habits of perception, largely based on Autonomous Man.

1. B. F. Skinner, *Beyond Freedom and Dignity* (New York: Alfred A. Knopf, 1971), 201, 202.

2. *Ibid.*, 203.

3. *Ibid.*, 79, 94.

4. *Ibid.*, 118.

5. *Ibid.*, 12.

6. See *ibid.*, 34.

7. *Ibid.*, 37.

8. *Ibid.*, 190.

9. *Ibid.*, 191; 194, emphasis added.

10. *Ibid.*, 196, 20, 174, 157, 201.

11. Leslie White, "Individuality and Individualism," in Gordon Mills, ed., *Innocence and Power* (Austin: University of Texas Press, 1965),17, 19, 32.

12. Clarence E. Ayers, in Mills, ed., 49.

13. Walker Percy, *The Message in the Bottle* (New York: Farrar, Strauss and Giroux, 1954), 22, 108.

14. Willard Gaylin and Ethel Person, eds., *Passionate Attachments: Thinking About Love* (New York: The Free Press, 1988), viii.

15. Christopher Lasch, *The Minimal Self: Psychic Survival in Troubled Times* (New York: W. W. Norton and Company, 1984), 205.

16. *Ibid.*, 215.

Thirty-Six

That Old-Time Religion

While scholarly writers debated aspects of will and determinism, the implications of naturalism in its various forms, of pragmatism and behaviorism, most Americans continued to live on the assumptions of self-reliance, character, and will-power. Intellectuals talked about individuality and individualism in relation to Feuerbach and Nietzsche, Marx and Mill and Freud, but New Thought was as philosophical as most people felt any need to be, especially with reinforcement from major native figures like James and Royce. American literature in the first decades of the twentieth century, both inspiring and expressing the life of the people (as Santayana put it), presented individualism in forms that set the stage of public attention for such inspirational popular moralists as Harry Emerson Fosdick in the 1920s and Norman Vincent Peale in the 1950s. Fosdick would explain that personal "integration and self-realization had replaced salvation."[1] Peale would go so far as to advocate the general attempt to practice magic, invoking supernatural intercession in natural processes, besting one's rivals and succeeding in material matters by prayer and faith.[2] One could imagine John Dewey or B. F. Skinner in his last years, shaking his head in dismay.

Theodore Dreiser notably exemplified literary devotion to New Thought ideas of individualism. He also became acquainted with Nietzsche, through H. L. Mencken, and his enthusiasm for the acquaintance showed in his tough, lonely, individualist heroes, defiant toward conventional morality. More importantly, Dreiser held the conviction, as Kenneth S. Lynn remarks, "that knowledge, direction, and control of life were within the grasp of the strongminded individual . . ."[3] In this he resembled Jack London when London glorified competition rather than socialism, and individual will as power. David Graham Phillips provides another important example of this mind-set, not only because he dwelled on the theme of work as the only course to salvation but because, as Lynn says, his confidence in self-reliance and "inner strength" were so perfectly representative of his time.[4]

People often seem to assert beliefs that repudiate what they experience, or simply to claim more importance for something as they feel the lack of it more. Americans talked more and more about equality in the nineteenth century, as there was less and less of it, and they talked a great deal about individual control of circumstances as they experienced less of that in the twentieth. The culture overtly elevated and celebrated the "team player," but the team never lost its primary purpose of "show-casing the talents" of individuals, as sports jargon puts it.

In the 1920s, character was still much admired as a key to success, but foreshadowings of change appeared in the increasingly widespread appreciation of pragmatism's efficiency. At the same time, what seemed personally efficient in many lines of endeavor was "personality," that catchword of the 'thirties and 'forties, when preteen children went so far as to circulate rating sheets in school every day, to record incessantly the vagaries of popularity on various criteria of appearance and behavior. Personality "development" as self-improvement evidently drew upon the philosophical claim by Royce that if we focus our attention on a possible act, considering it as an option, we are likely sooner or later to do it or attempt it. Huber quotes Coué as saying "Every thought entirely filling our mind becomes true for us and tends to transform itself into action." The second part of this claim is true to Royce's argument, but the first part is a peculiar twist of pragmatism that was made to end up in the Ronald Reagan absurdity, "Everything will be fine if you just say it is."

The success mentality of the 'twenties relentlessly pressed the claim that equality of opportunity constituted equal opportunity, at least for those who were disposed to "get ahead." Exactly what such a "disposition" means is hard to say. This word comes to mind because of a phrase ubiquitous in German advertising, "gut gelaunt geniessen," well disposed to enjoy; and no more precise word than "disposed" offers itself. There is no sense of some individuals deserving success because they are qualified on the basis of something like Jefferson's "virtue and talents"; success somehow "depended upon the individual" and at the same time offered itself to virtually everyone as a possibility. Herbert Hoover, for example, never gave up this sort of description of "equal opportunity" as American reality. When he accepted the nomination in 1928 he said, "This ideal of individualism based upon *equal opportunity to every citizen* is the negation of socialism . . . . It is as if we set a race." Hoover's use of the word "race" here seems almost poignant.

Writers who presented success or failure as a matter of individual choice flourished, even as the failure to understand consequences of technological change brought well over half of American households below a subsistence level of income by the spring of 1929, before the crash. (Brookings figures showed about sixty percent.) Bertrand Russell said that even science was "politically conservative." Daniel J. Kevles writes in *The Physicists*, "He might have added that in the era of Harding, Coolidge, and Hoover, the leading exponents of science had . . . become vigorous advocates of the day's conservative syllogism -- that science was good for business, business good for America, and, in consequence, science good for the nation's economic and spiritual well-being."[5] Leo Marx is one of the scholars who has pondered how America maintained a creed of progress but forgot to ask "progress towards what?" But even if "what" was in question, "how" was not, as far as most people were concerned. It was up to the individual to get ahead.

The 1960s were a watershed decade with regard to the equation of individualism and success, as in other regards. From the vantage point of 1971, Richard M. Huber surveyed the literature of success in *The American Idea of Success*, identifying and explaining its chief characteristics over several decades. The "spirit" of this genre was anything but Social Darwinist, exhibiting instead a "Christian and humanitarian" conception of competition. In this new Christianity, character developed from inner struggle, much as Jonathan Edwards might have envisioned it. Fulfillment entailed giving as well as getting, which was "why one little word -- 'service' -- was surrounded with such reverence." Did an epidemic of hypocrisy sweep the country? Certainly not, since most people found opportunity to do good while doing well, if not always to do well while doing good. The classical capitalist doctrine of Adam Smith evolved into a "doctrine of service" under which, as Andre Siegfried put it, "Money . . . became not only the symbol of creative power, but a sort of moral justification." Bishop Lawrence, who had claimed, back at the turn of the century, that godliness was in league with riches, would undoubtedly have been pleased with ". . . a 'package deal' of comforting reassurances about their *raison d'etre* for which most modern Americans must have felt grateful."[6]

The literature of success was a "package" of rationalizations for egoism, and in itself so successful that egoism not only got justified, but could be taken for granted as established. As that process advanced, justifications were no longer urgently needed, because people found no reason to remember that there had ever been any question about the compatibility of Christian ethics and a value system centered on competitive material acquisition. After a time, justifications were no longer needed at all, because even if the historical doubt were remembered, the union was no longer open to question. The most ordinary occurrence in America was the camel passing through the eye of the needle.

From the 1930s, with Dale Carnegie and Dorothea Brande, an avalanche of self-help literature descended upon the public. Crude distortions of James's pragmatism and unwitting adaptations of Hans Vaihinger's "philosophy of 'as if'" abounded. In retrospect the veneration of will-power through the first half of the twentieth century looks like Arminianism gone mad; but the gospel of self-improvement surely ran amok in its "personality" phase after that decade of depression. Popularity was success, because "The way to get ahead was by a pleasing personality and the manipulation of other people." Kant's great ethical teaching, that a human being must always be regarded as an end in him- or herself, and never a mere means to an end, was totally inverted. Success was good, and manipulation was the high road to it. Huber writes, "The personality ethic, and the forces which it articulated, enforced a creeping conformity which was subtly tyrannous in its pressure to play the game according to the most effective rules, even though the rules might violate a person's ethical principles."[7] A good salesman could sell anything, for example; because what a good salesman sold was not a product, but *himself*!

With the prevalence and dominance of this attitude, egoism no longer required justification in the guise of morality, but for the first time openly eclipsed or actually *became* morality: an adumbration or a warning of ethical confusion and deterioration.

Huber notes that under the "personality ethic" the individual could be moral in solitude, bringing to mind a fulfillment of Tocqueville's apprehension about "idiotic" withdrawal of individuals into exclusively personal and private concerns. In his description of what alienation would be necessary to such a life, if indeed it is possible at all, Huber concludes that people would not choose solitude in any case; for ". . . it is only through people that the self-alienated product of the personality ethic can find his sense of identity."[8] In other words, for those who are drawn into such an orientation to life, *no integrity is possible in society and no sense of identity in isolation.*   Perhaps deliberately, Huber sounds like Tocqueville, considering how ". . . forces surrounding the personality ethic contributed to feelings of emotional isolation while they increased the need for affection. Many turned to the family unit to meet this need. The family became a refuge . . . ."[9]

The chief motivation to be ethical was that unethical behavior might lead to unpopularity and failure. As with Benjamin Franklin's humility, the *appearance* of virtue was desirable because it was advantageous, and any counter-productive inclination signalled the need for Mind-Cure. For some years after 1952, the Supreme Pontiff of New Thought was Norman Vincent Peale, heading the best-seller lists with enormous numbers of readers. *The Power of Positive Thinking* was orthodox New Thought, but the term was never used and no indication was given to late-comers into the fold that the same message had been gaining institutional status in the culture for more than half a century. In Peale's version, the individual's initiative took him or her to success by a simple route, a primitive religious version of Coué. If you want something to be accepted, to be true "to all intents and purposes," say that it is true, and pretend that it is, and insist that it is. Reverend Peale probably had no more conspicuously "successful" follower than Ronald Reagan.

The popularity of believing what you wish, or wishful thinking, is certainly not new or American, but it may have reached new degrees of influence in recent experience. Huber sees a "paradox" in "increased church membership . . . in the midst of a weakening religious influence over values . . . ."[10] Americans have become more and more adept at making religion mean whatever is most useful and convenient for it to mean, that's all. There is no paradox. They wanted it to be comforting, so they made it say what they find comforting. In the therapeutic culture described by Philip Rieff, the question would become, What other utilitarian value could religion have? Religion, claiming God as Love, easily permitted and encompassed racism.

Huber in fact formulates a fine explanation of New Thought behavior (unlabelled by the 1950s). He calls it "the law of affirmation," which considers Christianity ". . . a self-service supermarket where you could take what suits your fancy and leave the rest." It is of course a form of self-apotheosis, self-deification, and hence ". . . always tiptoeing along the borders of blasphemy . . ." as he amusingly puts it. "The distortion is the application of the pragmatic test to Christianity. The pragmatic test makes the absolute value of God something to be valued primarily for its consequences." Huber observes that people have always ". . . been trying to push God around and get him to do their will. For such a purpose, the law of affirmation is hard to beat."[11] That is undeniable.

This super-Arminianism is what Paul Zweig calls subversive individualism, restricted in earlier times to a tiny minority of extremists like the Gnostics, the Brethren of the Free Spirit, and certain religious and literary self-worshippers. Meister Eckhart exemplifies it in the thirteenth century: "I can do all things by my will."[12] Scarcely a twentieth-century American could be found to utter such a claim; and scarcely a culture could be found since the dawn of time that so lived by that religious assumption.

Self-improvement gradually became self-worship on a mass cultural basis. By the twentieth century, not only rare subversive characters like Rousseau appeared, but "ego-morphic" individualists by the million. "Mass individualism" sounds like an antithetical coupling, and in a sense it is; but it also became a reality in which Americans perceived no inherent contradiction. God needed everybody who had any interest in God, and He was diminished by every lack of interest. Religion in an age of skepticism continued to affirm the supreme value of the individual, and it imputed more importance than ever to the individual will, even as science challenged all traditional understandings of both "individual" and "will."

1. See Paul C. Vitz, *Psychology as Religion: The Cult of Self-Worship* (Grand Rapids: William B. Eerdmans Publishing Company, 1977), 73, 72.

2. Lynn, *The Dream of Success*, 47; cf. 42-43.

3. *Ibid.*, 47.

4. *Ibid.*, 139.

5. Daniel J. Kevles, *The Physicists* (New York: Vintage Books, 1979), 184.

6. Huber, 222, 224, 225.

7. *Ibid.*, 290.

8. *Ibid.*, 294.

9. *Ibid.*, 433.

10. *Ibid.*, 323, 332.

11. *Ibid.*, 335, 336, 333-334, 337.

12. See Zweig, *Heresy of Self-Love*, 34.

Thirty-Seven

Will-Power After Modernism

Only since the Great Depression, as social philosophy has been systematized and as the social sciences have matured, have the limitations and contradictions of individualistic materialism become evident. *Inter*dependence in material matters becomes increasingly undeniable and impossible to ignore. It has fallen to moral philosophy to remind us that *access* to security and comfort is not the same as happiness or fulfillment: but the voices of moral philosophy have often lacked clarity or conviction or both. Moral philosophy is historically individualistic -- concerned with individual salvation or fulfillment -- and idealistic. *Social* philosophy is concerned with interdependence and cooperation, but it is materialistic, focused on general access to happiness, not its attainment by the individual. Of the possible eclectic uses theoretically open to Americans, "liberals" would presumably choose to combine moral philosophy's idealism with social philosophy's awareness of interdependence and commitment to a cooperative commonwealth: something like the Social Gospel, seeking a Kingdom of God on earth. But the actual combination has more typically been an inversion, moral philosophy's individualism with social philosophy's materialism -- producing a national way of life emphasizing individual, material access to happiness. Our strongest traditions are, after all, individualistic; and our solutions to problems are habitually not just material but capitalist.

America's popular social commentators forged their own distinctive accommodations to the modern awareness of determinism and interdependence. In the 1950s, for example, none was more noticeable than Bishop Fulton Sheen, who had become a television celebrity as an oratorically accomplisheded monsignor. His central message was that the individual should surrender himself to God's will.[1]   At first glance, that seems unremarkable, orthodox and traditional. The individual should will God's will. But in fact this simple message accomplished an adaptation of individualism to the era of the Organization Man and mass society. It meant to be in tune with the music of change, to "go with the flow" or, as Speaker Sam Rayburn said in politics, "to get along, go along." In a word, it meant to conform to the authoritative interpretation of the way the world works, in this case that of the Roman Catholic Church; but it was always *voluntary* as well. Faith in free will remained majestically on course, as if none of the philosophical questions of the past century had arisen at all: with one exception. Communism, often redundantly characterized as both atheistic and godless in the same sentence, was the devil's own work: collectivist as opposed to the divinely ordained individualism of the West, and an unprecedented menace to civilization. The individual must *choose* the Word of God, and *will* it to prevail in the world. Action remained voluntary, individualistic, but its proper direction was in harmony with a world-wide crusade of righteous individualists against collectivist tyranny. Mass movements of individualists, chosen by themselves, differed implicitly from mass movements of "brainwashed" individuals, to recall a confused and controversial word of the 'fifties.

Bishop Sheen's message was similar to that of Reverend Billy Graham, perhaps the most successful deliverer of television sermons. Graham also warned incessantly against the minions of the devil, and he too exhorted the individual to make the right individual choice and commitment. The flavor of traditional Christianity survived in the goal of "neighborly" association, kindness and so forth, but the basis of action remained individualistic. Planning was somehow immoral, although a few people always wondered, like Senator Jacob Javits of New York, why it was good for American Telephone and Telegraph to use long-term, centralized planning, but not good for the United States. What commonly passed for reasoning seemed to be that Communists believed in public planning, and they are perverse or wrong-headed about everything, so public planning is clearly not for us. American planning, understandably enough, tended to be concerned with how American individualism could be safeguarded and perpetuated. In

1962, Columbia University Press published a study edited by Eli Ginzberg, *The Optimistic Tradition and American Youth,* summarizing a major project of the university. This statement introduced its Foreword:

> The Conservation of Human Resources Project was established by General Dwight D. Eisenhower at Columbia University in 1950 to undertake basic research in human resources. It has been supported by grants from corporations, foundations, and the federal government. The vice-president of the University exercises administrative supervision over the project.

The term "human resources" inevitably brings to mind Adam Smith's worries about how human work would be reduced to a commodity, and Karl Marx's claim that industrialization "dehumanized" the workers. Now the term has long been standard for designating "personnel," who were "processed" by the military, not having been persons or even people since some time before World War Two. "Modernist" attitudes toward human beings had crept into the thinking of individualists through the marriage of Herbert Hoover's "rugged individualism" to Frederick Winslow Taylor's mania for efficiency in the 1920s; and mid-century individualists worried about a diminution of "drive," of ambition and initiative among the young. The "optimistic tradition" was the cultural habit of "getting ahead," and Professor Ginzberg's project addressed "The Individual" in summary.

The idea of perfectibility assumes that everyone wants to improve himself. In earlier generations, millions of people struggled against formidable obstacles to

> . . . tame the rugged environment and push . . . the economy . . . . They were willing to put forth this great effort because they saw that their own salvation, or at least their opportunity for vast improvement, was intimately linked to this undertaking. American history, therefore, supports the belief that men are not only willing but eager to improve themselves.[2]

However, some Americans

> . . . like people in every society, *because of limited intellectual endowment were simply not able to take more than limited advantage of the opportunities available to them.* While they were able to improve themselves somewhat . . . . *limitations arising at birth* have limited the accomplishments of a significant segment of the total population . . . .

In short, some people are congenitally stupid or unable to see their own interests. Those with dark skin tended to fall into such categories.

Others are handicapped by the environment of early life: the unavoidable mid-century acknowledgement that not all determination is exercise of will. The

> . . . early years of life may bring so many emotional scars that a large number of young people . . . *will never be able to take advantage of the opportunities open to them* . . . . It is necessary to recognize that *because of their emotional instability many young people will be unable to take anything like full advantage of their environmental opportunities.* Nor is there any reason to expect that if society substantially increased these opportunities the outcome would be much different. Unfortunately *a person's defects themselves usually make it impossible for him to avail himself of opportunities,* whether limited or expanded.

> While intellectual shortcomings and emotional instability represent the major qualifications of the doctrine that each individual wants to improve himself, there is a third limitation. *Lack of motivation, an outgrowth frequently of intellectual limitation or emotional instability, may sometimes be independent of them and requires recognition as an additional factor.*

> The belief [in . . .] a universal desire for self-improvement [seems open to question]. But whatever the truth may be for generations past, it cannot be seriously questioned that a sizable proportion of today's young people are not

motivated -- for whatever complex reasons -- to do their
best.   Lacking such motivation, they cannot take
advantage of the opportunities our society has to offer
them.   And *if the available opportunities were increased,*
there is no reason to believe they would respond very
differently.

In brief, the assumption that every individual will try to
do his best does not always hold true. *There are, and there*
probably always will be, a large number of young people
who, lacking the necessary intellectual capacity, emotional
stability, or strong motivation, will be unable to take full
advantage of the opportunities open to them.   It follows
from this that a marked expansion of those opportunities
would not seriously alter the outcome.[3]

Something along the lines of "benign neglect" seemed in order for
such an identifiably deficient population.

Ginzberg, a professor of economics, had a large staff with
impressive credentials, and the Foreword of the study makes clear the
massive support from Columbia, and from corporations, foundations,
and the federal government. The conclusions so emphatically stated
and repeated suggest that nobody involved thought to ask what the
word "opportunities" means, or how it might be related to
"possibilities," for example. Evidently, nobody thought to ask what
"take advantage of" means, or how it might be related to certain kinds
of options.   The study suggests how strong the assumptions of
individualism were in the second half of the twentieth century. Those
assumptions were obviously sacred, in the literal sense: not open to
question.   Individuals of normal intellectual capacity, emotional
stability, and motivation could do what they *willed* to do. The
Arminian tradition of will-power and self-determination remained
powerful, to say the least.   It has the limitless appeal of self-
congratulation.

These social scientists noted that, while the

belief is widely held that what happens to an individual
depends *entirely* on him . . . . it simply is not true that the

> serious failure of so many deprived children is due to
> their own personal shortcomings and deficiencies . . . . .
> An indiscriminate doctrine of personal responsibility can
> be very discouraging. It can weaken still further what
> little motivation deprived youngsters may have acquired
> to better themselves, by creating not only frustration but a
> deep sense of guilt.

If an "indiscriminate doctrine of personal responsibility" could not reasonably be applied to deprived children, then what doctrine of responsibility could be applied? "Society wisely places the primary responsibility on *parents* for the care and nurturing of their offspring . . . ."[4] "Society" placed an indiscriminate doctrine of personal responsibility "on parents" initially, and then this responsibility was gradually shared between parents and children, before being shifted to the children. *That* was settled. If social scientists could make such individualistic assumptions, what could be expected in the society at large? The assumption of "individual responsibility" is not racist, but it sometimes has much the same effects as if it were.

The Columbia people apparently thought that the "optimistic tradition" was the mind-set that "you can't keep a good man down." Interestingly, when William James used the term "optimistic" in his description of the "tender-minded" person resistant to the implications of science (more than fifty years before the Columbia report) he explained that it meant optimistic about the Romantic idea of imposing individual will on the world! Ginzberg and his staff may have thought they were lamenting the passage of America's optimistic tradition; but what they actually did was illustrate its persistence and strength, long after scholars and intellectuals had supposedly been disabused of such Romantic notions.

Will is a constant, vital factor in American suppositions and dispositions, but expressions and applications of it vary with the sense of power to affect life. The cross-currents of the 1960s illustrate a sense of powerlessness over individual fate, shared by a great many people; and they illustrate how desperate the need for effective will is felt to be when will-power is threatened. Middle Americans have never stopped wanting economic security, material self-reliance, or to be let alone by bureaucracies and organizations they do not perceive as furthering their individual aims. Jefferson's ideas are very much alive, and continue to show the validity of Tocqueville's apprehensions about withdrawal into private concerns. Herbert Gans talks about "organizational avoidance" as a noticeable characteristic of recent decades. Donald B. Meyer noted in the 1970s what he called the "implacable rise of individualism," meaning egoism; and, like Gans, he points to the diminished importance of organized religion in more people's lives.[5]

It seems likely that many people were changing "religions" in the sociological sense, looking for usable messages or instruction or guidance. Individualism of various kinds flourished, including no end of "Dr. Feelgood" and "Reverend Feelgood" prescriptions, restating the most popular tenets and attitudes of New Thought, Mind-Cure, and other variants of will-power doctrine. Behaviorism declined, even as Skinner in his eighties continued to insist that "there is nothing inside the behaving organism but the organism itself. It is the whole organism that behaves."[6] Cognitive psychology gained adherents, drawing on computer analogies and treating the "mind" as software, or programs run on the brain. Yet the conviction of self-determination remained, as Peter Clecak summarized in his discussion of the "custom-designed, well-crafted self."[7] Such a notion was probably more fun to talk about in Scarsdale than it was in East St. Louis.

1. See Lawrence Chenoweth, *The American Dream of Success* (North Scituate, Mass.: Duxbury Press, 1974), 125.

2. Eli Ginzberg, *The Optimistic Tradition and American Youth* (New York: Columbia University Press, 1962), 128.

3. *Ibid.*, 129-130, emphasis added.

4. *Ibid.*, 131, emphasis added.

5. Donald B. Meyer, *The Positive Thinkers* (Middletown, Ct.: Wesleyan University Press, 1988). Cf. Herbert J. Gans, *Middle American Individualism* (Glencoe, Ill.: The Free Press, 1988).

6. B. F. Skinner, *The New York Times*, Sept. 13, 1987, E 6.

7. Clecak, *America's Quest for the Ideal Self*, e.g.

Thirty-Eight

Individualist Ethical Theory

Michel Foucault attempts to identify a change around the end of the seventeenth century, in how people could think about similarity and difference, order and discontinuity. This change made possible relativistic thinking,[1] and it was also a sort of culminating shift in the awareness of large numbers of people, from viewing themselves as members to proclaiming themselves separate and unique. In America, David Potter looked at Jacob Burkhardt's nineteenth-century description of such a shift, taking shape from the Renaissance, and decided that ". . . it is questionable whether modern psychology would accept the view that the nature of the psyche in Western man experienced a basic transformation between the fourteenth and the sixteenth centuries."[2] Of course there was no such "basic transformation." What occurred was the emergence of a system of institutions, attitudes, and philosophical persuasions conducive to our remarkable historical form of "awareness": or arrogance, one might say, in the literal sense of arrogating importance to oneself. Individualism developed from Promethean, heroic, or eccentric claims of uniqueness to widespread and even universal claims.

Subversive individualists attacked authority with the weapon of intuition, and they brought about both individualistic and universal claims that came together in mass individualism. Intuitionism, Richard Price's new term in the late eighteenth century, flourished. Shortly intuition could be seen as not only respectable but even necessary to all claims of knowledge except in mathematics and symbolic logic.[3] It was not necessary to know how it works. Gerald Dworkin suggests an analogy even in mathematics, when Frege wrote to Bertrand Russell that "arithmetic totters." Dworkin says, "But we no more need foundations in order to count correctly than we need them in order to act correctly."[4] We know intuitively when we are on the right track.

Not that intuition is the same in all endeavors. Bernard Williams, for example, notes that people who have used intuition in ethics ". . . all supposed that the way in which we grasped . . . ethical truths was significantly like the way in which we grasp mathematical and other necessary truths." This idea of intuition has been thoroughly discredited and the ruins of it are hardly worth explaining.

> Above all, the appeal to intuition as a faculty explained nothing. It seemed to say that these truths were known, but there was no way in which they were known . . . . So intuition in ethics, as a faculty, is no more. But *intuitions* -- the beliefs which, when there was supposed to be a faculty, were supposedly given by it -- are very much part of the subject.[5]

The moral sense has been abandoned, but the beliefs about good and bad conduct which used to be credited to it remain alive and well in discussion about ethics: and they are still intuitive, having nothing else to be, or choice in the matter.

Intuition led to universal claims because the moral faculty or moral sense had to be regarded as a part of basic human equipment; and so, before evolution was established, moral intuitions were virtually "self-evident." Intuition permitted individualistic claims as evolution was demonstrated, because the later nineteenth century world gradually closed out closure. Truth about human behavior was scientific, but the scientific truth was that the meanings of behavior are situationally determined. All categories of value judgments, normative and prescriptive pronouncements, and beliefs not susceptible of empirical or mathematical demonstration are conditioned by time and culture. Soon individual capacities and sensibilities acquired unprecedented authority *as a widespread phenomenon.* An age of individualism dawned, as opposed to earlier ages in which some individualists lived.

When the moral sense as a universal faculty was successfully challenged, everything previously inferred from it was inevitably called into question. If there was no general intuition, no Intuitive Reason or Moral Faculty, then little basis remained for ethical judgments except, in our culture, the pervasive utilitarian spirit. That spirit was, however, sharply divided into egoistic and universalistic ideologies; and in America, all circumstances conduced towards the prevalence of the former, the individualistic, competitive ethos. Science offered little help to those who sought it, like John Dewey. He wrote that, from the "evolutionary standpoint . . . there is no separate body of moral rules; no separate system of motive powers; no separate subject-matter of moral knowledge, and hence no such thing as an isolated ethical science."[6]

Utilitarianism began as an anti-individualist doctrine, with its assumption that happiness is measurable or somehow at least homogenized. From a characteristic American point of view, this "measured" happiness left out some important, time-honored elements: the sense of meaning and satisfaction that attends effort, the peace of well-spent leisure, the pleasurable sense of achievement, the sense of security, or of excitement and adventure, the feeling of freedom, or of insouciance, or of responsibility assumed and well met, among others. In ethical theory there are three basic criteria by which actions are judged: consequences, intentions, and motives. As A. J. Ayer emphasized, it is not self-contradictory to say that it is sometimes wrong to perform the action which would actually or probably cause the greatest happiness, or the greatest balance of pleasure over pain, or of satisfied over unsatisfied desire. And since it is not self-contradictory to say that some pleasant things are not good, or that some bad things are desired, it cannot be the case that the sentence "X is good" is equivalent to "X is pleasant" or to "X is desired."[7] Santayana commented most eloquently on one important reality: "The necessity of rejecting and destroying some things that are beautiful is the deepest curse of existence." If all choices were between good and bad, children could make them. The toughest ones are between wonderful and wonderful, choices of the greater good: and that is the kind posed by the *desiderata* of equity on the one hand, and self-esteem through the assertion of individual responsibility on the other.

Sidgwick argued that egoism and utilitarian morality are incompatible, but G. E. Moore countered that it is quite possible to be both an egoist and a utilitarian. One could claim that adding to his own pleasure added to the general happiness, or he could be an altruist as a means of making himself happier. Westermarck concluded that John Stuart Mill's argument "would lead to egoistic hedonism, not to utilitarianism or universalistic hedonism."[8] Then Sidgwick rested the utilitarian rule of seeking the general happiness on a fundamental moral intuition, returning to the ideas of Hutcheson and Price; but America was unconvinced. In a sense, utilitarianism always led back to Hobbes and Spinoza, and the equation of "right reason" with the most efficient calculation of advantage. As Lester G. Crocker puts it,

> . . . if virtue is defined in terms of happiness, and if it is assumed that there is no natural impulse or reason to prefer the interest of others to our own, the amoralist must perforce triumph, unless it can be shown that there is an indissoluble, invariable identity between the two terms, virtue and happiness. This became the central problem of ethics for nineteenth-century thinkers, one with which they were faced as a result of their analysis of human nature and their reduction of moral experience to reactions of pleasure and pain.[9]

The pursuit of happiness as goodness proved to be destructive of itself when the attempt was made to cast it in systematic form. Why? Because it never really escaped egoism, and never succeeded in making egoism into a social code either. Egoism cannot be a *system* of ethics. It is capable of systematic formulation, but it is not an ethical theory: rather, it dismisses all ethical theory as irrelevant.[10] When all intuitions were created equal, and utility constituted the sole or unquestionably dominant criterion of value, ethics became unprecedentedly vulnerable to egoistic eclipse. Utilitarianism meant in America mainly what it had always meant in France (where its universalistic version was generally viewed as English nonsense): "good" meant "good for me." It might mean more than that, to be sure, but it had to mean that.

David Riesman succinctly summarized the prevalent American view: "I am insisting that no ideology, however noble, can justify the sacrifice of an individual to the needs of the group."[11] A practical philosophical problem for pragmatic ethical naturalists like John Dewey was that groups are also composed of individuals. The practical problem faced by African-Americans was that they *were* a group in an ethical context that only dealt with individuals.

Many devotees of citizenship, Christianity, civic virtue and the common weal tried to show that individuals should not always act on self-interest. Significantly, almost nobody in America proposed that the choice belonged to anyone but the individual. Above all, individualistic America stood united against the State. J. M. T. E. McTaggart is funny as well as incisive on that subject: "Compared with worship of the State, zoolatry is rational and dignified. A bull or a crocodile may not have great intrinsic value, but it has some, for it is a conscious being. The State has none. It would be as reasonable to worship a sewage pipe, which also possesses considerable value as a means."[12]

Ethics rested upon obligation; obligation was decided intuitively; and intuition served individual interest, expressed through will. If survival of ideas, like organisms, depended upon adaptation, then the odds still favored moral autonomy in the age of science. The rise of relativism, first cultural and then situational, posed no threat to ethical individualism, or to racism.

1. See Anthony Pagden, *The Fall of Natural Man* (Cambridge: Cambridge University Press, 1982), 2.

2. Potter in Fehrenbacher, ed., 327.

3. See A. C. Ewing, *The Definition of Good* (New York: The Macmillan Company, 1947), e.g.

4. Gerald Dworkin in Daniel Callahan and H. Tristram Engelhart, eds., *The Roots of Ethics: Science, Religion, and Values* (New York: The Plenum Press, 1981), 28.

5. Bernard Williams, *Ethics and the Limits of Philosophy* (Cambridge, Mass.: Harvard University Press, 1985), 84.

6. Dewey, in Miller, ed., 238.

7. A. J. Ayer, *Language, Truth and Logic* (1936) (New York: Dover Publications, 1946), 28.

8. *Ibid.*, 31.

9. Lester G. Crocker, *An Age of Crisis: Man and World in Eighteenth-Century French Thought* (Baltimore: The Johns Hopkins University Press, 1959), 34.

10. *Ibid.*, 35.

11. Riesman, *Individualism Reconsidered*, 27.

12. J. M. T. E. MacTaggart, *Philosophical Studies* (Freeport, N. Y.: Books for Libraries Press, 1934), 109.

Thirty-Nine

Individualism and Justice

From the eighteenth century, moral theory has slowly moved toward a universe without purpose, a non-teleological universe. With the conspicuous exceptions of Utilitarianism and some tenacious forms of natural law philosophy, normative and prescriptive judgments in the age of individualism have been chiefly based upon appeals to will rather than claims of knowledge. If moral choices are not dictated by God's Will or its secular equivalent, Natural Law, they can only be made by human will. Nothing was more central to the rise of individualism than the need to posit autonomous individual will in order to have a universe in which moral meaning is possible.

In America the principal moral theory meeting that need was clearly religious: the Arminian departure from Puritanism. Its secular parallel was moral sense philosophy, leavened with the fundamental utilitarian perspective which we associate with Franklin. Moral theory anchored in autonomous individual will, the ethical individualism of the free moral agent, served the culture almost without challenge until the wave of naturalism and deterministic social science that surged through Western thought after the era of Marx and Darwin. Since the latter part of the nineteenth century moral theory has been hard pressed to adapt further, not only to a universe without purpose but to a universe in which individual will and choice may be severely limited or even largely illusory. Behaviorism and Freudian psychology, for example, cast profound doubts upon the idea of autonomy, and therefore upon voluntaristic moral theory. Like Sartre, we have been forced to ponder "the implications for action of a meaningless universe," and one in which the very possibility of moral meaning is open to question.

John Rawls, the author of *A Theory of Justice* (1971), came to the center of such discussion because he proposes a moral social philosophy and also salvages as voluntaristic a moral theory as is tenable in light of twentieth century understandings. That is to say, his position is as individualistic as it can be, although that is very much less individualistic than earlier prevailing assumptions. Rawls says that individuals are "self-originating sources of valid [moral] claims."[1] But "self" after Freud and Skinner is not what it used to be, and the claims it can make are proportionately diminished. Rawls's moral agent is, as Michael Sandel says in a brilliant analysis, "epistemologically impoverished" and "conceptually ill-equipped to engage in the sort of self-reflection capable of going beyond an attention to its preferences and desires . . ."[2] The individual Rawls sees is "free to plan his life as he pleases," but certain to choose in accord with interests not chosen but determined; or else to act from ignorance, which amounts to much the same thing. An individual choosing from fantasy crashes head on into his situational limits, and Rawls recognizes those limits as described by Skinner.

By now almost nobody disputes the assumption that "the self is realized in the activities of many selves."[3] What Dewey had to argue vehemently for, Rawls can and must take for granted. "Only in the social union is the individual complete."[4] In that social union, capacities and inclinations are determined, but specific uses of capacities, or actions based on inclinations, are volitional. The self is originally naked, so to speak, not a *tabula rasa*, but an arbitrarily occurring set of potentialities, dispositions, and propensities. The self does not possess itself in the sense of C. B. MacPherson, but it acquires and possesses traits. Although this sounds something like existentialism, self-chosen interests and commitments do not *constitute* the self; the self just includes them at any given time. Through the exercise of will and the acquisition of self-knowledge the self emerges and changes through time, defining, refining and altering its ends and its perceptions and conceptions of appropriate ends. If the given organism, the raw self, is to become much of a person, it has to be dynamic. What is given is only the opportunity to acquire traits, not any proprietary right to them. *Nobody deserves anything, because nobody can determine what attributes he can choose.* There is no choice of choices one confronts. Nor does the original, prior-to-ends self choose its inclinations to choose as it does.

Rawls departs from the tradition of Hobbes and Mill and all the others who have sought a "science of man" to answer the question "What are we?" as a basis for ethics. It's not what we are but what we *have* that serves as a foundation for justice as fairness; and individualism is the expression of the primal self in its choices of what to have, given its possibilities. Rawls posits a sort of sentiment of benevolence for the twentieth century, a desire for "fairness that includes me" that is quite common if not quite universal.[5] He wants to avoid egoism along with all other theories of motivation, and he attempts to accomplish that by adopting utilitarianism as well as benevolence. Yet there is no escaping the assumption of self-interest as the general principle of motivation. "[T]he principle for an individual is to advance as far as possible his own welfare, his own system of desires."[6]

Social awareness saves this position from egoism: "To be sure, there is one formal principle that seems to provide a general answer . . . the principle to adopt that plan which maximizes the expected net balance of satisfaction."[7] Observe that I am altruistic for self-interested reasons: I find it satisfying. But, as Jefferson said, that means I am a benevolent sort of being, to find altruism satisfying. Why do I find it satisfying? The circle closes: Because it serves my interest. Or, perhaps, because I am what I am, and it is "in the nature of my being," deontological. Rawls, in the tradition of Kant, adopts the latter explanation. Utilitarianism serves him no better than it has anyone else attempting to oppose it to egoism. When his deontological argument seems to accept utilitarianism, it really adopts consequentialism on an individual basis, or socialized egoism. Good is once again good for me as I see it. But since I am a social product, I am obliged to see that I do not deserve anything that everyone else does not also deserve, and any extraordinary benefits accrue to my situation, not to me as a self.[8]

Rewards come to positions, not to abilities or "merits." A bungling fool or a genius gets the rewards set for the office he or she occupies. Circumstance plays for Rawls the role of Divine Favor in predestination: it cannot be earned, but its presence or absence ensures "success" or "failure." Justice is therefore distributive: benefits should be distributed equitably, without regard for individualistic claims of privilege (Cf. "private law") or deserving. Individuals inevitably advance such claims, and they "should" pursue their interests, consistent with their nature; but their individualism does not dictate the material arrangements of society. Such is the peculiar setting of individualism in Rawls's thought. He provides a launching platform for an indirect assault on racism through its effects in the social phenomenon of discrimination.

The deontological position, from Kant, is that freedom is given in our nature, and rights are therefore given in the nature of things. Ordinarily, this persuasion denies consequentialism in ethics, whether egoistically or universally utilitarian. To make any sense at all, rights have to be absolute in the sense of being unqualified, rather than inferred from conditions as in utilitarianism.   This has been the prevalent view of rights in America, as evidenced by our veneration of natural rights in our political history.

> [R]ights, as we Americans understand them . . . are not given to us by the state. We have them, as we have life, independent of any gift from the state. We consent to be governed on the understanding that we have entrusted no power to the state to abridge those rights. We owe nothing to the state for those rights because we did not get them from the state.[9]

And yet, an alleged

> . . . right to autonomy can be had only if the interest of the right-holder justifies holding members of the society at large to be duty-bound to provide him with the social environment necessary to give him a chance to have an autonomous life . . . .[10] [The] . . . human rights associated with . . . liberalism . . . . imply a correlative duty on the part of all individuals, and particularly the state, not to interfere with individual behavior. Thus, the power of the state is limited by the rights of its citizens.

In the seventeenth century sense, in fact, a right was a moral claim which the law could enforce on behalf of an individual or a group.[11] Such claims had appeared in some Greek city-states, and then in Rome; and some modern thinkers, from MacPherson to Maritain, contend that all ideas of human rights must be founded in natural rights doctrine.[12]

But Jeremy Bentham scorned what he called the "nonsense" of natural rights; Hume as well as Burke opposed such claims as inflammatory, raising false expectations; and John Stuart Mill simply did not use the idea at all. More recently, Alasdair MacIntyre says that belief in natural rights is "one with belief in witches and unicorns."[13] Rawls depends upon a particular individual *right to exercise the natural capacity to choose purposes*. This "choice" theory of rights preserves moral agency by vesting the right in the subject rather than in what the subject claims by way of entitlement or benefit, or in the nature of the claim itself. Rawls presents a universalistic individualism, in which each necessarily and legitimately pursues his own interest, but extraordinary benefits revert to the society because the individual can be what he is only in the social context.

This protective disposition toward individuals appeared early in the century in the liberalism of L. T. Hobhouse, arguing for a right *to* property as well as traditional rights *of* property. Hobhouse thought that "a certain minimum claim on the public resources" ought to be recognized for each individual in society, much as Franklin D. Roosevelt argued (with help from Adolph Berle and Gardiner Means) in 1932 that the right to life includes the right to make a living. Both Steven Lukes and Michael Walzer argue that meaningful equality is equality of entitlement to respect. Does respect for persons imply equal opportunity, regardless of rights theory? Steven Lukes says yes, inescapably, in the sense of providing what is needed for fulfillment.[14] Lukes incisively notes that Rawls has constructed individuals with "a certain fixed range of modern liberal beliefs and wants built into them."[15] These are mainly and disturbingly materialistic: there just isn't much *to* Rawls's individual, except what is "given" in human nature, traits acquired in social experience, and the *de ontos* right to make self-interested choices. That is, it is hard to see just what this individual's fulfillment might consist in, other than security and comfort. As Lukes puts it, "the interests which the political individualist sees the government as representing, protecting and promoting are, from Locke to Hayek, characteristically individual economic interests."[16] Respect for individuals is ironically impersonal. The same may be said of the individual considered in relation to Rawls's distributive justice: he or she is not a rounded-out person.

Rawls illustrates what Robert N. Bellah and his colleagues described in the mid-1980s as occurring in our culture of individualism. We experience "a moral vacuum" in which

> . . . it has been tempting to translate group claims and interests into the language of individual rights, a language that makes sense in terms of our dominant individualistic ideology. But if large numbers of individuals and groups or categories of individuals begin to insist, as they have . . . that they are owed or are entitled to certain benefits, assistance, or preference as a matter of right, such claims are not readily treated as matters of justice. They begin to be treated instead as simply competing wants.[17]

The language of individual deserving and entitlement remains solidly entrenched in religious as well as secular institutions, as is often noted regarding the complementarity of Protestantism and capitalism. Catholic positions are equally illustrative. For example, Pope Leo XIII wrote in 1891, in *De Rerum Novarum*, "of new things," that every individual

> makes his own that portion of nature's field . . . on which he leaves . . . the impress of his individuality; and it cannot but be just that he should possess that portion . . . and have a right to hold it . . . . Hence it is clear that the main tenet of Socialism, community of goods, must be utterly rejected, since it . . . is directly contrary to the natural rights of mankind.

So John Locke spoke for the Church until 1931, when Pius XI made the position even stronger in *Quadregesimo Anno*, the fortieth year after Leo: "Society . . . as socialism conceives it, is impossible and unthinkable without the use of obviously excessive compulsion."[18]

Not only is individual deserving generally regarded as self-evident, distributive justice is perceived as denying natural rights to both personal property and civil liberty. In fact, secular justifications for extraordinary material benefits depend much less upon rights to property than on arguments basing individual freedom on private ownership, freedom being the incontestable right, in some sense, to virtually everyone.

There are two kinds or levels of individual fulfillment or success in America, and while material equity of the sort Rawls addresses is a necessary condition, "true success" or meaning in life requires something more, which Rawls not only does not address, but which the individual he portrays may be incapable of grasping. Rights theory protects and assaults the dignity of the individual at the same time, alternately envisioning person and object, depending upon whether the point of view is individual or social, resting on agency or entitlement. Rights theory, presented in the deontological tradition from Kant to Rawls, conflicts with the social justice Rawls seeks to establish.[19] A secular Arminianism set out the premises that the individual has a right to fulfillment, and the power of will to attain it; but it developed in a period of unprecedented material change, and inevitably acquired a materialistic emphasis.

Economic Man still casts a long shadow. The very subject of deserving raises assumptions about property at once. When Rawls rejects the traditional idea that virtue deserves reward, that one can merit advantage, what does he mean? We need to distinguish between material and non-material rewards -- fortune and due recognition, for example. They need not go together. If a Chinese head of surgery receives no more pay than a new janitor in the hospital, that doesn't mean that the surgeon has no greater rewards. "Gifted" and accomplished people can surely hold reasonable expectations of appreciation of their contributions to the general welfare. Pride and satisfaction are the just rewards of the individual who does something especially valuable, even though he can't take credit for having the ability to do it, or claim that he deserves tens of millions of dollars, like many American entertainers and financial manipulators.

In a sense current moral theory returns to pre-Romantic realism. Before the Romantic era, for example, there was no deserving in French folk tales -- just random disaster and good fortune.[20] Both were caused, of course, in an orderly and purposeful universe. A deontological view like Rawls's could appear only in a non-teleological age, open to choice and not determined, with the individual as radical subject, choosing the good for himself.[21] But America did take shape in the non-teleological Romantic era, and Americans generally have taken for granted the validity of "deserving." God and the government were simply supposed to be "impartial." Justice was an inherent feature of the universe, as Jesus taught, and people usually got their just deserts, as in the Hollywood ending. Not only were the rich and the poor equally free to sleep under bridges, but there was nothing about that situation that required question or challenge.

A deontological ethic asserts both epistemological and moral priority of the individual: individual interests before common, social interests. Its distinguishing individualistic feature is that the self has the ability to choose its own ends. But just because ends are chosen does not mean that they are chosen from the range of all conceivable alternatives. Not everyone is eligible for everything that can be imagined: only for what comes to his attention and falls within the scope of his capacities. One doesn't face a choice of either discovering ends or choosing them, or constructing or inventing them. Rather one discovers what evidently can be chosen, decides on that basis what to choose, and chooses. To follow inclinations is to choose, rejecting the putative choice of not following them. And when it is objected that this is pretty weak "choice" on which to claim moral agency and individual dignity, the haunting question of Peggy Lee may come to mind: "Is that all there is?"

In Rawls's version of no-desert justice and individualism, there are still legitimate expectations of fair shares which accommodate individuals' material needs and wants. Michael Walzer's version attempts to reach the same ends on the basis of membership rights in a political community, and material shares also dominate his reflections, which are less thought-provoking than Rawls's. The "fair shares" doctrine is conducive to individualism in the sense of nobody having to consider others, a rather unattractive sort of inference from self-interest and freedom to make choices. The "complex equality" Walzer seeks to establish entails freedom from domination on the basis of any "social good," on reasoning of the kind that makes Bellah apprehensive regarding rights claims leading simply to power struggles over wants. For Walzer, individuals come together in society because they have to. "But they can live together in many different ways."[22] The deeper questions of what a self is, and what if any kind of individualism remains morally viable and logically tenable in a world understood as Rawls understands it to be, remain unanswered. So, of course, does the question of how racism might be expected to fade from a popular culture in which individualism dictates what ways of living together are morally viable. Racism says that what can be chosen is limited by inherent traits, and the consequences of such traits. Individualism recognizes choices within such limits.

1. John Rawls, "Kantian Constructivism in Moral Theory," *Journal of Philosophy*, 77, 1980, 543.

2. Michael Sandel, *Liberalism and the Limits of Justice* (Cambridge: Cambridge University Press, 1982), 153.

3. Rawls, *A Theory of Justice* (Cambridge, Mass.: Belknap Press, 1971), 565.

4. *Ibid.*, 525n.

5. Cf. Sandel, 160, 172.

6. Rawls, *Theory*, 23.

7. *Ibid.*, 416.

8. Cf. Robert Heilbroner's explanation of *The Making of Economic Society*.

9. Goldwin, "Rights Versus Duties: No Contest," in Arthur L. Caplan and Daniel Callahan, eds., *Ethics in Hard Times* (New York: The Plenum Press, 1981), 140.

10. Joseph Raz, *The Morality of Freedom* (New York: Oxford University Press, 1986), 247.

11. Andrew Levine, "Human Rights and Freedom," in Alan S. Rosenbaum, ed., *The Philosophy of Human Rights* (Westport, Ct.: Greenwood Press, 1980), 137.

12. See Maurice Cranston, "Are There Any Human Rights?", *Daedalus*, 112, 4, Fall 1983, 3, 16.

13. Alasdair Macintyre, *After Virtue* (South Bend: University of Notre Dame Press, 1981), 67.

14. Steven Lukes, *Individualism* (Oxford: Basil Blackwell, 1973), 134-135.

15. *Ibid.*, 139, n.3.

16. *Ibid.*, 141.

17. Robert N. Bellah *et al.*, *Habits of the Heart: Individualism and Commitment in American Life* (Berkeley: University of California Press, 1985), 207.

18. See Richard Schlatter, 278-279.

19. See R. S. Downie in Rosenbaum, ed., "Social Equality," 135.

20. See Robert Darnton, *The Great Cat Massacre and Other Episodes in French Cultural History* (New York: Vintage Books, 1985), 53-54.

21. See Sandel, 175.

22. Michael Walzer, *Spheres of Justice: A Defense of Pluralism and Equality* (New York: Basic Books, 1983), xiv; 65.

Forty

Individualist Ethics: A Further Note

Robert Nozick, Rawls's conservative counterpart, takes a position more recognizable as individualist, most notably developed in *Anarchy, State, and Utopia* (1974). Nozick accepts the absence of deserving by individuals, but with a radical difference from Rawls. He holds individual rights to be unquestionably prior to society's, with the state obligated to observe and protect those rights against any collective aims such as social justice. Nozick argues that, although I have no exclusive right-by-deserving to the apparent fruits of my talents and efforts, that does not mean that society at large *does* have a proprietary claim on them. I have the abilities naturally, as by God's will, and I have the benefits they produce. They are part of me, aspects of myself, inviolable, and their rewards come naturally to me. In justice, society is obliged to recognize my entitlement. There is no valid competing claim. I don't deserve to be so fortunate, but that doesn't mean everyone else is entitled to share my good fortune.

Both Rawls and Nozick follow Kant's dictum that each individual must be treated as an end, never a means, and they are anti-Utilitarian on "individualistic" grounds. Rawls protects the individual's inviolability *as a self*, but views the traits acquired by that self as appropriately shared or used as means to the common good. According to Nozick, as Sandel says, "for the community as a whole to deserve the natural assets in its province and the benefits that flow from them, it is necessary to assume that society has some *pre-instititional* status that individuals lack, for only in this way could the community be said to possess its assets in the strong, constitutive sense of possession necessary to a desert base."[1] Rawls's position is that society needs only a *pre-individual* status to make such a claim, and it always has that status. The individual appears at a particular time, exercising the self's choices of ends presented to him or her by society in a particular situation. He or she has a right to choices and their pursuit, and society has a right to absorb the consequences while treating the individual with due respect and fairness.

Voluntarism is now much contracted, in light of social science, but the more precious perhaps for being less than hoped for, or "all there is." Nobody is deserving, any more than anyone was deserving under God's mysterious will in the days of Michael Wigglesworth. All individual traits are determined and arbitrary, whether genetic or cultural in seeming origin. There is no justice in nature, just facts, and that extends to society as well. Justice is up to us, Rawls maintains, and we have barely enough choice to seek it, to do right. The difference principle, under which all individual traits are common possessions -- resources or liabilities -- provides the key to rightness and justice for Rawls. Like Edwards, Rawls attempts to reconcile individual will with determinism. Nozick, like Chauncy, claims more for the will, that it can be self-determining and free in a richer sense.

Nozick retains some Romanticism, the imposition of will upon the world, as opposed to Rawls's base in Skinner's behaviorism. Rawls, like Edwards or Royce meeting earlier challenges from Locke and Spencer, tries to save whatever can be saved, while accepting the new as valid. Nozick flatly insists on rightful claims from natural rights. One arrives intuitively at rights to participate in society and assume obligation as the basis of individual dignity; the other intuits rights to assert priority of individual claims over society's. Rawls associates himself with equal opportunity as justice, Nozick with equality of opportunity.

Rawls uses Skinner's psychology as Edwards used predestination. Nozick represents the more optimistic line of thought regarding how distinctive the self can be, how individualistic in the sense of autonomy. He thinks that Rawls virtually erases the self; and in fact, Nozick has the same objection to determinism that Chauncy had: it does not permit enough dignity, or attach sufficient importance to the reality of our differences, even conceding that they are random.

(Ronald Dworkin, notably in *Taking Rights Seriously,* 1977, seeks to combine Nozick's rigid natural rights with a compelling demand for social justice more like Rawls's.) Rawls's individualist is morally obligated to "do his fair share" and support others' getting their *fair shares.* Nozick's is obligated to recognize others' *right to their random lot,* and to support that right against interference, a basic libertarian position. Nozick's version of justice is far more congenial to both American traditions and popular American views -- and also more conducive to perpetuating the effects of racism.

1. Sandel, 101.

Forty-One

Moral Subjectivism

Cultural relativism is indisputable. Every culture has its own norms and expectations, although, as Clyde Kluckhohn observed, a common "moral value" runs through them all: conformity to whatever *their* norms and expectations are. Anthropologists no longer claim that all patterns of life are equally valid; rather, "recent developments in the behavioral sciences have tended to narrow the areas of indeterminacy while still affirming the necessity of ethical relativity in certain contexts."[1] Indeterminacy is the condition of having no definite propositions available, attainable, or indeed possible; and the "ethical relativity" implicit in it is quite a different matter from cultural relativism. It is the circumstantial uncertainty already very noticeable in the eighteenth century, when American culture was taking shape.

As systematic historical and comparative studies developed, before anthropology had its name, examination of moral beliefs from culture to culture and in the light of individualist orientations was conducive to a generally skeptical attitude toward moral teachings with absolutist claims.[2] This skepticism not only confirmed cultural relativism but gave rise to the second meaning, that "what is right in one set of conditions may be wrong in another." But a third persuasion arose from the second of these two meanings: a subjectivist interpretation of circumstance, harkening back to our primary knowledge of our "subjective experiences." Morris Ginsberg wrote: "The two meanings," circumstantial ethical relativity, and moral validity relative only to the subjective states of the actor, "are frequently confused when morality is said to be relative . . ." Our "variations in moral judgment . . . due to circumstances . . . cannot be used in support of ethical relativity *in the sense of ethical subjectivity*." Ginsberg is perfectly accurate in his reminder: ". . . that historically the recognition of moral diversity has not always led thinkers to commit themselves to doctrines of ethical relativity."[3] Again, the examples from the eighteenth century suffice to show the point. Jefferson clearly inclined toward circumstantial determinants of moral validity while also adhering to "self-evident truths."   But as pragmatism has dominated American attitudes, cultural and circumstantial relativism has often been assumed to imply subjectivism.

Ginsberg writes, "it might be argued that the diversity of moral judgments affords no more proof of their subjectivity than the diversity of judgments regarding matters of fact throws any doubt on the possibility of valid scientific judgments about them." There is, he says, "no necessary connexion between the diversity and the relativity of morals." But in the culture of individualism, one tends to suggest the other. The pursuit of happiness is justified in every conceivable way.   Prevailing "concern is ultimately with the liberation of personality," as Ginsberg puts it; but not so much, as he thinks, with "the equalization of conditions under which different personalities may develop." Americans have not generally felt morally obligated to bring about "what can be done by organized effort to assure equal freedom in a common life,"[4] as Rawls advocates, but rather entitled to bring about what they feel is most advantageous to themselves and those they perceive as like them. Our twentieth-century mainstream drift has been subjectivist in ethics.

Quantum thinking, in which "muddle" is the normal and inescapable situation, has enabled non-scientists to draw some misleading analogies -- just as evolution did. Because objectivity does not produce certainty or full explanation, the inference is drawn that subjectivity is called for: "All bets are off," and "every man for himself." In the elementary world we can see order, of course: all electrons are identical, or we would not have our clear color television pictures, for example. The reality of that mysterious world is "neither subjective nor objective, but *interactive*," as Michael Riordan puts it.[4] In that, perhaps, lies whatever useful potentiality physics offers for analogies. As Einstein explained, we might well regard the most fundamental physical realities, not as objects, but as relationships.

Subjectivism already held great appeal before relativity appeared and relativism gained momentum. We might say that science seemed to reinforce a tendency already present in the thought of William James, for example, to combine empiricist rigor in some areas of knowledge with radical subjectivism in others, where values are concerned. James's "radical empiricism" prominently included radical subjectivism. But a new subjectivism also gained currency, as Brand Blanshard described.[5] This new kind was emotivism, which holds that ethical judgments are like the most ordinary aesthetic judgments, statements regarding attractiveness and repulsion. "This is good" means "I like this, approve it, find it agreeable," and "This is bad" means "I dislike this, disapprove it, am repelled by it." Such statements make a truth claim based only on the feeling of the person making them. (If I say "I feel that barking dogs are silent," you can show that I am illogical, but not that I do not feel this way.) Blanshard thinks that logical positivism's revisions of epistemology required such a departure in ethical thought. In any case, emotivist judgments regarding behavior are disguised imperatives. "It is wrong to do X" means "Don't do X," expressing an attitude and urging the adoption of that attitude. Emotivism may be the most widely held theory in the English-speaking part of the world in this century.[6]

Santayana commented on Bertrand Russell's observation that philosophers "often fail to reach the truth" that "they do not desire to reach it." He wrote that "professional philosophers are usually only apologists: that is, they are absorbed in defending some vested illusion or some eloquent idea . . . . They do not covet truth, but victory, and the dispelling of their own doubts." There would be no philosophical systems if people just wanted to know what is true. "What produces systems is the interest in maintaining against all comers that some favourite or inherited idea of ours is sufficient and right."[7]

Emotivist subjectivism gives *any individual* the same capacity to do this as a philosopher with a system. A more individualistic orientation could hardly be imagined. Russell, like many other thinkers in the twentieth century, has remarked that science "cannot contain any genuinely ethical sentences, because it is concerned with what is true or false," not desirable or obligatory. "That is to say, when we assert that this or that has 'value,' we are giving expression to our own emotions, not to a fact which would still be true if our personal feelings were different." Ethics, Russell said, "consists of desires."[8]

Hume had argued that the will is guided by instinct and passion, not by reason, and that instinct and passion grow out of tradition and established routine rather than deliberation. In America it was William James more than anyone else who brought the tradition and "routine" of romanticism into the thought of the twentieth century, by arguing so forcefully for the priority of the will and even its capacity to shape reality individually by denying what we do not like and affirming what we do.[9] James was not an emotivist, but he laid the foundations for acceptance of emotivism. In ethics, no logic and no evidence could be adduced to show that I do not or should not feel that something is good, or that it is not in fact good, on such a basis. Nor can it be shown that anyone should not set such terms, or is obligated to accept any other terms. It can only be shown that an action or belief has characteristics the critic finds illogical or otherwise objectionable. Emotivist or subjectivist claims can be denied or rejected, but not refuted. Their prevalence constitutes a foundation in moral theory for the continuing legitimacy and respectability of racist attitudes.

E. M. Adams says simply that moral subjectivism generates moral confusion, and that we need to recognize the Common Good.[10] This is not a readily definable project, unless common good is taken to mean *democracy* or perhaps the greatest happiness of the greatest number. But democracy and utility, as democratically interpreted, seem to offer little but support for racism. Adams writes, "When the assumptions, beliefs, and values embodied in a social structure come to be progressively questioned and rejected by its people, it gives way and may collapse."[11] In America, such linked assumptions and beliefs involve democracy, egoistic utilitarianism, competitive individualism, individual responsibility, individual rights over group needs, pragmatism, moral subjectivism, and racism. Since they are so linked, there seems little danger that any of them will be rejected, or that the social structure they form will collapse.

1. Clyde Kluckhohn, "Ethical Relativity: *Sic et Non*," *Journal of Philosophy*, 52, 1955, 663.

2. See W. D. Ross, *The Right and the Good* (Oxford: The Clarendon Press, 1930), esp. chapters 1 and 2.

3. Morris Ginsberg, *On the Diversity of Morals* (London: William Heinemann, Ltd., 1956), 98, 100, 99, 113.

4. Michael Riordan, *The Hunting of the Quark* (New York: Simon and Schuster, 1987), 41, 39.

5. See Brand Blanshard, "The New Subjectivism in Ethics," *Philosophy and Phenomenological Research,* 11, 3, 1949.

6. See James Rachels in Caplan and Callahan, eds., 12.

7. Santayana, "The Genteel Tradition in American Philosophy," in *Winds of Doctrine* (1913); e.g., *Winds of Doctrine and Platonism and the Spiritual Life* (New York: Harper Torchbooks, 1957).

8. Bertrand Russell, *Science and Religion* (Oxford: The Clarendon Press, 1935), 26.

9. See Frederick J. Hoffmann, "Dogmatic Innocence . . ." in Gordon Mills, ed., 115.

10. E. M. Adams, "The Individual and Society," *The World and I,* 6, 1, Jan. 1991, 561-573.

11. *Ibid.,* 568.

Forty-Two

Self-Referential Validation

W. D. Ross represents those who maintain that emotivism lacks a vital feature of ethical theory, in that it provides no basis for generalizing obligation. Insofar as beliefs can be shown as the result of wishes, hopes, and fears, "as being the product of purely psychological and non-logical causes of this sort . . . you remove their authority and their claim to be carried out in practice."[1] Granting this, the practitioner of self- referential validation, who can bring discussion to a halt by saying "I don't feel that way about it," does not care about his claim lacking authority for anyone but himself. When Blanshard says that such emotivism is a new subjectivism, he probably means that its widespread adoption is recent: a very recent aspect of widespread individualism itself. There have been individualists employing self-referential validation (or rejection) for centuries, but not very many of them until recently.

Paul Zweig explains: "The subversive 'egotist' responds to authority by disqualifying it, drawing out of his idiosyncrasy another, better authority before which all else must give way. In its most extreme form, this attitude is not only anti-authoritarian, but anti-social as well." Yet "all else must give way" *only* within the range of the actor's will; he is not attempting to posit a universal system. Zweig shows that we have "traditions whose common insight exalts the authenticity of 'inwardness' over all outward authority."[2] His description is similar to that of Joseph Campbell, who traces modern "narcissism" to ideas of love in the twelfth and thirteenth centuries, citing such figures as Tristan and Wolfram von Eschenbach's Parzeval in relation to love that is not Agapé, not "casting the mote from thine own eye" to understand the other, not Christian love, learning to love your enemy, but egotistical love, self-love. This is love of one's own will.

Santayana found it "truly American" to believe "that Will [is] deeper than Intellect." He meant that the widespread belief is truly American, not that the belief is uniquely American. The Transcendentalist or subjectivist of any sort provides the meaning, truth, and beauty of the universe for himself: "My nature produces my Nature," so to speak. Santayana calls Transcendentalism "systematic subjectivism," treating knowledge as always having "a station, as in a watchtower; it is always seated here and now, in the self of the moment." He says the German Transcendentalists were "colossal egotists," solipsists in effect. But this was no mere case of Kant's *de gustibus non est disputandum*, there is no arguing about "taste"; rather, "the terrible weapon . . . got out of hand, and became the instrument of pure romanticism." In America the terrible weapon of self-referential validation went beyond the moral sense altogether, as in Thoreau: "The only obligation which I have a right to assume is to do at any time what I think right." What I *think* right: the moral faculty assumed by Jefferson had now become completely confounded with reason itself. And yet, "since the expression of a value judgment is not a proposition, the question of truth or falsehood does not here arise," as A. J. Ayer puts it.

Self-referential validation brings to value judgment the endorsement of reason without any corresponding liability to challenge by evidence or logic. As Ayer says, "it must be admitted that if the . . . person persists in maintaining his contrary *attitude*, without however disputing any of the relevant facts, a point is reached at which the discussion can go no further. And in that case there is no sense in asking which of the conflicting views is true."[3] Racist attitudes easily persist, not only because they are convenient and gratifying, but because attitudes cannot be shown to be untrue or illegitimate. The culture of individualism and pragmatism supports racist attitudes simply by conferring legitimacy on them.

With the spread of emotivism, the way was opened to go beyond self-referential validation as justification of one's own individualism.

Ross's point remained valid, that emotivism could not *compellingly* persuade others; but there was less and less to discourage the emotivist from saying "You *ought* to validate self-referentially" -- either *a priori*, deontologically, or simply for lack of alternatives. Self-referential validation came to seem instinctive to many; and, as C. S. Lewis laments, "the Innovator would have to say not that we must obey instinct, nor that it will satisfy us to do so, but that we *ought* to obey instinct."[4] The kind of self-awareness that attended new claims of inner authority tended toward treating "the individual (together perhaps with a few partners in direct interaction) as some kind of closed system. The stimuli to which one becomes open are largely one's own."[5]

The literature of self-improvement continues to appeal to vast numbers of readers, but what was formerly discussed in terms of character, and then "personality," has turned inward. In *How to Be Your Own Best Friend*, a notorious title, one learns:

> Your genuine self does not want to do things that are utterly foreign to it . . . . When we use our will power to achieve goals that do not spring out of us, but which we set for the sake of pleasing others or to fulfill a fantasy about who we are, we create a kind of monster, a mechanical man in which our living self is trapped. We have all seen people who are held together by sheer will-power; the effort is enormous, but the result is hardly worth it.[6]

Here some of the standard foundations of individualism are discarded: will, usually claimed in the Arminian discipline of self-definition; personality, "for the sake of pleasing others"; and character, the ideal self, "a fantasy about who we are." Individualism is placed upon altogether new grounds, not really superseding or eclipsing the older versions, but adding a new version which contradicts the more traditional ones, while extending the "positive thinking" self-construction of the nineteen-fifties.

> The first thing is to realize that we've probably been looking in the wrong place. The source is not outside us;

it is within . . . . We are accountable only to ourselves for what happens to us in our lives. We must realize that we have a choice: we are responsible for our own good time.[7]

In its romantic emphasis on feelings, self-referential validation also extends a mood of the nineteen sixties, when "I feel" began to be so often substituted for "I think" or "I believe." Students often *felt* that Benjamin Franklin was too boring to warrant reading, or that languages and science were irrelevant -- and felt that their feelings were authoritative.

In their illuminating and widely discussed *Habits of the Heart* (1985), Robert N. Bellah and his colleagues write: "The American understanding of the autonomy of the self places the burden of one's own deepest self-definitions on one's own individual choice." They observe that "it is a powerful cultural fiction that we not only can, but must, make up our deepest beliefs in the isolation of our private selves."[8] Contrary to some of its own most cherished traditions of morality, individualism in America seems now to mandate self-referential validation. Only those individualists who emphasize reason and social responsibility continue to be uneasy with the notion that all opinions are created equal.

It is as if the contemporary witness can only testify: "I swear on my holy feelings to act on what I feel, all that I feel, and nothing but what I feel, so help me Personal Gratification." The new individual, sentenced by his culture to solitary confinement of a sort, is encouraged by that culture to regard this as a form of fulfillment, like Ibsen's Peer Gynt. What was once the sin of selfishness can be advocated as the pursuit of self-fulfillment or even salvation. From "I think, therefore I am," we have reached "I feel, therefore I am right." And I can be "right" in feeling aversion or contempt toward others if that pleases me.

1. W. D. Ross, 13.
2. Zweig, 243-244, 246.
3. Ayer, 22.
4. C. S. Lewis, *The Abolition of Man* (New York: The Macmillan Company, 1947), 46.

5. Edwin Schur, *The Awareness Trap: Self-Absorption Instead of Social Change* (New York: The McGraw-Hill Book Company, 1976), 25.

6. Mildred Newman and Bernard Berkowitz, with Jean Owen, *How to Be Your Own Best Friend* (New York: Random House, 1971), 22.

7. *Ibid.*, 7.

8. Bellah *et al.*, 1985, 65.

Forty-Three

Egoism

At least in their stated opinions, Americans have generally handled subjectivism and self-referential validation with equanimity. If nothing is sacred and we can validate self-referentially whatever we wish, we tend simply to affirm the same values formerly held to be sacred. We self-referentially validate what were held, before the disintegration of authority, to be truths and virtues above questioning. For a very large proportion of Americans, this has simply meant a return to "that old-time religion," a reaffirmation of familiar beliefs. But the *most* familiar beliefs and values, the most firmly established attitudes, are utilitarian and individualistic. The "new dispensation" of the twentieth century, problem-solving as The Good, has endorsed a quest for whatever is most comfortable. As inertia undergirds an adamant Fundamentalist religious posture, self-interest dictates a private exceptionalist stance. Each of us can feel righteous (which is notoriously agreeable) in affirming traditional moral teachings, truly wishing that they would prevail; and also free to rationalize them so that they are convenient in light of our own interests. The "problem" of egoism is finally solved in "post-modernist" times, i.e., since the impact of modernism has been absorbed by the culture. There is no longer any need to check, restrain, deny or resist egoism for oneself, because we can posit truth and rightness subjectively, emotively, self-referentially. At the same time, it is devoutly to be wished that others behave by traditional ethical standards, which will presumably make them restrained and benevolent.

Egoism, or egoistic hedonism, is, in G. E. Moore's words, the persuasion that "my own greatest happiness is the only good there is; my actions can only be good as means, in so far as they help me to gain this." Publishing his thoughts in England in 1903, Moore said that this view is not much held by modern writers: an opinion that few in America could now share. The intervening decades have impressed upon our society the incapacity of reason to ordain obligation, and the claim that everyone is entitled to personal, private "truth" regarding morality. In the age of pragmatism, there is no necessary Truth, no Idea of the Good, so overwhelmingly appealing that you cannot help willing to pursue it. And if you do claim such a beacon, it is your own discovery or invention, its authority derived from or conferred by you. Ethics is overwhelmingly naturalistic, experimental in character, equating expediency to good.

Dewey wrote in the first third of the twentieth century, "It would be difficult to find in history an epoch as lacking in solid and assured objects of belief and approved ends of action as is the present." That seems more accurate as one comes closer to the present. Now "firm" commitments are constantly broken, "loyalties" betrayed, apparently without a second thought. There is virtually nothing that is not open to revision or renegotiation at all times, because the sovereign individual may choose a position and validate it self-referentially, and he may also reject any past or present position or commitment in like manner. As the isolation of the individual in a world without reliable values, truths, or general standards (to say nothing of absolutes) has been more widely recognized, the implications of that isolation have been elaborated in terms of right and will to act "autonomously."

In modern American experience we see a widespread inclination to adopt, consciously or not, the assumptions of solipsism, that "the individual self and its states [are] the only possible or legitimate starting point" in epistemology; of subjectivism in axiology, the belief that "moral and aesthetic values represent the subjective feelings and reactions of individual minds and have no status independent of such reactions"; and of ethical egoism, the position that "each individual should seek as an end only his own welfare."[1] Authority devolving upon ourselves brings an exhilarating feeling of freedom which, understandably, has been widely welcomed. Celebrants of sovereignty exhort us to awaken to possibilities, to discover the promise of self-realization and self-expression. Their critics meanwhile call for a return to lost ideals of the past: confusingly, often the same ideals that literally apotheosized the individual and left him lonely as a god. We are "liberated," or "thrown back upon ourselves," like it or not. The individual who wants an authoritative tradition gives authority to a tradition of his choice rather than acknowledging the authority of one. Non-egoists now deviate from the cultural norm.

In the past, egoism has been held in contempt by moral philosophers. Egoism is not a system, because it is private, not interpersonal or public. It is, however, tenable as a "coherent practical theory of conduct."[2] It has been regarded as "an attitude . . . of mere contempt for all moral considerations whatsoever."[3] In fact it does break down if it is treated as a theory of obligation, because obligation is to others, despite all talk of what we "owe" to ourselves. Egoism is not a theory of obligation in the same sense as other theories, but a denial of all others. It is a relativist assertion about the right to judge what is desirable, and to reject obligation and all assessments of obligation. C. D. Broad describes five types of egoism, and he says that the ethical hedonist, as he calls the egoist, "has to show that nothing is intrinsically good or bad except experiences" and so forth;[4] but the egoist is not obliged to show anything. He merely says that he does not find these notions of good or intrinsic value compelling.

R. B. Brandt argues that a principle is not truly "ethical" if it contains a proper name or substitute for one, e.g., "me";[5] but the egoist is uninterested in whether his position is called "ethical." It does not meet the conventional minimum standards to qualify as moral theory. However, as J. A. Brunton shows, one can be an egoist without wishing that others would be.[6] (In fact, a rational egoist would prefer that others *not* be egoistic, out of self-interest, his one fundamental standard.) It is perhaps safe to say that egoism has gained respectability, or at least acceptability, in recent American experience -- even though a vast majority would say, and presumably think, that they reject it. For most Americans, who are white and fairly comfortable with their beliefs and attitudes, egoism obviously has nothing to say against racism. Egoism endorses racism, as long as the egoist does not see self-interest as coinciding with common interests.

1. Ledger Wood and Charles A. Bayles, in Dagobert Runes, ed., *Dictionary of Philosophy*, 295, 303-304, 88.

2. See Jesse Kalin *contra* Brian Medlin in David P. Gauthier, ed., *Morality and Rational Self-Interest* (Englewood Cliffs, N. J.: Prentice-Hall Company, 1970), 84-85.

3. Medlin in Gauthier, ed., 58.

4. C. D. Broad, *Five Types of Ethical Theory* (London: Routledge and Kegan Paul, Ltd., 1930), 152-153.

5. R. B. Brandt, *Ethical Theory* (Englewood Cliffs, N. J.: Prentice-Hall Company, 1959), 369 ff.

6. J. A. Brunton, "Egoism and Morality," *Philosophical Quarterly*, VI, 1956, 289.

Forty-Four

Pragmatic Individualism's Therapeutic Appeal

Even Francis Hutcheson, strongest of the moral sense philosophers, had to acknowledge the power of egoism in ordinary behavior. He approached the matter diffidently, not prepared to talk about innate depravity or original sin, but writing indirectly, that "we do not positively condemn those as evil who will not sacrifice their private interest to the advancement of the positive good of others, unless the private interest be very small, and the public good very great." Beyond trivial sacrifices for great ends, self-interest could be expected to prevail. Hobbes cast a huge shadow over the century following *Leviathan*, with Mandeville illustrating in 1714 the secular counterpart of Calvinism which proved more durable than Calvinism itself. In *The Fable of the Bees* he assumed "that most natural passions, and especially the pursuit of wealth, are vicious . . . ." Only the variety of men's wants made it possible for them to act in a civilized manner, since they could generally recognize the advantages of cooperating to serve "the principle of the natural identity of interests."

More than a century later and an ocean away, Emerson held a position not remarkably different, a philosophical conviction that each individual "identified himself in just pursuits," working toward "private satisfaction." In fact, "Only such men were finally successful, for only they were engaged, only they were fulfilled. In the whole meaning of the national promise, only such men were free."[1] Whatever promoted "human growth" was morally good, and the clearest, most effective promotion of human growth was promotion of one's own individual interests. Americans found conformity and cooperation useful just in proportion as they served individual needs and purposes, so when David Riesman examined individualism yet another century later, he found "other-directed" and "inner-directed" persons both seeking autonomy. But now the implicit question arose, "What if nothing authoritative is available to be internalized?" What if the collapse of authority is so complete that people only "feel they must be able to adapt themselves to other people, both to manipulate them and to be manipulated by them"?

Riesman wrote that "This requires the ability to manipulate oneself, to become a 'good package'. . ." Both the inner- and other-directed man depended on others "for clues to the meaning of life," differing chiefly in their leanings toward team or group work as a means to their individual ends. Each type seeks the same kind of satisfaction. "Neither type is altogether comfortable in the world. But in different ways each finds the discomforts it psychologically needs in order, paradoxically, to feel comfortable. The inner-directed person finds the struggle to master himself and the environment quite appropriate; he feels comfortable climbing uphill. The other-directed person finds equally appropriate the malaise he shares with many others."[2] But the crucial point here is that the purpose is simply to feel comfortable.

Riesman wrote about autonomy as "a process, not an achievement. Indeed," he said, "we may distinguish the autonomous [person] by the fact that his character is never a finished product, but always a lifelong growth." Autonomy in character is necessarily related to freedom in action.[3] Stuart Hampshire describes the individualist ideal:

> The man who is comparatively free in his conduct of his life is active in the adoption of his own attitudes and of his own way of life; his decisions and intentions are the best guide to his future actions; and just that is the significance of calling him 'free.' He is a free man, in so far as he is the authority on his own future actions as issuing from his decisions; then his self-knowledge is predominantly of the kind that comes, not from observation and induction, but from his making up his mind what his attitudes and actions are to be.[4]

Yet this ideal of the free, autonomous individual, reminiscent of Transcendentalists and pioneers, has soured for many thinkers in recent years. Philip Slater says, "We are too enamored of the individualistic fantasy that everyone is, or should be, different -- that each person could somehow build his entire life around some single, unique eccentricity without boring himself and everyone else to death." Slater thinks that the characteristic American "desire to be somehow special inaugurates an even more competitive quest for progressively more rare and expensive symbols -- a quest that is ultimately futile since it is individualism itself that produces conformity." American society gives much greater latitude than most to individuals pursuing their own ends, "but, since *it* defines what is worthy and desirable, everyone tends, independently but monotonously, to pursue the same things in the same way." We tend, he thinks, to generate "competition, individualism, and uniformity" rather than the "cooperation, conformity, and variety" of less determinedly individualistic societies.[5]

A central thrust of American life has been to "free" us "from the necessity of relating to, submitting to, depending upon, or controlling other people. Unfortunately, the more we have succeeded in doing this the more we have felt disconnected, bored, lonely, unprotected, unnecessary, and unsafe."[6] Our literature presents a picture of disintegrated selves, and we struggle to find effective therapy rather than self-knowledge. Christopher Lasch analyzes how "new therapies . . . intensify the disease they pretend to cure . . .";[7] and Peter Marin has made the same point still more forcefully, writing about ". . . the trend in therapy toward a deification of the isolated self." Marin worries about "the ways in which selfishness and moral blindness now assert themselves in the larger culture as enlightenment and moral health." He says that the self has come to replace "community, relation, neighbor, chance, or God. Looming larger every moment, it obliterates everything around it that might have offered it a way out of its pain."[8] This strong language, suggesting a sense of desperation, reflects the same sort of concern to be found in widely read studies of social change, such as Alvin Toffler's *Future Shock*. Toffler describes the phenomenon of "trying on," modifying and discarding "life styles" like garments, with no sense of commitment but only "shallow membership of various kinds, in which the individual consciously

holds back part of himself."[9] Every adoption of style or membership is
tentative, guarded, conditional, and experimental.

Whether Lasch and Marin are correct about the ineffectiveness
of various therapies, Philip Rieff is surely correct about the "triumph"
of the therapeutic *approach* to life in America. This is not only a recent
development. Since the time of Herbert Spencer's initial popularity in
the years following the Civil War, his "crudely hedonistic ethics"
brought a new "standard of morality . . . simply life itself, and the good
that which promotes survival."[10] Spencer taught that there is one
inevitable and "ultimate moral aim" which is "a desirable state of
feeling called by whatever name -- gratification, enjoyment, happiness.
Pleasure, somewhere, at some time, to some being or beings, is an
inexpugnable element of the conception. It is as much a necessary
form of moral inituition as space is a necessary form of intellectual
intuition."[11] Spencer preserved the moral sense and the utility of
Scottish Enlightenment thought, but this version so widely admired in
America denied "natural relations between acts and results," because if
there were any we could identify them. What we do in fact identify is
that some kinds of acts are conducive to happiness. We then call such
acts good, by "common sense" which is moral intuition.[12] Self-interest
acquired the status of revealed truth in an age when revealed truth was
increasingly rejected. The will to be good, or to be saved, became
simply the will to survive, to endure.

Psychiatry formulated its conceptions of self against this
naturalistic backdrop; and for Harry Stack Sullivan, for example, the
self is what avoids anxiety. That is the purpose and the meaning of the
self, to be satisfied and not anxious. For Sullivan, what was real was
defined by what could be studied empirically: a positivistic conception
obviously related to behaviorism. But now the estimation of the self as
something unique underwent radical revision. In the study of
personality, Sullivan wrote, "it is preposterous to talk about
individuals and to go on deceiving oneself with the idea of
uniqueness, of single entity, of simple, central being." We "find that it
makes no sense to think of ourselves as 'individual,' 'separate,' capable
of anything like definitive description in isolation, that the notion is
just beside the point . . ." and there is "no such thing as the durable,
unique, individual personality . . . ."[13]

Yet Sullivan and all the other behavioral scientists could not prevent the adaptation of their therapeutic understandings to the traditions of individualism and even egoism. Americans were pleased to be counseled against anxiety and encouraged to regard survival as the primary aim of life; but they took the counsel on their own pragmatic terms, accepting Sullivan's emphasis on will but interpreting it as interested will, Arminian will, or devotion to self in the spirit of Spencer. The pursuit of happiness was only confirmed in the interpretations of Freud, the guru of utilitarian egoism: life as a quest for "feeling good about yourself." The age of Romanticism and philosophical materialism had produced consensus: "that only an illusory history, or an illusory religion, or illusory politics, could lead human beings to a therapy of commitment."[14] "Psychological Man" preserved the individualism of motive, the preoccupation with self-interest and self-enhancement, and the culture of individualism spread more widely than ever in the twentieth century. Efforts toward democracy only extended and heightened claims to individual sovereignty and uniqueness; and if social science discredited the culture of individualism, so what? The very heart of the therapeutic approach is to believe what you wish to believe, what you need to believe to avoid anxiety and self-disapproval. Inconsistency troubles the pragmatic individualist in the twentieth century even less that it did his explicitly Romantic forebears. As Rieff puts it, the therapeutic objective is "to keep going,"[15] an objective which is widely discussed as "coping" with life. There are no more heroes, but people admire themselves as "survivors."

The question of direction hardly arises in a therapeutic context, any more than it is posed by any other pragmatic mind-set. The hippie limerick of the 1960s comes to mind: "God is dead; Drive, he said." God turns over the wheel to you, and it is up to you to determine where you are going, how fast, and in what style. "When so little can be taken for granted, and when the meaningfulness of social existence no longer grants an inner life at peace with itself, every man must become something of a genius about himself. But the imagination boggles at a culture made up mainly of virtuosi of the self."[16] We hear people say admiringly, "*He* knows who he is." Formerly the question might have been raised, "On what basis?" or "In terms of what?" But the "civilization of authority" has now become "dysfunctional."

Psychological man, ". . . understands morality as that which is conducive to increased activity. The important thing is to keep going."[17] Rieff says that the successful individual, therapeutically, "can only make himself his own vocation. To the extent of his intellectual and emotional capacity, he joins the negative community; he settles down to limit . . . the power of the culture . . . to sink deeper into his self."[18]

But the prototypical American self grows up in the potting soil of pragmatic individualism. It is anti-social, not in any overtly negative or hostile sense, but simply because it recognizes no interest in social responsibility. Truth and justice do not concern it, except as they appear in beliefs that maintain and enhance self-perception. The greatest happiness of the greatest number lies in being left alone, which evidently led Slater to his peculiar-sounding phrase, the "pursuit" of loneliness. Such therapeutic inertia offers a happy home in the majority psyche to comforting notions of deserving and superiority. Racist assumptions "work" pragmatically in the therapeutic era, at least as well as they ever did earlier.

1. Cf. John Morton Blum, *The Promise of America* (Baltimore: Penguin Books, 1967), 134.

2. Riesman, *Individualism Reconsidered*, 104, 110, 113.

3. *Ibid.*, 117.

4. Stuart Hampshire, *Freedom of the Individual* (New York: Harper and Row, 1965), 112.

5. Philip Slater, *The Pursuit of Loneliness* (Boston: The Beacon Press, 1970), 8-9.

6. *Ibid.*, 26.

7. Christopher Lasch, *The Culture of Narcissism* (New York: W. W. Norton and Company, 1978), 30.

8. Peter Marin, "The New Narcissism," *Harper's*, Oct. 1975, 45, 48.

9. Alvin Toffler, *Future Shock* (New York: Random House, 1970), 317-318.

10. Cynthia Eagle Russett, 213.

11. Herbert Spencer, *The Data of Ethics*, 46.

12. *Ibid.*, 55-56.

13. Harry Stack Sullivan, "The Illusion of Individual Personality," *Psychiatry*, 13, 3, 1950, 328, 329.

14. Philip Rieff, *The Triumph of the Therapeutic* (New York: Harper and Row, 1966), 119.

15. *Ibid.*, 7.

16. *Ibid.*, 32.

17. *Ibid.*, 41.

18. *Ibid.*, 33.

Forty-Five

Believing What Helps

In his brilliant work, *The Triumph of the Therapeutic*, Philip Rieff first describes a classical tradition of social theory in which "the sense of well-being of the individual was dependent on his full, participant membership in a community." A second traditional theory "was that men must free themselves from binding attachments to communal purposes in order to express more freely their individualities." Both of these theories assumed commitment, either to community or to an ideal self. A third view appeared in distinct form with Freud, and assumed that "there is no positive community now within which the individual can merge himself therapeutically." The older "therapies of commitment" are no longer satisfactory or even viable; and the Freudian theory not only assumed that individuals are not merged into a community, but that they cannot satisfactorily be so merged. Does this mean that commitment is ruled out, even as therapy? Liberals have expressed concern, since Tocqueville and Mill, "about what would happen in public life once individualism sapped its virtues. The individual would no longer feel "committed" to any version of community. The immediate question was: "Within such privacies" as might be substituted for community, "can a man feel well? This question has been debated ever since the beginnings of modern social theory. The standard answer has been that he cannot."[1] But what if people are smugly satisfied with an anti-social neurosis? As therapists know, it is not at all unusual to be fiercely proprietary about pain, to say nothing of a familiar and comfortable pattern of neurotic attitudes.

Introducing a new edition of Charles Horton Cooley's sociological classic, *Social Organization*, Rieff writes: "From . . . reciprocal imagining, both self and society achieve their unity; without this reciprocity, both self and society disintegrate internally, lacking the sense of obligation that makes life worth living."[2] Pervasive individualism of the sort rooted in autonomy, Arminian will, and institutionalized competition ostensibly based on character and deserving, virtually precludes "commitment therapies" in America. A new kind of therapy was needed and developed, in which the individual is not transformed but merely informed about himself. It is an "anti-culture" which "aims merely at an eternal interim ethic of release from the inherited controls." The individual practitioner of this new therapy and its ethic is Psychological Man. Where "Religious man was born to be saved, psychological man is born to be pleased."[3] His purpose is to be spared anxiety, to be secure in what he understands, and comfortable.

Rieff calls psychological man "the latest, and perhaps the supreme individualist . . ." because he is "opposed to earlier modes of self-salvation [which came about] through identification with communal purpose." Psychological man can work in any kind of organization or cooperative setting because he reserves his feelings, remains uncommitted and uninvolved beyond the level at which the communal endeavor serves his own purposes. He maintains the ideal of the autonomous man, using the organization rather than allowing himself to become part of it. "The therapeutic individual cannot conceive of an action that is not self-serving, however it may be disguised or transformed." Like Freud, he may view others, from "the fulness of his self-knowledge, as 'trash.' Freud used the word to summarize his general opinion of people." Yet such an individual is tolerant; he has "the ethic of a wayfarer rather than a missionary; it is the ethic of a pilgrim, who, out of his experience, became a tourist." The individual must free himself from the moral demand system of the culture in order to be "properly bedded in the present world" which no longer offers comfort through commitment.[4]

Jung's therapy is also intensely individualistic, but unlike Freud's it constitutes "an essentially private religiosity . . . . a religion for heretics in an age where orthodoxy no longer serves the sense of well-being." Freud abandons altogether the past notions of saint and sinner, but Jung looks back with regret that men can no longer "make their lives endurable without constant revivals of commitment." To Freud ". . . sin is almost incomprehensible . . . inasmuch as the moral demand system no longer generates powerful inclinations toward obedience or faith nor feelings of guilt when those inclinations are over-ridden by others for which sin is the ancient name." With no consequences beyond the therapeutic aim of personal adaptation, "religion becomes a form of edifying self-examination, calculated to distract the individual from what would otherwise be the meaninglessness of living . . . . *This modern form of quietism is a powerful answer to the question of how to live in the modern world. It is also an answer that denies, in principle, any significant social responsibility.*"

Rieff comments that "The strange new lesson we have begun to learn in our time is how not to pay the high personal costs of social organization." Our "cultural revolution" is "anti-political . . . representing a calm and profoundly reasonable revolt of the private man against all doctrinal traditions [which are] urging the salvation of the self through identification with the purposes of community." The latest version of reform "asks only for more of everything . . ." which is why distressed political theorists like Hannah Arendt have associated it with consumption as a goal in itself.[5]

In his introduction to the reissued 1911 work, Rieff quotes Cooley's traditional view: "It is a poor sort of individual that does not feel the need to devote himself to the larger purposes of the group." "Yet," he says,"just that poor sort has learned, the hard way [between 1911 and 1962, perhaps] to suspect all larger purposes and higher calls. More precisely, the American individualist demands of all higher calls that they . . . demonstrate *their usefulness to his personal sense of well-being.*"[6] One might say that managerial efficiency has done away with initiative and creative effort within organizations: the dedication and devotion of the individual to the firm, the agency, or the university, for example. In the age of Frederick Winslow Taylor, reduction of workers to a commodity proceeded beyond what Adam Smith or even Karl Marx imagined; and then the age of the computer made departures from managerial norms of efficiency simply undesirable. Working unusually well became a disturbance of forecasts, quite comparable with not working well enough. The Organization left individuals no intelligent choice but to function on that basis: to adapt, to survive, to continue. "Work to rule" became the rule.

Rieff describes how Cooley "was attracted to sociology by the size of its target, as he came to see it, that false antinomy between self and society by which men improved themselves at the expense of others."[7] They improved themselves materially and emotionally perhaps, not so much at the expense of other individuals as at the expense of what would formerly have been perceived as the interest of the organization. Organizations, which had claimed that they welcomed and appreciated extraordinary efforts by individuals, no longer provided much evidence that the claim was accurate. Unusual initiative became as unwelcome as malingering.

The age of systems is not only an age of *The Man Versus the State*, Spencer's title, but of The Individual Versus the Organization. Still, as Rieff writes, individuals "draw together . . . because they prefer any company to being alone. In the concept of the primary group, into which all men are born and which they always seek, Cooley proposed the eternal and unchanging form that would save the American individualist from demoralizing belief in himself alone."[8] Cooley's model, Georg Simmel, had adopted Hegel's "togetherness"; but this was not a communal spirit that solved the problem so frightening to Tocqueville. Identification in the primary group is not commitment in anything like the civic or communitarian sense; it is *exclusionist*, withdrawing from and shutting out the wider society and its culture: a "negative" society. Its disposition provides a snug fit with racism.

1. Rieff, *Triumph*, 71, 70.
2. Rieff, intro. to Cooley's *Social Organization*, xv, xvi.
3. Rieff, *Triumph*, 72-73, 23, 24-25.
4. *Ibid.*, 10, 61-62, 77.
5. *Ibid.*, 134, 137, 245, 138-139, 239, 242-243, emphasis added.
6. Intro. to *Social Organization*, xix, emphasis added.
7. *Ibid.*, vii.
8. *Ibid.*, xiv.

Forty-Six

Be What You Want to Be, Do What You Want to Do

As Christopher Lasch remarks, the traditional American idea of the society "open to virtue and talents" envisioned social mobility for anyone to reach the most desirable situation "deserved" or "merited." He calls it the idea that "you can be anything you want," presumably given a modicum of luck, or maybe the spectacular luck of a Horatio Alger hero. But the idea has changed in recent decades, Lasch says, and now means "that identities can be adopted and discarded like a change of costume" (the analogy also used by Alvin Toffler). "Ideally, choices of friends, lovers, and careers should all be subject to immediate cancellation: such is the open-ended, experimental conception of the good life . . . which surrounds the consumer with images of unlimited possibility."[1] This may seem extravagantly phrased, but it is not substantially different from the sober, restrained analysis of Ann Swidler, for example. The description does tend to bring home the implications of self-referential validation.

The philosopher Bernard Williams discusses Robert Nozick's troubling question about what inconsistency means to the individual who sees himself as psychological man and lives by the therapeutic ethic. Evidently it does not mean much, which is why a "firm deal" is so hard to find in recent times. If the "immoral man," as he is called, has to make a choice to be moral, or to stop claiming something he claims, or to be inconsistent, he is likely to consistently choose being inconsistent. His attitude is, in effect, "So sue me." There is no "knowledge" in question, upon which to base a judgment of right or wrong, after all; and it was a fast trip from Ralph Waldo Emerson to self-referential validation and the triumph of the therapeutic. Lionel Trilling says that the "conscious dissembler," who was a scandalous rogue in the sixteenth century, is now hardly noticeable. The hypocrite, playing a role, is no longer even interesting to us, because he is taken for granted.[2] Hannah Arendt depicts *animal laborans* as the new individual who lives for consumption, expecting and demanding to be happy.[3] "The last stage of the laboring society, the society of job-holders," she says, "demands of its members a sheer, automatic functioning . . ." in which their mindless conformity to organizational expectations is assumed, and departures are inconveniences to management, or worse.[4] The new individual is a hypocrite, playing the role of caring about the welfare of the organization and the wider society, of being dedicated to their "success" beyond their perceived usefulness to his individual welfare. This is rational, and we pretend that it is also appropriate, genuine, and commendable. It is "normal," with the normality that gave Sartre's protagonist *Nausea*.

John Morton Blum thinks that "Americans had no ideology" as "the promise of America" took shape.[5] A far more persuasive description is that of Robert N. Bellah and his colleagues, that "since the early nineteenth century, the network of kinship has narrowed and the sphere of individual decision has grown." In fact, these sociologists point back to the psychology of John Locke, to identify what Steven Lukes calls ontological individualism:

> The individual is prior to society, which comes into existence only through the voluntary contract of individuals trying to maximize their own self-interest. It is from this position that we have derived the tradition of utilitarian individualism. But because one can only know what is useful to one by consulting one's desires and sentiments, this is also ultimately the source of the expressive individualist tradition as well.[6]

There has been a very distinct ideology, compounding the kinds of voluntarism Lasch mentions, and some other kinds as well. Bellah *et al.* write: ". . . Americans tend to think of the ultimate goals of a good life as matters of personal choice." For us, ". . . . freedom turns out to mean being left alone by others, not having other people's values, ideas, or styles of life forced upon one, being free of arbitrary authority in work, family and political life." But it is not simply "to be left alone by others." By freedom we also mean "to be your own person in the sense that you have defined who you are, decided for yourself what you want out of life, free as much as possible from the demands of conformity to family, friends, or community." Ironically, ". . . present-day American individualism derives from the fact that while a high degree of personal initiative, competence, and rationality are still demanded from individuals, the autonomy of the successful individual and even the meaning of 'success' are increasingly in doubt."[7] We want to act "as if" we lived in the world of Emerson, and as if nobody like Marx or Freud or Skinner had ever spoken. We find the world more attractive without economic determinism, subconscious and irrational springs of action, or behaviorist analysis, and so we operate as if those elements were not present. In short, we make the world more comfortable for ourselves by taking advantage of therapeutic opportunities to deny the dominance of the therapeutic.

Bellah *et al.* express it in this way:

The ambiguity and ambivalence of American individualism derive from both cultural and social contradictions. We insist, perhaps more than ever before, on finding our true selves independent of any cultural or social influence, being responsible to that self alone, and making its fulfillment the very meaning of our lives. Yet we spend much of our time navigating through immense bureaucratic structures . . . manipulating and being manipulated by others.

Rather, we spend much of our time dealing with systems before or within which we are obviously incapable of functioning independently; while at the same time we stubbornly maintain that we are "finding our true selves independent . . ." and that we are responsible only to the self. Among American individualism's "most articulate defenders . . . . we find the fear that society may overwhelm the individual and destroy any chance of autonomy unless he stands against it, but also recognition that it is only in relation to society that the individual can fulfill himself and that if the break with society is too radical, life has no meaning at all."[8]

The most articulate defenders of individualism are those who know perfectly well the difficulty of rejecting a position like Skinner's, or Rawls's for that matter; but whose articulateness enables them subjectively to validate what science cannot. We use self-referential validation to validate "eternal verities" or "self-evident truths" about inherent worth and dignity, because we find those to have the greatest therapeutic value. No wider application of these values is required, or useful.

The sociologist Robin M. Williams, Jr., explained that goal-oriented behavior generates "long-run pressure toward high rates of individual deviation and nonconformity." Each individual accommodates himself to the norms perceived as generally effective by adopting them and feeling "guilt or shame if he deviates"; or by taking the norms "only as *conditions*" to be observed in utilitarian fashion, because of "the extraneous rewards or penalties attached"; or by rejecting them, in either "withdrawal or active attack."[9] This simple array of alternatives illustrates why Karl Mannheim found that "The more individualized people are, the more difficult it is to attain identification." In the first case, the individual submits to norms and subordinates himself to them, submerging his identity. In the second, the utilitarian, he holds himself back, uncommitted, in the manner described by Rieff. In the third, he withdraws and denies himself the social context in which to identify himself. What is left? Only the imposition of will, to insist upon identity as the old Arminian could insist upon salvation.

Rieff cites a letter from Coleridge, proposing an institution for persons suffering from "lunacy and idiocy of the will," and perhaps another rigid program for "a higher class of will-maniacs or impotents." Coleridge wrote, "Had such a house of health been in existence, I know who would have entered himself as a patient some five and twenty years ago."[10] When our best writers address the problem of pervasive sickness in society, even saying, as Rieff does, that we are all sick, this is what they mean: we have nothing but survival as selves to seek, nothing but will to rely upon, and no way to use the will for our purpose except in defiance of the reality presented to us by our religions of materialism and science. "God is dead; Drive, he said." You can be anything you want as long as you can make yourself believe that what you want is true or possible. You can do anything you want as long as you can believe that what you want to do is governed by your will.

Harriet Tyson-Bernstein finds that the philosophy of "as if" is now presented in school textbooks "as the fruit of inarguable scientific research." She reports, "Schema that classify human needs, personality types, developmental stages, and ego states are treated as though they were facts based in nature, not constructs . . ." For example, books in home economics "presented Abraham Maslow's 'hierarchy of needs' -- with 'self-actualization' at the pinnacle -- as a scientifically sanctioned prescription for living, rather than as his particular description of successful individuals." Ignoring other points of view or possibilities for the most part, "the ultimate authority on morals and ethics is assumed to be the student's own opinion. Family and religion might 'influence' one's values, but the books say each person must ultimately assemble his or her own lists of 'values.' The underlying message in these books is that 'you' are the most important thing in the world." She cites several examples of how everything important is "your decision," and notes "even a suggestion in one of the books that acting in accord with one's conscience might be neurotic . . . Too strict a conscience may make you afraid to try new ventures and meet new people. It may make you feel different or unpopular. None of these feelings belongs to a healthy personality."[11] Here is the therapeutic inversion: individualism against individuality, "you" against your conscience, to be "healthy." Americans can easily apply individual will to make racism pragmatically true and instrumentally moral, therapeutic and healthy.

1. Lasch, *Minimal Self*, 38.

2. Lionel Trilling, *Sincerity and Authenticity* (Cambridge, Mass.: Harvard University Press, 1972), 16.

3. Hannah Arendt, *The Human Condition* (Chicago: University of Chicago Press, 1958), 133-134.

4. *Ibid.*, 322.

5. Blum, 19.

6. Bellah *et al.*, *Habits*, 89, 143.

7. *Ibid.*, 22, 23, 149-150.

8. *Ibid.*, 50, 144.

    9. Robin M. Williams, *American Society: A Sociological Interpretation* (New York: Alfred A. Knopf, 1960), 378.

    10. Rieff, *Triumph*, 24.

    11. Harriet Tyson-Bernstein, "The Values Vacuum," *American Educator*, Fall 1987, 19.

Forty-Seven

An American Way: Individualism Beyond Commitment

Of course we have to have social context to have individual meaning. The individual can only mean something in relation to society and culture. But we reject as incomplete or unsatisfactory the possible meanings we can have in such contexts, and insist on some other meaning in addition to or as opposed to that kind of meaning. We find ourselves involved in "post-existentialist speculations about the human condition," to use the phrase of Wylie Sypher.

> The difficulty is the more bewildering because after all the identities, or possible identities, of the self are subtracted, there seems to remain some existence, however minimal -- some residue of a self that still causes us trouble, malaise, unhappiness. This minimal self, a nearly spectral identity that refuses to vanish, or that cannot vanish, is the cornerstone on which a new humanism must be based -- a humanism so strange that it seems not to be humanistic.[1]

Sypher says "Our need is not to seek a self -- much less to assert a self -- but to get out from under a self, to escape from the heavy burden of freedom." We can no longer accept the Arminian freight of responsibility and guilt that go with willing and deserving. "It is perhaps more than this: we want to get beyond the self, beyond personality . . . . "[2] Yes, Skinner does, and Rawls does, and perhaps we all do. It is just too tiresome to bear, that we are authors of ourselves;

and yet we have no relief in sight except to author our own exemption from the burden.

Celebrants and critics alike seem always to rely upon Dostoyevsky to demonstrate, especially in *Notes from Underground*, that men have a perverse passion to *choose* to do as they wish, contrary to reason. Men do not have any such compulsion to act against self-interest, and it is time this romantic nonsense was put to rest. Any individual takes it to be in his own best interest to act willfully, to assert his self as he understands it. His interest is in exerting his will, and then justifying or "explaining" it, if or as it suits him -- whether he determines his "will" or it is determined for him, or some comfortable or uneasy combination obtains. There is no possibility of willfully acting against interest *as perceived*. There are *infinite* possibilities for distorted perception of interest, and choices not to act which are actions: the proverbial sins of omission.

Robert Musil is something of a cult hero because his "man without qualities" sees, as Wylie Sypher says, "that we are continually destroying the moral self while we keep hoping that our old moral contrivances can hold our organizations together."[3] American individualism's old contrivances are relentlessly insisted upon: will, responsibility, autonomy, and above all, deserving. Schopenhauer only confirmed what already pervaded America in the early nineteenth century. The will *was* the world in the New World, but it never attained its aims; so there was no danger of Kierkegaard's "sickness unto death," despair.   "The entire universe was contaminated with an anthropomorphism that was inherent in Newtonian physics," Sypher says. No resignation to the dissatisfaction of the will was needed until the twentieth century demonstrated that *individualism requires society, and society cannot accommodate individualism satisfactorily.* In the nineteenth century there was "a surprising compatibility between . . . science and romanticism" because both "sprang from an anthropocentric view of the world. The romantic frankly created a world as his will or idea." It was a world in which he could will a self that suited him: that is, attain the secular counterpart of salvation.   But that salvation stemmed from commitment, an instrument of self-definition less durable than its faithful could then have imagined.

The culture clings to the irreducible person within the empirical self, Skinner's "homunculus." The homunculus is not always white in terms of pigmentation, but it always lives in the white culture of individualism, even when adopted by so unlikely a proponent as Louis Farrakhan. The homunculus dotes on self-help and self-improvement, because that way its only responsibility is for "feeling good about itself": its overriding concern. It takes credit for what pleases, and ignores or sullenly resents the rest, selecting consistency and even coherence only as needed. Good feelings lead to happy beliefs: success in what T. S. Eliot called "our endless struggle to think well of ourselves." In this struggle, what is most real or true is readily sacrificed to what is most agreeable, like superiority or special status in "creation." Our pragmatic and therapeutic version of reality makes possible Romantic pride of self without commitment: without respect for truth or for values beyond self.

1. Wylie Sypher, *Loss of the Self in Modern Literature and Art* (New York: Random House, 1962), 68.

2. *Ibid.*, 70.

3. *Ibid.*, 14.

Forty-Eight

Self-Importance: Individualism without Individuality

Daniel Bell exemplifies a host of social and political commentators who have lamented the loss of civic consciousness and devotion to public duty in an age pervaded by egoism and alienation. The danger of imagining some Golden Age in the past, or simply that earlier times were better, is ever present. People have always been opportunistic and exploitative; and yet there does seem a real basis for concern that true civic responsibility has declined. Now, Bell says, "each man goes his own way, pursuing his private vices, which can be indulged only at the expense of public affairs."[1] This is perfectly rational behavior if one makes the assumptions of utilitarian and expressive individualism, especially with the attendant self-referential validation. For civic responsibility, one can substitute egoistic patriotism similar to the claim of the sports fan, "We're Number One." "We" is important, in the service of "me."

In an essay on "Social Science as Practical Reason," Bellah reflects on Tocqueville's fears "that our citizens might ultimately withdraw their concern for the common good in pursuit of a purely private good and that structures of 'soft despotism' would almost unnoticeably replace our free institutions . . .", and he worries that those fears are "coming true."[2] Tocqueville did not understand either government or human behavior as well as, say, Hamilton and Madison did. They never assumed concern for the common good in what was already taking shape as a culture of individualism. Hamilton had plenty of company in thinking that the only way to make people act in the public interest was to convince them that their own interests coincided with it. This is not to say that Tocqueville, and Bellah, do not have a valid point: at least there were many leaders in former times who found fulfillment in service of the general welfare, rather than viewing public life as a vehicle for self-enhancement. It does seem in recent times that an alarming proportion of Americans accept the use of power and influence for personal aggrandizement, through formal and informal institutions that govern in various ways. Grover Cleveland's idea that a public office is a public trust now seems wistful, to say nothing of Franklin Roosevelt's idea that a private office is also a public trust. We tend to assume that individuals will use their positions personally if they are permitted to, and their performance generally bears out the assumption.

Peter Berger tells a story of the Roman Republic's late days, when the Republic was at war with the Greeks over some islands. A Roman emissary to the Greeks was entertained at dinner with an explanation of the Epicurean philosophy of the host seated beside him. When the Roman understood that the goal of this philosophy was individual gratification and happiness, he said "I hope you will continue to believe in this philosophy as long as you are at war against Rome." Berger imagines foreign leaders now, hoping in the same way that the recent and current versions of individualism in America will continue to prevail as long as the United States is in competition with them. Evidently they have little cause for concern. Daniel Callahan says,

> What we have not had, until recently, are cultures that systematically tried to forswear communal goals; that have tried to replace ultimate ends with procedural safeguards; that have resolutely worked to abolish the most profound questions of human meaning to the depths of hidden, private lives only; and that have striven to sanctify the morally autonomous agent as the cultural ideal. [Callahan wonders] Can that kind of a culture survive . . . . without the wanton violence, moral indifference, and callous self-interest that are the growing pathologies of life in the United States?[3]

Why is it that we see in America the undeniably growing legitimacy of egoism, when the whole tradition of moral philosophy militates against it? If one could hazard a general answer, perhaps it is simply that our whole tradition has only *seemed* to militate against egoism, but is really ambiguous with regard to it. Salvation, originally preached as communal, always carried individualistic implications; and they became dominant because they appeal to self-interest, the original sin from which salvation is sought! Happiness, originally civic in nature and unthinkable as a private condition, became widely understood as self-gratification, regarding others' welfare overwhelmingly in terms of self-interest. The utilitarian cast of mind, natural rights thought, the inward focus of entitlements and liberties, together with the host of historical factors here delineated, convinced Americans that, as Andrew Hacker says, every personality, however ordinary, is "a deep and unparalleled mechanism."[4] What began as the inherent worth and dignity of the individual became a religion of self-regard.

Much of the impetus for this secular belief system has derived from the seemingly irresistible and endless appeal of romanticism. George F. Will once wrote: "Romanticism holds that each young person contains a creative 'self,' and that the purpose of education is 'self-realization.'" He wondered, tongue in cheek, "by what standards does anyone judge anyone else's self-realization?"[5] This musing, in a year of bicentennial celebration, perfectly illustrated what self-adulation suggests as a rational approach to living -- in George Will as well as in his fellow citizens. Adaptation, accommodation, comfort are the goals of therapeutic individualism. In the nineteen-fifties, psychology professors were pontificating that intelligence is only another name for adaptability. In the 'seventies Herbert Hendin described one noticeable result: "In a culture that institutionalizes lack of commitment, it is very hard to be committed . . . . We subject even young people who are most apt for life to an extraordinary pressure to be less than they are by idealizing the forces that are pulling them apart."[6]

Neither self-sufficiency nor even the illusion of it is any longer necessary to the kind of individualism chiefly discussed since mid-century. What Aristotle called the ethical will has also become unnecessary, or impossible to exercise, if Erich Fromm is correct that "We have become automatons who live under the *illusion* of being self-willing individuals." All that is necessary is the *feeling* that we are meaningful individuals, even though the meaning we express is nothing but our egoistically utilitarian wills. Fromm says, for example, that the right of self-expression means little if we have nothing individual to express, no "thoughts of our own." He argues that most people do not know what they want, so their "wills" are not really individual. We operate by formula or game rules most of the time, because we can't give attention to everything. Custom, tradition, regulation, all generate manipulation, no doubt; but we cannot start over every day in every way. No doubt Fromm is correct: most of us cannot start over any day, in any way. However, most recent versions of individualism require only the subjective feeling that will is "ours" and operating.

The acerbic Andrew Hacker writes: "It is a symptom of our age that people invest themselves with grand attributes, even though they lack the talent or the perseverance to realize potentialities they have convinced themselves they have. Hence the need for the illusion of individuality. For this fragile myth is the only support that remains for uncertain spirits in their quest for self-respect." When he considers such "illusions of individuality," Hacker's view is very close to Fromm's. There are very few "real" individuals, few who do anything that is not entirely explainable and largely predictable from circumstances. In a witty note on this contention, Hacker distinguishes between mere idiosyncrasies, the affectation of eccentricities, and serious distinguishing characteristics.[7]

Much of what is best in American thought has also been most subversive of common values and of cultural community. Our most exciting and dominant thinkers have sought to confront the world as it is, to be relentlessly scientific; and the world they have led us to confront is indeed a "pluralistic universe," richly diverse, full of ambiguity and uncertainty. The strength of American thought has been its openness to experience, its readiness to adapt and change in light of new evidence, its devotion to the facts. Our serious thinkers have struggled to avoid ideology: a truism so common in the land of pragmatism that one risks banality in repeating it. But devotion to the facts turned out to be a kind of ideology in itself, an instrumental concentration on means at the cost of ends, on process without purpose, how rather than why. Our more elevated habits of thought seem free of dogma except anti-dogmatic facticity and utility. We are noted for resourcefulness and practicality as well as materialistic meliorism. Our instrumental cast of mind conduces toward egoism by default, as it were. Determined to resist all claims of authority over ourselves, we strive to author ourselves by a constant process of eliminating rival claimants.

If there is an American ideology further expressing instrumentalism, it must be capitalism: now as always a system of institutionalized egoism. For us, values are established by facts, and this system still appears most harmonious with the facts of human behavior as well as economic and political safety and comfort for most of us. Egoism remains unattractive if nakedly asserted, but we have long since become marvelously adept at presenting it to ourselves in acceptable attire. The dominance of the instrumental is broadly analogous to the triumph of the therapeutic. Both are descriptions of how commitment to over-riding ideals has been abandoned as an ideal. In place of values as conceived in other traditions, individualism in America tends to value what "counts," not only what can be counted but what can be counted upon for gratification. Such a disposition fits the facts as our culture presents them. Of course a huge number of Americans attend to values in their religious activity: but that too is utilitarian and therapeutic. The fundamental values, those in terms of which meaning gets established, are usefulness and satisfaction, fruits of the individual pursuit of happiness.

R. G. Collingwood explains that absolute presuppositions are not propositions. Absolute means "stands, relatively to all questions to which it is related, as a presupposition, never an answer." Absolute presuppositions are simply sacred, and if you challenge one, he says that the person who holds it "will probably blow up right in your face, because . . . people are apt to be ticklish in their absolute presuppositions." If you get an answer, it will be to the effect that something is simply assumed, self-evident, or obvious.[8] "Not verifiable" can mean that the notion does not program logically, but that will not suffice for everyone. With regard to individualism, the implication is that the perception of self must include deep feeling, not just a conception or something rational. It is a habit of culture, the disposition to perceive in certain ways -- one of Collingwood's absolute presuppositions.[9] As Murray G. Murphey says, when epistemology is in question, "all belief systems, religious and scientific alike, are attempts to give order and coherence to experience."[10]

Not all belief systems are created equal, and none has been equal to the complex individualisms of America. What we hear about are "attempts . . . made to rationalize the fact that consistency cannot be maintained in a way that avoids the imperative to reject all but one of the inconsistent theories."[11] Nor are Thomas Kuhn's "paradigm shifts" the whole story. New beliefs have to be reconciled with older ones, or the newer ones are rejected as a rule. In America, anything that is not reconcilable with conventionally understood individualisms is ineligible for general acceptance. Perhaps that's why people act as if Skinner never wrote, for example, or as if they did not understand what he said. Racist beliefs and attitudes are virtually unassailable so far.

In the United States now, neither ideologies nor belief systems effectively provide "a world view that relates man to time and space in some meaningful fashion and . . . . What common beliefs there are are insufficient to provide an understanding of American life . . . ."[12] For some, as Rieff says, "There is nothing, really, to believe -- except the utility of belief itself."[13] Most of us are tenaciously pragmatic, insisting that we deal with ideas in terms of their presumed effects, and not their origins or whether they were or are "tenable."[14] One of Kuhn's most thought-provoking observations in *The Structure of Scientific Revolutions* (1962) is that "mankind's most fundamental assumptions . . . are normally immune to the experiential evidence that might modify or falsify them." Those who are comfortable, thinking that they have autonomously chosen to be as they are, prefer to think that everyone chooses characteristics, and perhaps even conditions; and the assumptions that have "worked" for them should work for everyone. Our pragmatic individualism is a sort of anti-dogmatic dogmatism; and it perfectly accommodates our racism.

1. Daniel Bell, *The Cultural Contradictions of Capitalism* (New York: Basic Books, 1976).

2. Bellah in Daniel Callahan and Bruce Jenkins, eds., *Ethics, the Social Sciences, and Policy Analysis* (New York: The Plenum Press, 1983), 47-48.

3. Daniel Callahan, "Minimalist Ethics," in Caplan and Callahan, eds., *Ethics in Hard Times*, 64.

4. Andrew Hacker, *The End of the American Era* (New York: Atheneum Press, 1968), 168.

5. George F. Will in *Newsweek*, Feb. 9, 1976, 84.

6. Herbert Hendin, "The New Anomie," *Change*, Nov. 1975, 29.

7. Hacker, 172, 166.

8. R. G. Collingwood, *An Essay on Metaphysics* (London: Oxford University Press, 1940), 32, 31.

9. Cf. Paul Conkin in Higham and Conkin, eds., 231-232.

10. Murray G. Murphey in Higham and Conkin, eds., 152.

11. *Ibid.*, 138.

12. *Ibid.*, 123.

13. Rieff, intro. to *Social Organization*, xiv.

14. See Rush Welter in Higham and Conkin, eds., 70, e.g.

Forty-Nine

Individualism and Racism

Steven Lukes is our best analyst of individualism, brilliantly distinguishing and explaining several important meanings of the concept. In his conclusion to *The Category of the Person*, an extraordinary collection of essays, Lukes sketches out

an individualist mode of thought, distinctive of modern Western cultures, which, though we may criticise it in part or in whole, we cannot escape. It indelibly marks every interpretation we give of other modes of thought and every attempt we make to revise our own. Central to this mode of thought is a distinctive picture of the individual in relation to his roles and to his aims or purposes . . . . The will, choice, decision, evaluation and calculation are central to this picture; and the individual to whom these features are essential thinks and acts as an autonomous, self-directing, independent agent who relates to others as no less autonomous agents.[1]

On the next page Lukes writes:

This picture contrasts with that in which the individual is largely identified with and by his roles (though these may conflict) and who relates to his ends or purposes less by choice than through knowledge and discovery. This second picture is one in which self-discovery, mutual understanding, authority, tradition and the virtues are central. Conceptions of the good are not seen as subject to individual choice, let alone invention, but rather as internal practices within which individuals are involved by reason of their roles and social positions. Reason, innovation, criticism, argument can all be a part of this picture, but are differently understood within it, as operating within an accepted social framework. And, most important, that framework is seen as constitutive of the identity of the persons within it: *who* I am is answered both for me and for others by the history I inherit, the social positions I occupy, and the 'moral career' on which I am embarked.

Lukes then advances this enormously powerful conclusion: "My point is simply this: that *once the first picture has been imprinted upon the cultural tradition, we are thenceforth irrevocably transformed and can no longer live by the second.*"[2]

America presents a particularly graphic illustration of Lukes's incisive analysis -- and a remarkable exception to it at the same time. His first "picture" of individualism, in which the individual perceives and defines everyone's self as "autonomous, self-directing, and independent" is a picture of stereotypical American behavior. But in America that picture is undergirded, not opposed, by the second "picture" of self, as identified by involvement in traditions. The American who humbly concedes the inability of will to establish self, and who is reconciled to accepting definition by the history of the culture, arrives at the same place as the one who sets out to seize fate by the throat and make his demands. To "live by" the second picture is practically to live by the first.

The second picture of self in America provides an individual with authoritative traditions endorsing the first picture. An individual to whom "will, choice, decision, evaluation and calculation are central" is a *traditional* American. Such a person is indeed involved in society "by reason of . . . roles and social positions." But in America these are perceived as reflecting individual characteristics, including ethnicity, or whatever "works" toward the individual's satisfaction. Historically, Americans place responsibility on individuals for being as they are, or alternatively, for accepting their *lot*

-- a revealing word. Our fatalistic individualism elevates the "gifted" and holds "cry-babies" in contempt, even as activist individualism cheerfully insists that "where there's a will there's a way." Individualism focused on will is inescapable in America, because tradition and the "mode of thought, distinctive of modern, Western cultures" *both* dictate it in the same "picture": a picture based on egoistic utilitarianism, individual will and responsibility, pragmatism, and subjectivism. The chief difference between an American who is pleased to be self-defined and one who sees the self as culture-defined is that the latter has resources for validation by authority instead of having to rely upon self-referential validation. A typical behavioral adaptation invokes traditions and cultural norms to justify beliefs, *and* self-referential validation for attitudes not supported in that way.

For people with traditional American self-perceptions, convictions of self-reliance, will power, and individual responsibility support racist views, or at least make them plausible, acceptable, and reassuring. The pragmatic cast of mind permits such plausible views to function as truth. Popular approval moved easily from James's "right to believe," and the legitimate role of will in choosing or formulating belief, to "Believe what you wish" -- not in rebellion against norms, but casuistically, according to cultural norms. This is a perfect example of how ethical individualism can lead to unthinking conformity, despite Emerson and Thoreau. I have a right to believe what I will, as long as I don't reject compelling scientific evidence. In some regards I can will to select what I will treat as compelling, by saying that "the evidence is not yet all available or understood," for example. From there it is an easy step to "If it feels good, believe it": a version of Rieff's "triumph of the therapeutic." The therapeutic culture now values as truth claims whatever we can best "live with," not something we might live best with.

Precisely to the extent that Americans find racist beliefs and attitudes useful, racism persists. As it contributes to the greatest happiness of the greatest number, racism thrives. Presumably it will persist and thrive in proportion to how comfortable people find it. So far, a great many people find it very comfortable because their historically fashioned views of self are so familiar, convincing, and difficult to give up or even to modify.

The *expression* of racism in discrimination continues to diminish, as more African-Americans gain individual acceptance, approval, and admiration.   Negative generalizations about performance and innate deficiencies break down to some extent, in belief and then in attitudes.   However, to provide anything beyond individual opportunity is to threaten the self-perceptions of most Americans.   Paradoxically, categorical remedies fuel the fires of racism with resentment and hostility toward the "favored," and even reinforce racist steretypes.   This is the "perverse effect" of collective solutions, which worries Shelby Steele and many other people.

But America's individualist traditions are complex, and they do not have to militate *only* toward the self-perceptions that are so compatible with racism.   The most impressive thinkers dealing with individualism, from John Dewey to Steven Lukes, argue for individualism based on good sociology and genuine individuality: neither stubborn adherence to pre-scientific notions of free will nor rigid behaviorism.   Lukes cites George Herbert Mead, the social psychologist, for explanation of how "internalizing" institutionalized behavior forms personality; but integrity, the quality of one-ness that literally makes persons, also involves autonomy in some sense.   To respect ourselves as persons, we have to be not only social selves but capable of real choice.

Ethical individualism, drawn from idealism and used historically to justify economic individualism, can be subversive of individuality.   It can easily lead to anti-social egoism, with self-referential validation.   Lukes says that to take the *values* of equality and liberty seriously would require us "to abandon most of the *doctrines*" propagated about them.   We have to learn "to hold to these values while rejecting the doctrines . . ."[3]   He brings to mind the conclusion of Henry Alonzo Myers, that "the uniqueness of the self in no way contradicts the principle of equality."[4]   But in America the principle of equality seems to most people to contradict the uniqueness and importance of the self, unless equality be twisted into the peculiar natural rights form of "equality of opportunity."

Responding to Bellah *et al.*, Christopher Lasch advocates something like the communitarianism suggested by Royce, the polity understood by Dewey, and a sense made explicit in such diverse writers as Rawls, MacIntyre, Sandel, Spragens, Stout, and Walzer, that "the self is situated in and constituted by traditional membership in a historically rooted community." Few history professors would argue with that; but in drawing inferences from it, most of us exemplify it more often than we apply it. We adhere to what Lukes calls the "doctrines," rather than focusing clearly on the values of liberty and equality. Lasch says, "The left understands private life as primarily cultural, the right as primarily economic. When the left attacks individualism, it is 'acquisitive individualism' that is referred to. The right, on the other hand, specializes in condemnation of ethical individualism and cultural anarchy. A more comprehensive indictment of individualism is called for . . . ." which would "replace 'the distinction between private and public life' with discussion of practices and institutions."[5]

With nothing against such discussion, it is possible to wonder why "replacement" is the most desirable course, and why the language of condemnation and indictment is needed. The positive approach of Lukes is more appealing, and perhaps more promising. The left *promotes* individualism as ethical autonomy and diversity; the right *promotes* it as recognizing and protecting material self-interest. Are these mutually exclusive, irreconcilable programs? What does our cultural history offer us by way of unifying concepts? After the debate over the Fugitive Slave Law and the attempted accommodations loosely called the Compromise of 1850, John Greenleaf Whittier lamented the behavior of one distinguished public man in particular. In a poem called "Ichabod," he wrote, "When faith is lost, when honor dies, the man is dead." Our question in a time of "deconstructionist, post-modernist, ironic detachment" is "Faith in what? Honor in terms of what?" What the individualist culture offers us is integrity, and truly enlightened self-interest.

If individualism has any moral ground and continuing value, it would seem to be in the idea of the one, the integer. Some would say that unique integrity cannot be grounded now, because its only basis would be for its own sake. But no. It is for the sake of the possibility of enlightened living, for peace and dignity. The triumphant therapeutic ethic justifies integrity as much as commandments or conscience or moral sense or character ever did. Integrity rings true in pragmatic terms. It is the effective idea in common between those preoccupied with ethical individualism, emphasizing uniqueness and non-conformity, and those whose enlightened self-interest centers on economic concerns. The real values of the individualist tradition, as Lukes says, may guide us to abandon or at least radically overhaul the doctrines. The need for traditional assertive kinds of individualism, and therefore their usefulness, would diminish if we emphasized the worth and dignity of *others* as individuals. So would the need, the seeming usefulness, and the appeal of racism. Racism persists in proportion as *we need and attempt to validate cherished notions of ourselves* -- and as we fail to grasp that it is in the interest of everyone for everyone else to be productive, fulfilled and reasonably satisfied.

1. Steven Lukes, in Carrithers, Collins, and Lukes, eds., *The Category of the Person* (Cambridge: Cambridge University Press, 1985), 298.

2. *Ibid.*, 299, 300, emphasis added.

3. Steven Lukes, *Individualism*, 154.

4. Myers, 264.

5. Lasch, in Ralph V. Norman, ed., special double issue of *Soundings*, Spring-Summer 1986: Symposium on *Habits of the Heart*, 62, 74.

Fifty

A Note on the Future of Racism

It is important to understand how or why our assumptions work to perpetuate racism; but understanding does not mean that change will necessarily occur. Beliefs and attitudes about ourselves and others are not simply assumptions we have *chosen* to make, which we might abandon as a society by an act of general volition. They cannot be "corrected" by instruction about how claims of autonomy and individual responsibility have been exaggerated, for example.

Neither do our assumptions respond to "moral" persuasion, whether to uplift our character or to reject the very notion of character in favor of universal "deserving." Racism does not seem vulnerable to mere charges that it is morally wrong. Treasured convictions of individual character are, after all, main supports of racist dispositions. We may wish racism's supports were weak or easy to reject, but in fact they are strong and enduring.

One opportunity suggests itself, for change through enlightened self-interest. Racism has clearly been strongest where and when it has been most useful in meeting people's needs, interests, and wishes. But the intellectual model of competitive individualism, underlying such concepts as affirmative action, assumes that meeting someone's needs means frustrating someone else's needs. Competitive individualism, our national habit of perceiving one another as rivals, tacitly assumes a sort of "economy of scarcity," in which more opportunity for some means less opportunity for others. But is it necessary to assume that more opportunity for dark-complected people entails less opportunity for the rest? The premise seems valid *only if opportunity is limited in relation to demand for it.*

For example, if southerners are more healthy, that does not mean that northerners must become less healthy to compensate. If women enjoy more self-fulfillment, there is no penalty to men. Increasing the happiness of A does not mean that B's satisfaction must be diminished. Health, self-fulfillment and happiness are not, *in their nature,* limited commodities; and neither is opportunity. But the material basis for these welcome conditions seems to be limited because we still do not make basic health care and sound education, for example, available to everyone. Our culture does not prepare us for the realization that everyone's interest is wired to everyone else's: that anyone's legitimate gain can add a little to the advantage of everyone else.

The culture of competitive individualism keeps alive our historical assumptions about winners and losers. Its implicit premise is that if there are to be winners, there must be losers. The idea that everyone can be a winner, and "everyone must have a prize" strikes us as truly a Wonderland fantasy. The Puritans assumed losers, those who were ill-favored of God. The Arminian view that everyone had effective will, and therefore the individual responsibility to use it for salvation or success, assumed losers who did not use this God-given or natural will-power. Our popular literature of "self-improvement" has always reaffirmed that conviction. Capitalism assumes competition, and godliness has been presented as "in league with riches." We embraced various versions of "the fittest" as most deserving. As William James said, Americans insist upon having "real winners and real losers." Losers make the world morally comfortable and gratifying for those who count, the "successful."

Affirmative action rather mindlessly extended this idea that the success of some requires the disappointment of others, that gain for some entails loss for others. It sought impersonal rewards and penalties, defining interests on ethnic grounds, and fueling racism even as it sought to relieve some of racism's effects. In reality, *collective* competition is to be avoided in the common interest of all. And treating fairness as a limited commodity, as in a market, is what most tragically makes racism look useful. There is no general willingness to atone for past sins of others, and no general sense of guilt requiring expiation, despite silly statements like those of the New York State Department of Education about "victims." There is no need or use for such impositions or aggravations. But even our courts make the stunning error of taking for granted the opposition of minority interests to majority or common interests. This is a false assumption, perpetuated by intellectual habits and perceptions which are obsolete. In reality, we confront one of those cases for which Plato is quite right: what is good for the whole is good for its parts, and what is good for a part is good for the whole.

Competition among individuals certainly cannot be expected to diminish, but it can readily be imagined as proceeding on the understanding that everyone ought to have a chance for fulfillment. My opportunity depends upon yours -- not at all in the sense that yours threatens mine, but *only in the sense that a danger to yours is a danger to mine*. The pertinent analogy here is to the concept of rights. Our wisest forerunners saw that nobody's rights are any safer than everybody's. My right to free speech cannot possibly be served by denying or reducing yours. My right is safe and secure only if yours is the same: and so is my opportunity. When I protect yours, I defend my own; so I should protect yours, and you mine.

It is easy but not useful to say, as Professor Henry Louis Gates, Jr. does, that America is a "fundamentally racist society."[1] Deep convictions of individualism have given racism much of its persistent appeal, but individualism did not develop to support racism. Different applications of individualism offer ways in which we might live better. Recognizing how our cultural values have shaped perceptions of ourselves and one another, a familiar American point of departure appears: the acceptance of self-interest as legitimate, and nothing to be apologized for. Ask what your country can do for you, by all means. If being an American is not useful, how can Americans be expected to "love" their situation? Ask what you should do for your country, in your own self-interest, and everyone else's. A possibility that occurs at once is affirmative action for everyone, so that everyone succeeds and contributes as much as possible. In that case, racism might be expected to lose its usefulness and become the historical curiosity it ought to be.

Black *individuals* can be winners, heroes, even popular idols. Blacks in general are still seen as losers, and no small percentage of individual performances can invalidate that majority impression. In fact, individual performance reinforces comfortable individualist assumptions with regard to whole categories of people. Conventional white Americans say "Where there's a will, there's a way," and they use the success of individual blacks to support the claim that most blacks lack will, discipline, perseverance, character, or ability. African-Americans are *collectively* charged with *individual* responsibility for not being more successful. They are assumed to be less capable of succeeding in most areas, unless they receive special help as a category -- which commonly appears as unfair advantage, no matter how cleverly Ronald Dworkin or anyone else argues for it on the level of abstract justice. Individualist beliefs and attitudes militate against special treatment for any group except the successful -- who are *perceived as individuals* rather than as a category. The situation is further complicated by the fact that African-Americans are, after all, Americans, and share prevailing beliefs and attitudes. Black "conservatives" like U.S. Supreme Court Justice Clarence Thomas can cause terrible confusion by asserting traditional individualist beliefs about their own personal traits, and their presumably superior ability to "struggle" accounting for their being winners. Many of us struggle pretty well without notable recognition or reward.

Only the increasing success of many individuals, most or nearly all individuals, made possible by their believing that they can succeed, and seeing how they can succeed, offers real hope of breaking down wasteful, destructive, unjust ways of perceiving others. We see that opportunity for everyone is profitable, if only we look at the evidence. The Chase Manhattan Bank found that the original G. I. Bill was already a profitable effort for the government by 1960. It is obvious that smaller nations enjoy disproportionate success in competing with the United States, by trying to make available to everyone a kind and degree of education that leads to productivity and personal satisfaction: Germany, with no tuition, and a maintenance allowance for all students, for example. Even Uruguay offers free education to anyone who can pass qualifying examinations. Problems of lack of incentive, indifference, and discouragement would rapidly dissipate before such an approach. America has been as profligate in wasting lives as it has with other resources, largely because our culture makes convictions of our own superiority and deserving so useful and satisfying.

Nobody expects fair beliefs and generous attitudes to prevail anywhere; but neither is racism a necessary part of American culture. America's basic values, attitudes and beliefs have been made to serve racism, but racism does not serve our indispensable values. On the contrary, if we become *more* pragmatic, and *more* devoted to enlightened self-interest, the diminishing usefulness of racism should cause it to fade toward insignificance.

1. Henry Louis Gates, Jr., in conversation with Lynne V. Cheney, *Humanities*: XII, 4, July-August, 1991, 8.

Selected Bibliography

Part One: Works cited and works having to do with racism

Adler, Mortimer. *Ten Philosophical Mistakes*. New York: The Macmillan Co., 1985.

Arendt, Hanna. *The Human Condition*. Chicago: University of Chicago Press, 1958.

Ayer, Alfred Jules. *Language, Truth, and Logic*. New York: Dover Publications, 1946.

Becker, Carl L. *Freedom and Responsibility in the American Way of Life*. New York: Vintage Books, 1958.

Bell, Daniel. *The Cultural Contradictions of Capitalism*. New York: Basic Books, 1976.

Berghofer, Robert F. *The White Man's Indian: Images of the American Indian from Columbus to the Present*. New York: Alfred A. Knopf, Inc., 1978.

Berlin, Isaiah. *Two Concepts of Liberty*. Oxford: Oxford University Press, 1958.

Berofsky, Bernard (ed.). *Free Will and Determinism*. New York: Harper and Row, 1966.

Blauner, Bob. *Black Lives, White Lives*. Berkeley: University of California Press, 1989.

Blum, John Morton. *The Promise of America: An Historical Inquiry*. Baltimore: Penguin Books, 1967.

Boas, George. *The History of Ideas*. New York: Charles Scribner's Sons, 1969.

-- (ed.). *Romanticism in America*. Baltimore: The Johns Hopkins University Press, 1940.

Branch, Taylor. *Parting the Waters: America in the King Years*. New York: Simon and Schuster, 1988.

Brandt, R. B. *Ethical Theory*. Englewood Cliffs, N. J.: Prentice-Hall, Inc., 1959.

Broad, C. D. *Five Types of Ethical Theory*. London: Routledge and Kegan Paul Ltd., 1930.

Brooks, Van Wyck. *America's Coming-of-Age*. Garden City: Doubleday Anchor Books, 1958.

Callahan, Daniel, and Bruce Jennings. *Ethics, the Social Sciences, and Policy Analysis*. New York: Plenum Press, 1983.

--   and H. Tristram Englehart, Jr. *The Roots of Ethics: Science, Religion, and Values*. New York: Plenum Press, 1981.

Caplan, Arthur L., and Daniel Callahan. *Ethics in Hard Times*. New York: Plenum Press, 1981.

Carrithers, Michael (ed.), with Steven Collins and Steven Lukes. *The Category of the Person*. Cambridge: Cambridge University Press, 1985.

Cawelti, John G. *Apostles of the Self-Made Man*. Chicago: University of Chicago Press, 1965.

Collingwood, R. G. *An Essay on Metaphysics*. London: Oxford University Press, 1940.

Cooley, Charles Horton. *Human Nature and the Social Order*. New York: Schocken Books, 1964. Intro. Philip Rieff, Foreword G. H. Mead.

--   *Social Organization*. New York: Schocken Books, 1962.

Crocker, Lester G. *An Age of Crisis: Man and World in Eighteenth Century French Thought*. Baltimore: The Johns Hopkins University Press, 1959.

--   *Nature and Culture: Ethical Thought in the French Enlightenment*. Baltimore: The Johns Hopkins University Press, 1963.

Dewey, John. *Individualism Old and New*. New York: Capricorn Books, 1962.

--   *Philosophy and Civilization*. New York: Minton Balch and Co., 1931.

--   *The Public and Its Problems*. New York: Henry Holt and Co., 1927.

--   *The Quest for Certainty*. New York: Capricorn Books, 1960.

--   *Reconstruction in Philosophy*. Boston: Beacon Press, 1957.

--   *Theory of Valuation*. Chicago: University of Chicago Press, 1939.

Diggins, John P. *The Lost Soul of American Politics: Virtue, Self-Interest, and the Foundations of Liberalism*. New York: Basic Books, 1984.

Dunbar, Leslie W. (ed.). *Minority Report: What Has Happened to Blacks, Hispanics, American Indians, and Other Minorities in the Eighties*. New York: Pantheon Books, 1984.

Elkins, Stanley M. *Slavery: A Problem in American Institutional and Intellectual Life*. Chicago: University of Chicago Press, 1968.

Ewing, A. C. *The Definition of the Good.* New York: The Macmillan Co., 1947.

-- *Ethics.* London: English Universities Press, 1953.

Ehrenbacher, Don E. (ed.). *History and American Society: Essays of David M. Potter.* New York: Oxford University Press, 1973.

Frederikson, George M. *The Arrogance of Race: Historical Perspectives on Slavery, Racism, and Social Inequality.* Middletown, Ct.: Wesleyan University Press, 1988.

-- *The Black Image in the White Mind: The Debate on Afro-American Character and Destiny, 1817-1914.* New York: Harper and Row, 1971.

Fromm, Erich. *Escape from Freedom.* New York: Rinehart and Co., 1941.

-- *Man for Himself: An Inquiry into the Psychology of Ethics.* New York: Holt, Rinehart and Winston, 1947.

-- *Marx's Concept of Man.* New York: Frederick Ungar Pub. Co., 1961.

Furay, Conal. *The Grass-Roots Mind in America: The American Sense of Absolutes.* New York: Franklin Watts, 1977.

Gans, Herbert J. *Middle American Individualism: The Future of Liberal Democracy.* Glencoe, Ill.: The Free Press, 1988.

-- *More Equality.* New York: Pantheon Books, 1973.

-- and Nathan Glazer *et al.* (eds.). *On the Making of Americans: Essays in Honor of David Riesman.* Philadelphia: University of Pennsylvania Press, 1979.

Gauthier, David P. (ed.). *Morality and Rational Self-Interest.* Englewood Cliffs, N. J.: Prentice-Hall Co., 1970.

Gaylin, Willard, and Ethel Person (eds.). *Passionate Attachment: Thinking About Love.* New York: The Free Press, 1988.

Ginsberg, Morris. *On the Diversity of Morals.* London: William Heinemann, Ltd., 1956.

Ginzberg, Eli. *The Optimistic Tradition and American Youth.* New York: Columbia University Press, 1962.

Gossett, T. F. *Race: The History of an Idea.* Dallas: Southern Methodist University Press, 1963.

Gould, Stephen Jay. *The Mismeasure of Man.* New York: W. W. Norton Co., 1981.

Hacker, Andrew. *The End of the American Era.* New York: Atheneum Books, 1968.

Hampshire, Stuart. *Freedom of the Individual.* New York: Harper and Row, 1965.

Handlin, Oscar. *Race and Nationality in American Life.* New York: Doubleday Anchor Books, 1957.

Hawthorn, Geoffrey. *Enlightenment and Despair: A History of Sociology.* Cambridge: Cambridge University Press, 1976.

Higham, John, and Paul Conkin (eds.). *New Directions in American Intellectual History.* Baltimore: The Johns Hopkins University Press, 1977.

Hobhouse, L. T. *Liberalism.* London: Oxford University Press, 1964.

Hofstadter, Richard. *Social Darwinism in American Thought.* Boston: The Beacon Press, 1955.

Hollinger, David A. "The Knower and the Artificer," *American Quarterly,* Vol. 39, No. 1, Spring 1987, 37-55.

Horsman, Reginald. *Race and Manifest Destiny: The Origins of American Racial Anglo-Saxonism.* Cambridge: Harvard University Press, 1981.

Huber, Richard M. *The American Idea of Success.* New York: The McGraw-Hill Co., 1971.

James, William. All works. See the bibliography in McDermott, John J., (ed.). *The Writings of William James.* New York: Random House, 1967.

Jordan, Winthrop. *White Over Black: American Attitudes Toward the Negro, 1550-1812.* New York: W. W. Norton Co., 1977.

Kallen, Horace M. *Individualism: An American Way of Life.* New York: Liveright, Inc., 1933.

Kant, Immanuel. *Foundations of the Metaphysics of Morals.* New York: The Liberal Arts Press, 1959. Trans. and intro. Lewis White Beck.

-- *Kant's Political Writings.* Cambridge: Cambridge University Press, 1970. Trans. H. B. Nisbet, intro. Hans Reiss.

Kevles, Daniel J. *The Physicists.* New York: Vintage Books, 1979.

Kovel, Joel. *White Racism: A Psychohistory.* New York: Columbia University Press, 1984.

Kuhn, Thomas S. *The Structure of Scientific Revolutions.* Chicago: University of Chicago Press, 1970.

Lasch, Christopher. *The Culture of Narcissism: American Life in an Age of Diminishing Expectations.* New York: W. W. Norton and Co., 1978.

-- *The Minimal Self: Psychic Survival in Troubled Times.* New York: W. W. Norton and Co., 1984.

-- *The New Radicalism in America, 1889-1963.* New York: W. W. Norton and Co., 1965.

Lears, T. J. Jackson, and R. Fox (eds.). *The Culture of Consumption.* New York: Pantheon Books, 1984.

-- *No Place of Grace: Antimodernism and the Transformation of American Culture, 1880-1920.* New York: Pantheon Books, 1981.

Lewis, C. S. *The Abolition of Man.* New York: Macmillan Pub. Co., 1947.

Lora, Ronald. *Conservative Minds in America.* Chicago: Rand McNally and Co., 1971.

Lorenz, Konrad. *The Waning of Humaneness*. Boston: Little Brown and Co., 1983. Trans. Robert Warren Kickert.

Lovejoy, A. O. *The Great Chain of Being*. Cambridge: Harvard University Press, 1936.

Lukes, Steven. *Individualism*. Oxford: Basil Blackwell, 1973.

Lustig, R. Jeffrey. *Corporate Liberalism: The Origins of Modern American Political Theory, 1890-1920*. Berkeley: University of California Press, 1982.

Lynn, Kenneth Schuyler. *The Dream of Success: A Study of the Modern American Imagination*. Boston: Little Brown and Co., 1955.

MacPherson, C. B. *The Political Theory of Possessive Individualism: Hobbes to Locke*. Oxford: Clarendon Press, 1962.

McTaggart, J. M. T. E. *Philosophical Studies*. Freeport, N. Y.: Books for Libraries Press, 1934.

McWilliams, W. C., et al. *The Idea of Fraternity in America*. Berkeley: University of California Press, 1973.

Mead, George Herbert. *Mind, Self and Society*. Chicago: University of Chicago Press, 1934.

Meyer, Donald B. *The Positive Thinkers*. New York: Pantheon Books, 1980.

Mills, Gordon (ed.). *Innocence and Power*. Austin: University of Texas Press, 1965.

Montagu, M. F. Ashley. *Man's Most Dangerous Myth: The Fallacy of Race*. Cleveland: World Pub. Co., 1964.

Moore, Arthur K. *The Frontier Mind: A Cultural Analysis of the Kentucky Frontiersman*. Lexington: University of Kentucky Press, 1957.

Myers, Henry Alonzo. *Are Men Equal?* Ithaca: Cornell University Press, 1959.

National Institute of Mental Health. *Bibliography on Racism*. Rockville, Md.: NIMH, 1972.

Newby, I. A. *Jim Crow's Defense*. Baton Rouge: Louisiana State University Press, 1965.

Newman, Mildred, and Bernard Berkowitz, with Jean Owen. *How to Be Your Own Best Friend*. New York: Random House, 1971.

Noble, David F. *The End of American History*. Minneapolis: University of Minnesota Press, 1985.

-- *Historians Against History*. Minneapolis: University of Minnesota Press, 1965.

Norman, Ralph V. (ed.) *Soundings*, Vol. LXIX, No. 1-2, Spring-Summer 1986: Symposium on [Robert N. Bellah et al.] *Habits of the Heart*.

Pagden, Anthony. *The Fall of Natural Man*. Cambridge: Cambridge University Press, 1982.

Percy, Walker. *The Message in the Bottle.* New York: Farrar, Strauss and Giroux, 1954.

Persons, Stow. *American Minds: A History of Ideas.* New York: Holt, Rinehart and Winston, 1958.

Perry, Bliss. *The American Mind and American Idealism.* Boston: Houghton Mifflin Co., 1912.

Pocock, J. G. A. *The Machiavellian Moment.* Princeton: Princeton University Press, 1975.

Pole, J. R. *The Pursuit of Equality in American History.* Berkeley: University of California Press, 1978.

Putnam, Carlton. *Race and Reality.* Washington: Public Affairs Press, 1967.

--   *Race and Reason.* Washington: Public Affairs Press, 1961.

Rawls, John. *A Theory of Justice.* Cambridge, Mass.: Belknap Press, 1971.

Reichenbach, Hans. *The Rise of Scientific Philosophy.* Berkeley: University of California Press, 1951.

Rex, John, and David Mason (eds.). *Theories of Race and Ethnic Relations.* Cambridge: Cambridge University Press, 1986.

Rieff, Philip. *The Triumph of the Therapeutic.* New York: Harper and Row, 1966.

Riesman, David. *Individualism Reconsidered.* Glencoe, Ill.: The Free Press, 1954.

Riordan, Michael. *The Hunting of the Quark.* New York: Simon and Schuster, 1987.

Rischin, Moses (ed.). *The American Gospel of Success: Individualism and Beyond.* Chicago: Quadrangle Books, 1965.

Ross, W. D. *The Right and the Good.* Oxford: The Clarendon Press, 1930.

Rossiter, Clinton. *Conservatism in America.* Cambridge: Harvard University Press, 1982.

Russell, Bertrand. *Science and Religion.* Oxford: The Clarendon Press, 1935.

Russett, Cynthia Eagle. *Darwin in America: The Intellectual Response, 1865-1912.* San Francisco: W. H. Freeman and Co., 1976.

Sandel, Michael. *Liberalism and the Limits of Justice.* Cambridge: Cambridge University Press, 1982.

Santayana, George. *The Life of Reason.* New York: Collier Books, 1962.

Schur, Edwin. *The Awareness Trap: Self-Absorption Instead of Social Change.* New York: McGraw Hill Book Co., 1976.

Sennett, Richard, and Jonathan Cobb. *The Hidden Injuries of Class.* New York: Vintage Books, 1973.

Singal, Daniel J. (ed.). "Modernist Culture in America," a special issue of *American Quarterly*, Vol. 39, No. 1, Spring 1987.

--   *The War Within: From Victorian to Modernist Thought in the South, 1919-1945*. Chapel Hill: University of North Carolina Press, 1982.

Skinner, B. F. *Beyond Freedom and Dignity*. New York: Alfred A. Knopf, Inc., 1971.

Slater, Philip. *The Pursuit of Loneliness*. Boston: The Beacon Press, 1970.

Smith, Lillian. *Killers of the Dream*. New York: W. W. Norton, 1961.

Smith, T. V. *Beyond Conscience*. New York: McGraw Hill Book Co., 1934.

Spencer, Herbert. *The Data of Ethics*. New York: D. Appleton and Co., 1880.

--   *The Man Versus the State*. Indianapolis: Liberty Classics, 1981. Intro. Albert Jay Nock (1940).

Spiller, Robert E., and Eric Larrabee. *American Perspectives: The National Image in the Twentieth Century*. Cambridge: Harvard University Press, 1961.

Stanton, William. *The Leopard's Spots: Scientific Attitudes Toward Race in America*. New York: St. Martin's Press, 1960.

Steele, Shelby. *The Content of Our Character: A New Version of Race in America*. New York: St. Martin's Press, 1990.

Sumner, William Graham. *Earth Hunger and Other Essays*. New Haven: Yale University Press, 1913.

Sypher, Wylie. *Loss of the Self in Modern Literature and Art*. New York: Random House, 1962.

Thomas, Alexander, and Samuel Sillen. *Racism and Psychiatry*. New York: Brunner-Mazel Pubs., 1972.

Tocqueville, Alexis de. *Democracy in America*. New York: Alfred A. Knopf, 2 vols., 1945.

Toffler, Alvin. *Future Shock*. New York: Random House, 1970.

Trilling, Lionel. *Sincerity and Authenticity*. Cambridge: Harvard University Press, 1972.

Trine, Ralph Waldo. *The Power That Wins*. Indianapolis: Bobbs-Merrill, 1928.

Turner, Frederick Jackson. *The Frontier in American History*. New York: Henry Holt and Co., 1920.

Vitz, Paul C. *Psychology as Religion: The Cult of Self-Worship*. Grand Rapids: Wm. B. Eerdmans Pub. Co., 1977.

Walling, William English. *The Larger Aspects of Socialism*. New York: The Macmillan Co., 1913.

Walzer, Michael. *Spheres of Justice: A Defense of Pluralism and Equality*. New York: Basic Books, 1983.

Weiss, Richard. *The American Dream of Success*. New York: Basic Books, 1969.

Wellman, David T. *Portraits of White Racism*. Cambridge: Cambridge University Press, 1977.

Williams, Bernard. *Ethics and the Limits of Philosophy*. Cambridge: Harvard University Press, 1985.

Williams, Robin M., Jr. *American Society: A Sociological Interpretation*. New York: Alfred A. Knopf, Inc., 1960.

Williamson, Joel. *The Crucible of Race: Black-White Relations in the American South since Emancipation*. New York: Oxford University Press, 1984.

Woodward, C. Vann. *The Strange Career of Jim Crow*. New York: Oxford University Press, 1966.

Wooldridge, Dean E. *Mechanical Man: The Physical Basis of Intelligent Life*. New York: McGraw Hill Book Co., 1968.

Zuckerman, Michael. "The Fabric of Identity in Early America," *William and Mary Quarterly*, Vol. 34, No. 2, 1977, 183-214.

Zweig, Paul. *The Heresy of Self-Love: A Study of Subversive Individualism*. New York: Basic Books, 1968.

Part Two: Some other studies of America drawn upon in this work

Arieli, Yehoshua. *Individualism and Nationalism in American Ideology*. Cambridge: Harvard University Press, 1964.

Bailyn, Bernard. *The Ideological Origins of the American Revolution*. Cambridge: Harvard University Press, 1967.

-- *Origins of American Politics*. New York: Alfred A. Knopf, Inc., 1968.

Baldwin, Kenneth H., and David K. Kirby. *Individual and Community: Variations on a Theme in American Fiction*. Durham: Duke University Press, 1975.

Bellah, Robert N., et al. *Habits of the Heart: Individualism and Commitment in American Life*. Berkeley: University of California Press, 1985.

-- *Individualism and Commitment in American Life: Readings on the Themes of Habits of the Heart*. New York: Harper and Row, 1987.

Bellamy, Edward. *Equality*. New York: D. Appleton and Co., 1937.

Bercovitch, Sacvan. *The Puritan Origins of the American Self*. New Haven: Yale University Press, 1975.

Bledsoe, Albert Taylor. *An Examination of President Edwards' Inquiry into the Freedom of the Will*. Philadelphia: H. Hooker, 1845.

Boller, Paul E. *American Thought in Transition: The Impact of Evolutionary Naturalism, 1865-1900*. Chicago: Rand McNally and Co., 1969.

Brown, Richard D. *Modernization: The Transformation of American Life, 1600-1865.* New York: Hill and Wang, 1976.

Chauncy, Charles, *The Benevolence of the Deity Rightly and Impartially Considered.* Boston: Powers and Willis, 1784.

-- *The Mystery Hid From All Ages and Generations.* London: C. Dilly, 1784.

Chenoweth, Lawrence. *The American Dream of Success: The Search for the Self in the Twentieth Century.* North Scituate, Mass.: Duxbury Press, 1974.

Clecak, Peter. *America's Quest for the Ideal Self: Dissent and Fulfillment in the 1960s and '70s.* New York: Oxford University Press, 1983.

Croly, Herbert. *The Promise of American Life.* New York: The Macmillan Co., 1909.

Cronon, William. *Changes in the Land.* New York: Hill and Wang, 1983.

Curti, Merle. *American Paradox: The Conflict of Thought and Action.* New Brunswick: Rutgers University Press, 1956.

D'Emilio, John, and Estelle B. Freedman. *A History of Sexuality in America.* New York: Harper and Row, 1988.

Edgell, David P. *William Ellery Channing: An Intellectual Portrait.* Boston: The Beacon Press, 1955.

Faust, C. H., and T. H. Johnson (eds.). *Jonathan Edwards: Representative Selections.* New York: American Book Co., 1935.

Fried, Albert (ed.). *Socialism in America: A Documentary History.* New York: Doubleday, 1970.

Gabriel, Ralph H. *Traditional Values in American Life.* New York: Harcourt, Brace and World, Inc., 1963.

Girgus, Sam B. *The Law of the Heart: Individualism and the Modern Self in American Literature.* Austin: University of Texas Press, 1979.

Godkin, Edward Lawrence. *Problems of Modern Democracy: Political and Economic Essays,* ed. Gordon Keller. New York: Charles Scribner's Sons, 1896.

Greene, Theodore P. *America's Heroes: The Changing Models of Success in American Magazines.* New York: Oxford University Press, 1970.

Hassan, Ihab. *Radical Innocence.* Princeton: Princeton University Press, 1961.

Heimert, Alan, and Perry Miller (eds.). *The Great Awakening.* Indianapolis: Bobbs Merrill Co., 1967.

Heineman, Robert A. *Authority and the Liberal Tradition.* Durham: Carolina Academic Press, 1984.

Hofstadter, Richard. *Anti-Intellectualism in American Life.* New York: Vintage Books, 1962.

Kammen, Michael. *People of Paradox.* New York: Alfred A. Knopf, 1972.

Kenner, Hugh. *A Homemade World: The American Modernist Writers.* New York: William Morrow, 1975.

Lindner, Robert M. *Must You Conform?* New York: Holt, Rinehart and Winston, 1956.

Love, Glen A. *New Americans: The Westerner and the Modern Experience in the American Novel.* E. Brunswick, N.J.: Bucknell University Press, 1982.

Martineau, Harriet. *Society in America.* London: Saunders and Otley, 1837, 3 vols.

Matthews, Jean B. *Rufus Choate: The Law and Civic Virtue.* Philadelphia: Temple University Press, 1980.

May, Henry F. *Ideas, Faiths, and Feelings: Essays on American Intellectual and Religious History, 1952-1982.* New York: Oxford University Press, 1983.

Miller, Perry. *Jonathan Edwards.* New York: William Sloane Associates, 1949.

--   *Nature's Nation.* Cambridge: Harvard University Press, 1967.

--   *The New England Mind: From Colony to Province.* Cambridge: Harvard University Press, 1953.

Morgan, Edmund S. *The Meaning of Independence.* New York: W. W. Norton and Co., 1978.

Perry, Ralph Barton. *Characteristically American.* New York: Alfred A. Knopf, Inc., 1949.

--   *Puritanism and Democracy.* New York: Vanguard Press, 1944.

Pierson, George Wilson. *Tocqueville and Beaumont in America.* New York: Oxford University Press, 1938.

Powell, Thomas F. *Josiah Royce.* New York: Washington Square Press, 1967.

--   "Sozialismus in Amerika: *Eine Bewegung die Stillstand,*" *Geschichte in Wissenschaft und Unterricht,* Vol. 30, No. 5, 1979, 284-296.

Quinn, Arthur Hobson. *The Soul of America, Yesterday and Today.* Philadelphia: University of Pennsylvania Press, 1932.

Rapson, Richard L. (ed.). *Individualism and Conformity in the American Character.* Boston: D. C. Heath, 1967.

Robertson, James Oliver. *American Myth, American Reality.* New York: Hill and Wang, 1980.

Ryan, William. *Equality.* New York: Vintage Books, 1982.

Schneider, Herbert W. *The Puritan Mind.* Ann Arbor: University of Michigan Press, 1958.

Schuster, Eunice Minette. *Native American Anarchism: A Study of Left-Wing American Individualism.* New York: AMS Press, 1970.

Shaler, Nathaniel Southgate. *The Individual: A Study of Life and Death.* New York: D. Appleton, 1900.

Smith, Henry Nash. *Virgin Land: The American West as Symbol and Myth.* Cambridge: Harvard University Press, 1950.

Stannard, David E. *The Puritan Way of Death: A Study in Religion, Culture, and Social Change.* New York: Oxford University Press, 1977.

Stroh, Guy W. *American Ethical Thought.* Chicago: Nelson-Hall, 1979.

Townsend, Harvey G. (ed.). *The Philosophy of Jonathan Edwards from His Private Notebooks.* Westport, Ct.: Greenwood Press, 1972.

Twelve Southerners. *I'll Take My Stand: The South and the Agrarian Tradition.* New York: Harper Torchbooks, 1962.

Veblen, Thorstein. *The Theory of Business Enterprise.* New York: New American Library, 1958.

Wecter, Dixon. *The Hero in America.* Ann Arbor: University of Michigan Press, 1963.

White, David Manning. *Popular Culture in America.* Chicago: Quadrangle Books, 1970.

White, Morton. *Science and Sentiment in America: Philosophical Thought from Jonathan Edwards to John Dewey.* New York: Oxford University Press, 1972.

Wiebe, Robert H. *The Segmented Society: An Introduction to the Meaning of America.* New York: Oxford University Press, 1975.

Wilkinson, Rupert. *American Tough: The Tough-Guy Tradition and American Character.* Westport, Ct.: Greenwood Press, 1984.

Wills, Garry. *Inventing America: Jefferson's Declaration of Independence.* New York: Vintage Books, 1979.

Wilson, Robert J. *The Benevolent Deity: Ebenezer Gay and the Rise of Rational Religion in New England, 1696-1787.* Philadelphia: University of Pennsylvania Press, 1984.

Wiltse, Charles M. *The Jefferson Tradition in American Democracy.* Chapel Hill: University of North Carolina Press, 1935.

Wise, Gene. *American Historical Explanations.* Homewood, Ill.: The Dorsey Press, 1973.

Wise, John. *A Vindication of the Government of New England Churches.* Gainesville: University of Florida Press, 1958.

Wolfe, Don M. *The Image of Man in America.* New York: Thomas Y. Crowell Co., 1970.

Wolin, Sheldon S. *Politics and Vision.* Boston: Little Brown and Co., 1960.

Wood, Gordon S. *The Creation of the American Republic.* Chapel Hill: University of North Carolina Press, 1969.

Wright, B. F. *American Interpretations of Natural Law.* Cambridge: Harvard University Press, 1931.

Wright, Conrad. *The Beginnings of Unitarianism in America.* Boston: Starr King Press, 1955.

Wyllie, Irvin G. *The Self-Made Man in America.* New York: The Free Press, 1954.

Ziff, Larzer. *Puritanism in America: New Culture in a New World.* New York: The Viking Press, 1973.

Part Three: Important background works

Blackstone, William T. *Francis Hutcheson and Contemporary Ethical Theory.* Athens: University of Georgia Press, 1965.

Bolton, J. D. P. *Glory, Jest and Riddle: A Study of the Growth of Individualism from Homer to Christianity.* New York: Harper and Row, 1973.

Bourke, Vernon, Jr. *Will in Western Thought: An Historico-Critical Study.* New York: Sheed and Ward, 1964.

Bouwsma, William J. *John Calvin: A Sixteenth-Century Portrait.* New York: Oxford University Press, 1988.

Braudy, Leo. *The Frenzy of Renown: Fame and Its History.* New York: Oxford University Press, 1986.

Burckhardt, Jacob. *The Civilization of the Renaissance in Italy.* New York: Harper and Row, 1958, 2 vols.

Coate, Mary. *Social Life in Stuart England.* Westport, Ct.: Greenwood Press, 1971.

Cua, Antonio S. *Reason and Virtue: A Study in the Ethics of Richard Price.* Athens: Ohio University Press, 1966.

Darnton, Robert. *The Great Cat Massacre and Other Episodes in French Cultural History.* New York: Vintage Books, 1985.

Diderot, Denis. *Rameau's Nephew* and *D'Alembert's Dream.* Harmondsworth, Middlesex: Penguin Books, 1966, trans. L. W. Tancock.

Findlay, J. N. *Hegel: A Re-Examination.* New York: Collier Books, 1962.

Fowler, T. *Shaftesbury and Hutcheson.* London: 1882.

Fowles, John. *A Maggot.* Boston: Little Brown and Co., 1985.

Frazer, James George. *The Golden Bough.* New York: The Macmillan Co., 1922.

Gellner, Ernest. *The Legitimation of Belief.* London: Cambridge University Press, 1974.

Gibson, James. *Locke's Theory of Knowledge and Its Historical Relations.* Cambridge: Cambridge University Press, 1960.

Grave, S. A. *The Scottish Philosophy of Common Sense.* New York: Oxford University Press, 1960.

Graves, Robert. *Wife to Mr. Milton.* New York: Penguin Books, 1954.

Haldane, E. S., and G. R. T. Ross (trans.). *The Philosophical Works of Descartes.* New York: Dover Books, 1955.

Hallowell, John H. *The Decline of Liberalism as an Ideology, with Particular Reference to German Politico-Legal Thought.* New York: Howard Fertig, 1971.

Hamilton, Edith. *The Greek Way.* New York: W. W. Norton and Co., 1930.

Heine, Heinrich. *Religion and Philosophy in Germany.* Boston: Beacon Press, 1959.

Hill, Christopher. *The Century of Revolution: 1603-1741.* New York: W. W. Norton, 1961.

-- *Society and Puritanism in Pre-Revolutionary England.* New York: Schocken Books, 1967.

Himmelfarb, Gertrude. *The Idea of Poverty: England in the Early Industrial Age.* New York: Vintage Books, 1985.

Hobbes, Thomas. *Leviathan.* New York: E. P. Dutton and Co., 1950.

Holstein, Baroness Staël. *Germany.* London: John Murray, 1813, 3 vols.

Hume, David. *Essays: Moral, Political, and Literary.* London: Oxford University Press, 1963.

-- *An Inquiry Concerning the Principles of Morals.* New York: The Liberal Arts Press, 1957.

-- *A Treatise of Human Nature.* Oxford: Oxford University Press, 1978.

Hutcheson, Francis. *A System of Moral Philosophy.* New York: A. M. Kelley, 1968. Cf. *An Inquiry into the Original of Our Ideas of Beauty and Virtue* (1725), *An Essay on the Nature and Conduct of the Passions, with Illustrations upon the Moral Sense* (1728), and *An Inquiry Concerning Moral Good and Evil* (1729).

Kelley, Donald R. *The Beginnings of Ideology: Consciousness and Society in the French Reformation.* Cambridge: Cambridge University Press, 1981.

Krieger, Leonard. *The German Idea of Freedom.* Boston: Beacon Press, 1957.

Maccall, William. *The Elements of Individualism.* London: Jack Chapman, 1847.

Macfarlane, Alan. *The Origins of English Individualism.* Cambridge: Cambridge University Press, 1979.

Mackenzie, Henry. *The Man of Feeling.* New York: W. W. Norton, 1958.

Mill, John Stuart. *Utilitarianism.* Chicago: Henry Regnery Co., 1949.

Montesquieu, Baron de. *Persian Letters.* Baltimore: Penguin Books, 1973. Trans. & intro. J. C. Betts.

--   *The Spirit of the Laws*. New York: Hafner Press, 1949. Trans.
       Thomas Nugent, intro. Franz Neumann.

Moore, G. E. *Principia Ethica*. Cambridge: Cambridge University Press,
       1903.

Pico Della Mirandola, Giovanni. *Oration on the Dignity of Man*.
       Chicago: Henry Regnery Co., 1956.

Plamenatz, John. *The English Utilitarians*. Oxford: Basil Blackwell
       and Mott, 1958.

Price, Richard. *A Review of the Principle Questions of Morals*. Oxford:
       The Clarendon Press, 1948.

Robertson, H. M. *Aspects of the Rise of Economic Individualism*.
       Cambridge: Cambridge University Press, 1933.

Schlatter, Richard. *Private Property: The History of an Idea*. New
       Brunswick: Rutgers University Press, 1951.

Schneider, Herbert W. (ed.). *Adam Smith's Moral and Political
       Philosophy*. New York: Hafner Pub. Co., 1948.

Sidgwick, Henry. *The Methods of Ethics*. London: Macmillan and Co.,
       1893.

Smith, Adam. *The Theory of Moral Sentiments*. New York:
       Augustus M. Kelley Pubs., 1966.

--   *The Wealth of Nations*. Middlesex: Pelican Books, 1970.

Stewart, John B. *The Moral and Political Philosophy of David Hume*.
       New York: Columbia University Press, 1963.

Strauss, Leo. *Natural Right and History*. Chicago: University of
       Chicago Press, 1953.

--   *The Political Philosophy of Hobbes: Its Basis and Genesis*.
       Oxford: Oxford University Press, 1936.

Street, C. L. *Individualism and Individuality in the Philosophy of
       John Stuart Mill*. Milwaukee: Morehouse Pub. Co., 1926.

Tuchman, Barbara. *A Distant Mirror: The Calamitous 14th Century*.
       New York: Alfred A. Knopf, Inc., 1978.

Tyacke, Nicholas. *Anti-Calvinists: The Rise of English Arminianism,
       c. 1590-1640*. Oxford: Clarendon Press, 1987.

Ullmann, Walter. *The Individual and Society in the Middle Ages*.
       Baltimore: The Johns Hopkins University Press, 1966.

Unamuno, Miguel de. *The Tragic Sense of Life*. New York: Dover
       Press, 1954.

Vaihinger, Hans. *The Philosophy of "As If."* London: Lund
       Humphries, 1924. Trans. C. K. Ogden.

Voltaire. *Candide and Zadig*. New York: Airmont Pub. Co., 1966.

Westermarck, Edward. *Ethical Relativity*. London: Kegan Paul, 1932.

--   *The Origin and Development of the Moral Ideas*. New York:
       The Macmillan Co., 1906, 2 vols.

Part Four: Some further social science and social
commentary drawn upon

Argyris, Chris. *Personality and Organization: The Conflict Between System and the Individual.* New York: Harper and Row, 1957.

Aries, Philippe. *The Hour of Our Death.* New York: Alfred A. Knopf, 1981. Trans. Helen Weaver.

Beck, Lewis. *The Actor and the Spectator.* New Haven: Yale University Press, 1975.

Berger, Peter, and Brigitte Berger and Hansfried Kellner. *The Homeless Mind: Modernization and Consciousness.* New York: Vintage Books, 1974.

Borgmann, Albert. *Technology and the Character of Contemporary Life.* Chicago: University of Chicago Press, 1985.

Clifford, James. *The Predicament of Culture: Twentieth-Century Ethnography, Literature, and Art.* Cambridge: Harvard University Press, 1988.

Danto, Arthur C. *Connections to the World.* New York: Harper and Row, 1989.

Dumont, Louis. *Essays on Individualism: Modern Ideology in Anthropological Perspective.* Chicago: University of Chicago Press, 1986.

Duerr, Hans-Peter. *Dream Time.* New York: Blackwell, 1985.

Durkheim, Emile. *Montesquieu and Rousseau.* Ann Arbor: University of Michigan Press, 1960.

Fletcher, Joseph. *Situation Ethics: The New Morality.* Philadelphia, Westminster Press, 1975.

Fried, Charles. *Right and Wrong.* Cambridge: Harvard University Press, 1979.

Friedrich, Carl J. (ed.). *Liberty (NOMOS IV).* New York: Atherton Press, 1962.

Galbraith, John Kenneth. *The New Industrial State.* New York: Houghton Mifflin Co., 1967.

Gardner, John W. *Self-Renewal.* New York: Harper and Row, 1964.

Gaus, Gerald T. *The Modern Liberal Theory of Man.* Canberra: Croom Helm, 1983.

Geertz, Clifford. *The Interpretation of Cultures.* New York: Basic Books, 1973.

Gross, Donald, and Paul Osterman (eds.). *Individualism: Man in Modern Society.* New York: Dell Pub. Co., 1971.

Hadas, Moses, and Morton Smith. *Heroes and Gods.* New York: Harper and Row, 1951.

Hare, R. M. *The Language of Morals.* Oxford: Oxford University Press, 1952.

Kluckhohn, Clyde. *Mirror for Man*. New York: McGraw-Hill, 1944.

Kolenda, Konstantin. *The Freedom of Reason*. San Antonio: Principia Press of Trinity University, 1964.

Ladd, John (ed.). *Ethical Relativism*. Belmont, Cal.: Wadsworth Pub. Co., 1973.

Laing, R. D. *The Divided Self*. New York: Pantheon Books, 1969.

MacIntyre, Alasdair. *After Virtue: A Study in Moral Theory*. South Bend: University of Notre Dame Press, 1981.

McCloskey, H. J. *Meta-Ethics and Normative Ethics*. Den Haag: Martinus Nÿhoff, 1969.

Mannheim, Karl. *Ideology and Utopia*. New York: Harcourt, Brace and Co., 1951.

Maritain, Jacques. *The Rights of Man*. New York: Charles Scribner's Sons, 1944.

Matson, Floyd W. *The Idea of Man*. New York: Delacorte Press, 1976.

Midgley, Mary. *Beast and Man: The Roots of Human Nature*. New York: New American Library, 1978.

Milo, Ronald D. (ed.). *Egoism and Altruism*. Belmont, Cal.: Wadsworth Pub. Co., 1974.

Moore, Barrington. *Social Origins of Dictatorship and Democracy*. Boston: Beacon Press, 1966.

More, Paul Elmer. *The Religion of Plato*. Princeton: Princeton University Press, 1921.

Mulkay, Michael. *Science and the Sociology of Knowledge*. London: George Allen and Unwin, 1979.

Musil, Robert. *The Man Without Qualities*. London: Secker and Warburg, 1979, 2 vols. Trans. E. Wilkins and E. Kaiser.

Newman, Charles. *The Post-Modern Aura*. Evanston: Northwestern University Press, 1985.

Niebuhr, Reinhold. *The Children of Light and the Children of Darkness*. New York: Charles Scribner's Sons, 1944.

--   *Moral Man and Immoral Society*. New York: Scribner's, 1932.

--   *The Nature and Destiny of Man*. New York: Scribner's, 1941 and 1943, 2 vols.

Nisbet, Robert A. *History and the Idea of Progress*. New York: Basic Books, 1980.

--   *Twilight of Authority*. New York: Oxford University Press, 1975.

Norton, David L. *Personal Destinies: A Philosophy of Ethical Individualism*. Princeton: Princeton University Press, 1976.

Nunn, Clyde Z., and Harry J. Crockett, Jr., and J. Allen Williams, Jr., *Tolerance for Nonconformity*. San Francisco: Jossey-Bass Publishers, 1978.

Ogilvy, James. *Many-Dimensional Man*. New York: Harper and Row, 1979.

Oppenheim, Felix. *Dimensions of Freedom*. New York: St. Martin's Press, 1961.

Prichard, H. A. *Moral Obligation*. Oxford: The Clarendon Press, 1949.

Purcell, Edward A., Jr. *The Crisis of Democratic Theory: Scientific Naturalism and the Problem of Value*. Lexington: University of Kentucky Press, 1973.

Quine, W. V. *The Ways of Paradox and Other Essays*. Cambridge: Harvard University Press, 1976.

Rashdall, H. *Theory of Good and Evil*. Oxford: Oxford University Press, 1924.

Raz, Joseph. *The Morality of Freedom*. New York: Oxford Univesity Press, 1986.

Rosenbaum, Alan S. (ed.). *The Philosophy of Human Rights: International Perspectives*. Westport, Ct.: Greenwood Press, 1980.

Stout, Jeffrey. *Flight from Authority*. South Bend: University of Notre Dame Press, 1981.

Taylor, Charles. *Sources of the Self: The Making of the Modern Identity*. Cambridge: Harvard University Press, 1989.

Telfer, Elizabeth. *Happiness*. New York: St. Martin's Press, 1980.

Wallace, Anthony F. C. *Culture and Personality*. New York: Random House, 1961.

Whitehead, Alfred North. *Science and the Modern World*. New York: The Macmillan Co., 1925.

Index of Names

Index of Subjects

Absolute presuppositions, 295

Absolutism, 208

Affirmative Action, 305-307

African-American(s): after Reconstruction, 94; American attitudes and beliefs shared by, 308; attitudes and philosophies disadvantage, 25, 46, 51, 79-80, 83, 157; character, personality and, 167, 208; class or categorical treatment of, 37, 45, 55-56, 104, 202, 239, 306, 308; deficiency (inferiority) of, 4, 23-24, 68, 94, 104, 108, 120, 157, 199, 208-209, 302; education and, 49; "election" of white over, 45; humanity of, 18, 24, 68, 105; identity, 203; individual acceptance, 302, 308; individualism and, 177, 202; interests "vs" common, 307; justifications of behavior toward, 10, 18, 37, 45, 50, 67; majority impression of, 62, 114, 208, 308; opportunity and, 45, 49-50, 55, 94, 98, 198, 208, 230; organization, 202-203; performance and, 109, 114, 120, 208-209, 302, 308; persistence of racism toward, 102; poverty and, 134, 202; progress of, 49, 94, 199, 202-203; "progressive" disenfranchisement of, 119; retaliatory racism of, 115; science, history, religion and, 116; slavery and, 10, 19, 51; will, success, deserving and, 23, 29, 34-35, 38, 45-46, 68, 103-104, 120, 157, 167, 183, 308

See also Race, Racism, Racist

Alienation, 190, 196, 223, 291

Altruism, 36, 80-82, 238, 243

Ambition, 81, 90-91, 94, 130, 142, 151, 170, 190, 192, 197, 201, 208, 223, 229, 243, 320-232

American: attitudes, assumptions and values, 4-5, 24, 28, 82, 86, 90-94, 106-109, 113, 120, 142, 164, 171, 182, 201, 207-208, 211-213, 219, 253, 256, 309; beliefs, 15-16, 22-23, 29, 61, 83-84, 102, 131, 133, 135, 141, 159, 197, 202, 221-224, 248, 262, 267-269, 282, 293-294; culture, 123, 126, 150, 165, 167, 174-177, 179, 181, 199, 205, 215-216, 220, 237, 249, 255, 264, 273, 293-294, 300, 306, 308-309; democracy, 118; equality, 37, 39, 42, 45-46, 49, 54, 59-60, 67, 302; experience, 82, 151, 166-167, 170, 179, 189, 268; goals, 94,

305-307, 309; brutality of, 114; conformity and, 151; defined, 1; democratic, 5, 106, 118-119; egoism and, 269; European, 111; expressions of, 1, 302; history of, 2; immigration and, 119; individual will and, 285; liberal and progressive, 111, 120; mind-set of, 11-12; national identity and, 100; "natural" disposition of, 45; patriotism and, 107, 112; performance and, 70; political thought and, 46; pragmatism and, 128, 134; proto-, 21, 24, 50; psycho-social aspects of, 109, 114; relativism and, 239; religion and 67, 115-116, 224; respectability of, 119, 258; "rhetoric of freedom" and, 103; "scientific" or systematic, 50, 67, 70, 74-76, 103, 107-109, 112, 116, 118-119, 128, 142, 167, 171; self-referential validation and, 264; slavery (exploitation) and, 11, 103; Social Darwinism and, 87; social philosophy and, 138-139, 142, 145, 147-148; success, failure and, 61, 84, 151; support of, 119-120, 123, 249, 258, 280, 301-302, 304-305

See also African-Americans, Race, Racist

Racist: assumptions, 12, 102, 111, 114-116, 120, 217, 232, 276, 301, 305; beliefs, norms and attitudes, 2-6, 208, 262, 296, 301; characterizations, 6-7, 302; history, 112-114; justification and rationalization, 12, 68, 103; literature, 112-114; science, 114; "society," 307

See also African-Americans, Race, Racism

Rationality, 145-148, 173

Realism, 248

Reason: actions and attitudes based on, 27-28, 31, 48, 52, 156, 174, 183, 187, 207, 213, 238, 258, 264, 268, 288, 300; belief and, 2, 4, 11, 18, 21, 171-172, 262; intuitive, 39-42, 44, 78, 150, 237; lack of, 157; success and, 159; truth and, 42, 135, 145; understanding through, 40-43, 59, 132-133; values and, 187

Reconstruction, 113, 119

Red River, 187

Relativism, 146, 194, 196, 235, 239, 255-257, 269

Religion: African Americans and, 18; attitudes toward, 16, 224, 233; beliefs and values, 82, 139, 213, 224, 246, 285, 295-296; differences, 185-186; Jamesian idea of, 133, 155, 171-172; national, 171, 181; philosophy synthesizes from, 166; racism and, 67, 115-116, 224; science and, 84, 92, 172, 196, 284; self and, 51, 57, 125, 156, 176, 279, 285, 293; types of, 16, 23, 37, 61, 82, 92, 132, 140, 153, 190, 267, 275, 278, 284

See also, Christianity, Faith, Fundamentalism

Requirimiento, 101

Responsibility: African-Americans, racism and, 6, 23, 58, 83, 94, 308; freedom and, 34-35; individual, 3, 6, 22-23, 28, 44, 48, 79, 83, 94, 107, 120, 126, 128-133, 138, 141, 159, 175, 181-182, 185, 188-189, 192-193, 201, 203, 205, 207-209, 212, 231-232, 237, 258, 264, 287-288, 300-301, 305-306; moral, 5, 205, 216; other kinds of, 38, 232, 289; property and, 38; self-interest and, 35; social, 79, 148, 197, 206-207, 216, 264, 276, 278-279, 291